RAISED BY WOLVES

Raised by Wolves

The Story of Christian Rock & Roll

John J. Thompson

With photographs by
Dinah K. Kotthoff

The publication of *Raised by Wolves* has been generously supported
by the Government of Canada through the
Book Publishing Industry Development Program.

CANADIAN CATALOGUING IN PUBLICATION DATA
Thompson, John J. (John Joseph), 1970-
Raised by wolves: the story of Christian rock & roll
ISBN 1-55022-421-2
1. Christian rock music – History and criticism. I. Title.
ML3187.5.T473 2000 781.66 C00-9317200-1

Front cover image courtesy of SuperStock.
All interior photos by Dinah K. Kotthoff (www.dinahphoto.com).
Cover and interior design by Guylaine Régimbald – SOLO DESIGN.
Typesetting by Yolande Martel.
This book is set in Dante and Loyalty.

Printed by AGMV L'Imprimeur, Cap-Saint-Ignace, Quebec.
Distributed in Canada by General Distribution Services,
325 Humber College Boulevard, Etobicoke, Ontario M9W 7C3.

Distributed in the United States by LPC Group,
1436 West Randolph Street, Chicago, IL 60607, U.S.A.

Distributed in Europe by Turnaround Publisher Services, Unit 3,
Olympia Trading Estate, Coburg Road, Wood Green, London, N2Z 6T2.

Distributed in Australia and New Zealand by Wakefield Press,
17 Rundle Street (Box 2266), Kent Town, South Australia 5071.

Published by ECW PRESS
Suite 200
2120 Queen Street East
Toronto, Ontario M4E 1E2.
ecwpress.com

PRINTED AND BOUND IN CANADA

To Michelle, Jordan, Wesley, and Trinity

IN MEMORY OF

Keith Green
Lonnie Frisbee
Danny (D-Boy) Rodriguez
Mark Heard
Vince Ebo
Rich Mullins
Chris Wimber
Gene "Eugene" Andrusco

Contents

Preface

What is "Christian rock"? It has been called everything from Jesus music to righteous rock to the devil's handiwork (the church can't sit idly by and let some waywards peddle "jungle music" in the name of the Lord without casting a little brimstone). But whatever it's called, it's a strange mix indeed, and to many people the term is an oxymoron.

Christian rock melds faith and culture. It is called Christian because of the messages in the lyrics, or at least because of the faith backgrounds of the artists, yet it explores every subject from politics to sex to cars to friendship. It is full-on rock and roll with the volume and the syncopation and the downbeats and the noise, yet it is used for worship, evangelism, and the entertainment of abstinent youth-group members and 50-year-old biker pastors. It features every nuance of rock, from techno, house, and disco; to metal, punk, hardcore, and emo; to singer-songwriter acoustic folk and americana, yet once the artist is identified as a follower of Jesus it is, unfortunately, simply called Christian rock.

The idea that rock and roll must be synonymous with rebellion was promoted by both the marketers of the music (sin sells better) and the conservative majority in the church. (Convincing believers that something is "of the devil" has often been the quickest way to protect the status quo within the church.) Certainly, rock has been a powerful tool for the spread of drug abuse, rebellion, lasciviousness, violence, and materialism, but over the past 30 years it has also been an effective tool for positive social change, education, inspiration, and even evangelism.

In fact, rock and roll is a direct descendant of blues, which is a direct descendant of gospel music. Rock really combined the sonic tension of the blues, the rhythm and groove of black gospel, and the melodic and lyrical simplicity of vocal pop music. So rock and the church are not as far apart as Marilyn Manson or the local antirock evangelist wants you to believe.

And what about the image of the rebel? Who was more rebellious than Jesus of Nazareth? He railed against authority, spoke against personal and religious corruption, and took a stick and a whip to the temple. He healed the sick on the Sabbath, and he encouraged people to walk away from their jobs, sell their belongings, and give their money to the poor. He even refused to remain dead, according to the account of the resurrection. He owned only the clothes on his back, had no home of his own, and got his tax money from the mouth of a fish. He was such a rebel that the religious leaders had him executed. Find one rocker with even a tenth of that rebellious fire. Yet Jesus has been reimagined in our postmodern world as a slow-moving, gentle, cryptic, and painstakingly polite rabbi, not the ruffian whom the San Hedrin thought was so dangerous. And what could be more risky in today's politically correct climate than to be labeled a Bible-believing Christian? From a certain perspective, Jesus and rock music are perfectly suited to each other.

Despite the seeming conflicts, the relationship has spawned over 30 years of strangely compelling yet mostly unheard music. There are hundreds of solo artists and bands; there have been thousands of concerts in venues from small clubs to church halls to parks to 50,000-seat arenas; and millions of eight-tracks, albums, cassettes, and CDs have been sold, yet most people have little knowledge of Christian rock. Some might remember Stryper, the multimillion-selling, yellow-and-black-spandex-clad, pop-metal band from the late 1980s. Others might think of multiplatinum-selling artist Amy Grant, who, though she has mastered the pop genre, would not consider herself a rocker. Or they might have heard of Jars of Clay, a more recent multiplatinum-selling alterna-pop band with Christian roots whose biggest hit, "Flood," draws on the imagery of baptism and Noah's Ark. Maybe they will recall the recent breakout success of the hard-music band POD, who have toured with Korn and many other big names in rock. Or maybe they will remember Bob Dylan's "Christian phase" or Joan Osbourne's hit "What If God Was One of Us?" or the Rolling Stones's "Shine a Light."

Most fans of rock would claim to know about Christian rock, but only about two percent would recognize names such as Smalltown Poets, Third Day, Burlap to Cashmere, The Waiting, All Star United, or Plumb — and those are the *big names*. Of that tiny minority, perhaps only five percent would own albums by Larry Norman, Resurrection Band, The Seventy Sevens, Daniel Amos, The Lost Dogs, or Stavesacre. Nonetheless, that five percent of fans has been enough of an audience to support Christian rock since it first appeared in the mid-1960s.

So how did Christian rock come about? Why has it been so marginalized by the larger pop culture? Will it ever reach larger audiences? *Raised by Wolves* answers these and other questions in detail. The personalities, foibles, and secret stories of Christian rock are discussed. The conflicts, as well as the miracles, fellowship, and growth, are explored. Whether you count yourself among the faithful or are just curious about these Jesus freaks who just won't fit in, this account will put you in the know.

I approach the history of Christian rock from a few angles. I have been exposed to this music since I was a small child. My mother became a Christian at the tail end of the Jesus Movement in 1973. Thus, from the age of three, I was exposed to the music of Love Song, Honeytree, Maranatha, and even a little Larry Norman. After a fairly tumultuous childhood, I found great solace in the rock strains of Resurrection Band, Petra, Jerusalem, Daniel Band, Daniel Amos, and DeGarmo and Key (among many others). When I "discovered" this underground scene, I couldn't believe it. Here were dozens of amazing bands that none of my friends had heard of, and I made it my agenda to let them know. I dragged them to concerts, I played tapes at school and church, and I even started writing my own songs. I had wanted to be the next Bob Dylan or John Lennon, but now I found myself looking up to artists such as Terry Taylor, Glenn Kaiser, Steve Taylor, and Mark Heard, who consistently cranked out amazing music knowing full well that they would not be heard by the world at large. It was the closest thing I had seen to artistic purity in rock and roll, and it rocked me to the core.

I remember with great fondness listening to WCRM nearly every night from nine o'clock to midnight when the station played rock and roll. I recall listening to the *Harvest Rock Show* and calling in requests. I remember bumming rides from my youth leader to the bookstore in Carol Stream (a few towns over from my home) that Mike Delaney stocked with hard-to-find music. I recall buying Charlie Peacock's *Lie Down in the Grass,* After the Fire's *ATF* (on a secular label no less), Weber and the Buzztones, and The Altar Boys' self-titled release from Mike in 1984. His store was worth the drive.

In 1986, I got a job at Wheaton Religious Gift Shop in Wheaton, Illinois. I did all the jobs required of me: I delivered candles, lifted merchandise from high shelves, cleaned the bathrooms, and vacuumed the floors. When I was done, I managed the music department, and that's what kept me going. The owner, Phil Taschetta, gave me great latitude in how I managed the department. I believed that it was the rock music, not the adult stuff, that would connect with most people, certainly most younger people. I seem to have been right. My predecessor, Matt Wielgos (also a fan of Delaney's department), had laid the groundwork, and I built on it. Within two years, the music department grew beyond its confines, and I approached Phil with my idea for an all-music store focused on the most progressive elements of the Christian music scene. It was called

True Tunes, and in 1989 it opened for business. We went on to launch a magazine, a mail-order catalog, and even a concert venue, Upstairs at True Tunes, that would host over 500 concerts. We have since settled on the Internet as our best way to keep telling this story. TrueTunes.com continues to dig deep into the underground to find the latest gems and to give honest critiques of the bigger names. We have also launched an Internet radio station that plays the best music from the past 30 years, including the earliest tunes to the brand-new stuff. In fact, you may want to tune in to www.truetunesradio.com and listen while you read.

I have also been writing, performing, and recording my own music since I was 16. I am a Christian and a musician. At times, various aspects of life, from romance to anger to politics to fear, have all found their way out of me through music. Yet I realized early on that no matter what I did I would be labeled a Christian artist as opposed to a songwriter who happens to be a Christian. I saw that in order to pursue a professional career in music I would have to either hide my faith or sign up for the farm leagues in the Christian market forever. I couldn't make that choice. Thus, I kept my music as an active side project and focused my professional efforts on breaking Christian music out of the "ghetto" in which it had become ensconced.

This book is a further effort to give Christian rock greater exposure. There are artists in the underground whom every fan of quality rock music should hear. Names such as Michael Roe, Terry Taylor, The Choir, and many others should be right up there with Brian Ferry, Tom Petty, and U2. With the success of Sixpence None the Richer, Creed, POD, Jars of Clay, and MxPx, maybe that time has come. The time has certainly come for the pioneers to get some long-overdue credit. There is a lot wrong with Christian rock, just like there is a lot wrong with mainstream rock, but there is a lot right with it too. This is the story of people of faith making rock and roll, music raised by wolves.

Acknowledgments

I owe thanks to many people: Mom for raising me with this music; Grandma Holton for buying me DeGarmo and Key's *Straight On* when I was eight; Dad for teaching me to play; the rest of the family for tolerating my obsession for music; Glenn Kaiser, Charlie Peacock, Randy Stonehill, Steve Taylor, and Dave Bunker for being examples and inspirations; Phil Taschetta for the chance to pursue this dream; Brian Heally, Mike Knott, Joe Taylor, Mike Pritzl, Matt Spransy, Bruce Brown, Marc Ludena, and Jeffrey Kotthoff for feedback, fact checking, and guidance; David Di Sabatino for his excellent unpublished thesis on the history of the

Jesus Movement; Randy Schoof, Dave Miller, and Scott Groleske for friendship and good counsel; Quincy Newcomb and Paul Emery; and the True Tunes readers and customers who have kept the dream alive all these years. Also, to all the artists, writers, players, and poets who "sew your heart onto their sleeve and wait for the axe to fall," as Bill Mallonee put it, thank you. Your work has made a difference whether or not the world knows it. Someone higher than us is watching, and I'm sure He is appreciative too.

Chapter 1

White Blossoms from Black Roots

What is rock and roll? What sonic or lyrical elements are required to cook this musical soup? How much is in the rhythm, the melodic structures, the attitude? Is it the devil's music? Did rock crawl out of some primordial swamp and evolve, or was it injected into humanity's bloodstream like a dose of speed? To discuss such a transformative and ubiquitous power as rock, a bit of sociological archaeology is required.

Because rock and roll is a relatively recent phenomenon, the answers are somewhat hard to come by. It's a challenge to rise above the din long enough to get any sort of historical perspective on it. What any fan does know is that rock is an almost magical synthesis of beat, melody, countermelody, and, of course, volume. But these elements alone will get us only halfway there. The drums can pound, the vocals wail, the bass pop, and the guitars shimmer, chunk, or soar. But what really sets rock apart as a genre of music is a mystical ingredient. What makes it so important is its heart.

Although rock and roll has spread to influence every part of the globe, it bears the immutable influence of its homeland. In a way, the birth and explosion of this "new music" parallel the American experience. In the United States, many cultures and peoples came together,

The "father" of Christian rock, Larry Norman, remains one of its most enigmatic figures.

often not without a fight, and created a new culture based on values such as liberty and equality (as well as greed and fear, to be honest). In a similar fashion, in the middle of the 20th century, in the middle-southern part of the country, art imitated culture. Suddenly, the music of the urban and southern African American community intersected with the commercial opportunity and yearning for identity growing within the increasingly disaffected white youth of America. In a way, this cultural collision and assimilation foreshadowed the integration of the white and black communities, which, as with the music, would not happen without a certain amount of fireworks.

Mass media were anathema to the status quo American Dream. Through radio and television, young white audiences gained access to the music of other social circles. Free radio offered popular music to all classes, not just the elite who could afford parlor musicians and cotillions. Just as the New World had allowed multiple cultures to melt into one, so too had broadcasting allowed people to hear music they wouldn't have had the option to listen to before. At the turn of the century, Scott Joplin laid the groundwork with a musical phenomenon known as ragtime. His music combined his classical training with a distinctively black feel, and, armed with the advent of the widespread distribution of sheet music (the first time that Americans in New York and San Francisco could hear and play the same new songs at the same time), he single-handedly created a new sound. As influential as sheet music was, no one was prepared for the enormous cultural shifts that took place when Edison perfected the phonograph or when Marconi invented the radio. Coupling Americans' desire for entertainment with easy-access radio and later television was like striking a match in a gas tank. Almost overnight, the vapors caught on fire.

During World War II, music bonded Americans who waited prayerfully for the safe return of their loved ones. The patriotic fervor that a war (almost) always brings on was heightened by the birth of pop anthems. Citizens huddled around radios for updates from Europe or the South Pacific. When the war ended, the party commenced. As an unexpected upside, the war effort brought the United States out of the Great Depression. Soldiers came home, jobs were plentiful, and cities belched millions of people into surrounding suburbs. Many people had their own cars, yards, and marital bliss. The result was obvious: 3.5 million more babies were born between 1946 and 1950 than in the five years prior. The baby boom was under way and would last until 1960. Prosperity ran rampant through the country, and national pride escalated to a fever pitch.

However, just before the end of the war, there was a handful of people too young to fight but old enough to notice what was happening around them. As the unbridled joy of mass consumerism gripped their parents' hearts and time, they found themselves with their own culture, their own worldview, and more time, freedom, and money than ever with which to pursue their interests. These young people laid the groundwork for what was to come: a cultural phenomenon whose impact would be rivaled in this century only by similar technological advances in war making.

Popular music, now easily available on radio, television, and wax, exploded. Genres splintered and merged. Big-band swing music made a comeback as dance halls filled to capacity. As public education became the norm (reducing the influence of churches) and parents busied themselves with the "pursuit of happiness," the generation gap was born. Everyone worried about the Korean War and the bomb, but adults and youth dealt with their fears very differently. Adults built bomb shelters and chanted patriotic mantras to themselves, while youth crammed into school gyms for sock hops. Youth had found their voice — or at least a voice that they could latch onto as their own.

The burgeoning entertainment industry tripped over itself with glee. A whole new market had been born. These youngsters had learned consumerism from their parents well. A new demographic was placed squarely on the lap of the relatively young entertainment industry. The movie producers and record companies just had to find something to sell.

Meanwhile, in the years since Joplin's ragtime entered the American soundscape, black music had blossomed. It's easy enough to trace all American black music to the spirituals sung by slaves in the fields. Although white people never respected the different African cultures enough to notice the differences, African American artists knew full well where their sounds came from. All the different voices of Africa, combined with Jesus' message of hope, endurance, and the meek inheriting the Earth, created a type of song known as the spiritual. Often improvised call-and-response songs, spirituals were aptly named, years later, because they were a direct manifestation of the human spirit. They proliferated throughout the country after the end of slavery. They took on different flavors in the north and south, but they always retained their basic character. When slavery ended and blacks were allowed more freedom to travel and to congregate, spirituals became infused with more earthy and secular lyrics and performance styles. Throughout the country, wherever large groups congregated, music clubs began to spring up. Dancing was the major pastime, and blues bands cranked out the tunes. Upbeat styles would become jump blues (largely inspiring the swing style uptown), and the slower, story-based songs that had been spirituals became lamentations. Freedom from slavery had only led to another kind of bondage. It had not brought the happiness that many had expected. The music became a document of social injustices as well as the more fleshly pursuit of fulfillment and fun. Thus was born the blues. Gospel music (spirituals) was for church on Sunday morning; the fun stuff was for Saturday night.

The advent of various recording and broadcasting technologies had a profound impact on the music of African Americans as well. As widespread print distribution had done for Joplin, records and radio brought the strains of blues and gospel music face to face with each other and the world. For the first time, people other than touring musicians could hear the differences between Chicago and Delta blues. Jazz music jumped from city to city, well beyond the small clubs that had nurtured it for decades. Perhaps most significant was that other people were listening. When a radio station in Chicago played Howlin' Wolf or Muddy Waters, it wasn't just blues fans on the south side who listened; many white kids listened too. At last, the "spirit" that had been missing from most white pop music could be heard in the suburbs. Records could be purchased and listened to again and again. The soulful music of blues and then R&B spread through America like a brush fire. Once it made its way from Memphis, New Orleans, St. Louis, and Chicago to the east and west coasts, it wasn't long before it jumped the ocean and caught the attention of British kids such as Mick Jagger, John Lennon, Jimmy Page, Eric Clapton, and Pete Townsend. But first it would fall on ears back where it started.

Bill Haley, a pudgy country singer playing the high school circuit, reinvented his style to keep up with the energy of the kids he was entertaining. By mixing boogie-woogie, country shuffles, and jump 'n' jive music and co-opting teen slang of the day such as "crazy, man, crazy" or "rock the joint," Haley connected with youth. His song "Shake, Rattle, and Roll" went on to sell more than a million singles.

Little Richard knew the music of the church and the juke joints. He combined the fervor of a Pentecostal preacher with the sexuality of a blues man. He added just enough showmanship to get the attention of the folks on the other side of the tracks. After a string of hits such as "Tutti Fruiti" and "Good Golly Miss Molly," Richard Penniman faced the conflict between his flamboyant rock and roll identity and his Christian faith by going to seminary and becoming a minister. Over the next 30-plus years, he frequently reappeared as Little Richard, but the gospel message was never far from his lips. He claimed to have taught John Lennon, Mick Jagger, and James Brown everything they knew. . . .

Chuck Berry followed (though who followed whom admittedly depends on the storyteller). Berry's lasting influence stemmed from his gritty double entendre lyrics (Berry was often referred to as a poet of the new generation) and what he did with his Gibson electric guitar. He took standard blues licks invented by cats such as Robert Johnson, Bo Diddley, and Muddy Waters, sped them up to sock hop speeds (Pentecostal church choirs sang fast and clapped along, whereas blues audiences danced slowly and nodded their heads), and formatted them into two-and-a-half-minute pop songs. His musical influence cannot be overstated. His own influences were plainly the music of his church and of the blues men.

These artists were the first to package the music of the African American community in a way that was attractive to both races. White kids, growing up in an increasingly integrated society (also thanks to broadcasting technology), were quick to embrace this new music with no name. First Jerry Lee Lewis brought the style of Chuck Berry and Little Richard to white schools and concert halls with a show that left people shocked. Then Buddy Holly took the basic rock and roll sound and added a vocal approach that had more in common with Texas country music. His nice-boy looks and horn-rimmed glasses connected with the suburban crowd easily. By the time Elvis Presley blended the vocal approach of the white southern gospel and pop stars with the energy and charisma of the blues and jump bands, the new genre was firmly ensconced in American culture. Alan Freed, a DJ in Cleveland, referred to the new music as rock and roll, borrowing the term from a 1947 R&B tune by "Wild Bill" Moore. Thus, to the dismay of parents everywhere, and to the delight of some shrewd businesspeople, rock and roll was born.

It soon went from rebellious social force to bankrollable institution to prepackaged commercial tripe. But no matter how many Wes Farrells there were cranking out Partridge family songs, or how many cheesy movies Elvis made, the spirit of rock and roll lived on. Although not always (or even often) the most commercially successful, each new morphing of rock music (at some point in the 1970s, we lost the "and roll" part) has had transcendent moments. That magic is still there. As the 20th century turned to the 21st, the world paused to look back on the previous 100 years. The "Song of the Century" (according to VH1) was "Satisfaction" by The Rolling Stones. How perfect that after 50 years of rock the defining song is among those that kicked it off. And how telling that the song echoes a spiritual tone similar to those of the old blues men and the spirituals. The longing for satisfaction (of one kind or another) is one thing that all people have in common.

The 1960s: The Perfect Incubator

By 1950, the United States was being pulled in many directions. World War II, the war to end all wars, was immediately followed by a new war in Korea. The Cold War with Russia had children learning to "duck and cover" in the event of a nuclear attack. Bomb shelters outnumbered swimming pools in many neighborhoods. The allure of the American

Dream was questioned in the early 1950s by a small but influential group of professors and students known as Beatniks. Although their answers came in the form of marijuana and LSD use and ultraprogressive art, the beat of their poetry found favor within the evolving youth culture.

The 1960s brought unprecedented social turmoil. And, as baby boomers developed a more sophisticated type of rock and roll, they moved from penning simple songs about chicks and cars to tackling the weightier issues of politics, race relations, war, and the general state of humanity. Boomer youth were not at peace with the world, and, empowered by new technological tools and the greater global awareness that they provided, they took matters into their own hands. Bonded by their music, many flatly refused the status quo American Dream. The bloom was off the postwar rose. The conflict in Vietnam made no sense to them and provided the perfect dividing line between one generation and its predecessor. Even the previously "safe" folk music became infused with the rebelliousness of the rock scene. Millions of young people believed that music and love would save the world. The gap between the generations became the size of the Grand Canyon.

Music became more important to the youth culture and more desperate sounding. Folk singers, who had always been lightheartedly subversive, stopped pulling their punches. The art scene, namely music and eventually movies, became the collective voice of a multiethnic generation bonded by anger and fear. In the black scene, James Brown brought intensity to R&B music, tackling social issues and love in the same breath. The white crowd listened to Bob Dylan, Joan Baez, Donovan, The Rolling Stones, and, of course, John Lennon and Paul McCartney. But even if a particular artist rose from one racial camp or another, for the first time on any widespread basis skin color blurred. Black kids dug the Stones, and white kids thrilled to James Brown, Stevie Wonder, Marvin Gaye, and The Temptations. Again art reflected the increasing integration forced on an often reluctant country. The music reflected the tension and at times amplified it.

This cultural mix gelled in 1967 with what became known as the Summer of Love. Music festivals such as the Newport Jazz Festival became the new church for kids coming of age in a strange world. The common enemy was identified as "the system." A government that sent young citizens off to die in the rice paddies of Southeast Asia, was wracked with political corruption, and was slow to implement its promises of racial integration and equality had let the boomers down. Leaders such as Martin Luther King Jr., Malcolm X, and Bobby Kennedy inspired the unsatisfied to carry on with patience and love. The thinnest thread of hope held the kids of Camelot together. But again shots rang out, and bullets hit their marks.

With their role models dead, the disillusioned generation turned to various sources for comfort. For some, it was activism; for others, it was drugs. The Vietnam War became the perfect focus of discontent for thousands. When troopers killed four students at a demonstration at Kent State University in Ohio, a distraught Neil Young saw the news on television and within minutes composed the song "Ohio," recorded immediately by Crosby, Stills, Nash, and Young. Within days, the song was heard on the radio. For the first time, rock music participated in the dissemination of, and the reaction to, a news item.

As the 1960s came to a close, rock was the biggest influence on baby boomers. The Woodstock festival in August 1969, replete with drug overdoses, free sex, and some of the most passionate and important music ever made, represented the zenith of the decade. By the end of that year, The Rolling Stones concert at the Altamont Speedway in California saw violence and death as one unfortunate result of the anarchy that youth seemed to want. As "Sympathy for the Devil" (ironically, not a pro-Satan song) played from the stage, a Hell's Angel who was part of the security team stabbed a fan to death. The 1960s closed with more questions than answers, and the despair would only increase in the early 1970s as all the protests did nothing to stop the war and prevent further political crookedness.

The 1960s provided many icons of deeper meaning. The film *Woodstock* shows a weary Jimi Hendrix playing a twisted version of the national anthem at dawn to a field littered with strung-out, mud-covered hippies. The young people were familiar with television stations beginning the broadcast day with a picture of the flag and the strains of "The Star-Spangled Banner." The irony was not lost on the crowd, no matter how stoned they were. The famous *Life*-magazine photo of a student placing a flower in the barrel of a soldier's rifle captured the story of the decade. The proliferation of visual and audio images had trained a generation to look for icons.

Throughout the 1960s, many youth looked to spirituality for answers. Some embraced "New Age" movements or the Nation of Islam. In 1967, The Beatles sought the wisdom of the guru Maharishi Mahesh Yogi and his Spiritual Regeneration movement. In fact, *Sergeant Pepper's Lonely Hearts Club Band* was intended to promote the New Age spiritualism and LSD fixation that they had picked up from the guru and would soon renounce (with the exception of Harrison). The album may be the most successful example of rock and roll being used to endorse a socio-spiritual agenda. It was both lambasted by some as a blatant ad campaign for drug use and praised by some as the same. History has been kind to the album and has focused more on the technical and musical accomplishments than on the lyrical or spiritual shortcomings. Fans eagerly bought it, making it one of the best-selling albums in history. Itself influenced by the Beach Boys' *Pet Sounds*, *Sergeant Pepper's Lonely Hearts Club Band* had a huge influence on pop music and even fashion.

What about the place of Christianity in the music scene of the 1960s? In the previous decade, it was common for gospel-based songs to be heard on the radio. Pop music in the 1950s was diverse: listeners could hear Tennessee Ernie Ford, Elvis Presley, Chubby Checker, and Montovani on the charts simultaneously. It was common for pop artists to record religious songs. Elvis did it, Checker did it, and Pat Boone did it. It was part of the 1950s mind-set. That all changed by the time 1960 rolled around.

Between 1960 and 1964, no significant inspirational hits, with the exception of Christmas songs, were found on the pop charts. Then came the mop-tops. Arriving in America like an invading army, The Beatles seemingly changed pop music overnight. The new music was still the "feel-good" variety, but the borders were being stretched. As the protest movement gathered steam, and the new spirituality gained a foothold, Jesus began to reappear, though not always in complimentary ways.

In 1964, The Impressions had a hit with "Amen" and then in 1965 with the seminal "People Get Ready." Also in 1965, Elvis sang "Crying in the Chapel." But the biggest moment was when The Byrds covered Pete Seeger's version of Ecclesiastes 3. "Turn Turn Turn" made it to the top spot in October of that year. It has had an amazing life since then, being covered dozens of times by both secular and Christian artists. Its most significant contribution at the time may have been that, for the first time in years, the Bible was being sourced for answers. Many hippies didn't recognize the source of the words as they sang along, but Christians did. Since the music industry was largely about copying other hits, a string of religious-based songs soon followed (one standout was "Get Together" by The Youngbloods).

In the late 1960s, several pop songs actually used the name of Jesus. Until then, inspirational songs referred to him as "Lord" or "Him" or some such substitute. In 1968, Simon and Garfunkle had a hit with a song from the controversial movie *The Graduate*. "Mrs. Robinson" contained the verse "Here's to you Mrs. Robinson, Jesus loves you more than you will know." The reference was certainly tongue in cheek, but the precedent had been set, and many bands rushed to keep up with it. Norman Greenbaum's "Spirit in the Sky" boasted "I've got a friend in Jesus" (though it also contained the theologically suspect "never been a sinner, I never sin"). Greenbaum explained in interviews that he was not a Christian and had just used a common phrase. That renunciation didn't keep Jesus freaks from claiming the song as their own, though.

Perhaps the grandest example was the musical *Jesus Christ Superstar*.

In the early 1960s, two Brits composed a 15-minute piece for a boys' choir. The piece was called *Joseph and the Amazing Technicolor Dreamcoat*. The composers, Andrew Weber and Tim Rice, further mined the Bible for material when they tackled the story of Jesus in 1969. Both had grown up attending the Church of England, but neither accepted the truth of the Bible, so they adopted the perspective of Judas Iscariot as the narrator. The musical basically served as a sort of nihilistic passion play, ending with Christ dead, not resurrected. The title song, "Superstar," was recorded by Murray Head and asked the question "Jesus Christ, Superstar, do you think you're who they say you are?" Although the composers' answer seemed to be a resounding no, *Jesus Christ Superstar*, after selling millions of copies and being performed to both critical and commercial success on Broadway, again brought Jesus into the vernacular of the hippie scene. The success continued with a movie, and its momentum carried it well into the 1970s.

At the same time, FM radio stations began to pop up around the country, bringing with them the advent of album-oriented radio. No longer were listeners limited to a handful of top-40 songs. This format, inspired by the deepening of lyrics in rock and roll, was perfectly suited for more complex and noncommercial developments in the music. Groups such as Pink Floyd may not have had many top-40 hits, but their album *Dark Side of the Moon* remains one of the top selling of all time. During this deepening of the rock waters, several major artists dabbled with Jesus in their lyrics just as they dabbled with the occult. Possibly sarcastic jabs at those who decried the amoral rock lifestyle, possibly genuinely searching songs, these tunes became a dominant force on AOR radio (Album Oriented Radio) in the early 1970s.

The influence of The Beatles on almost every aspect of pop culture in the 1960s cannot be overstated. But the band didn't present a united front when it came to Jesus. First, John Lennon flippantly commented on the hysteria over his band by saying "We're bigger than Jesus." When his comment blew up in his face, he explained that he'd meant no offense. In retrospect, he was probably right. At that point, all of pop culture, over which The Beatles reigned, was bigger than Jesus. It was just that polite society didn't want to admit it. Later, for his first solo album, Lennon wrote and recorded the song "God," in which he declared all the things he did not believe in, including God and The Beatles.

Then, in "The Ballad of John and Yoko," he repeated the line "They're gonna crucify me." Then, of course, there was "Imagine." Paul McCartney penned "Let It Be," which, when enhanced by the live performance from the film of the same name, conjured up many religious images. "When I find myself in times of trouble, Mother Mary comes to me. . . ." Of course, he explained that he was not referring to the Holy

Mother, but he might as well have been. While Ringo Starr was satisfied to get by with "a little help from his friends," George Harrison found his spiritual inspiration in the teachings of Maharishi Mahesh Yogi and penned "My Sweet Lord." Although full of the word *hallelujah*, popularized by some of the praise choruses of the 1960s, the song was in homage to the Indian god Krishna.

The Rolling Stones, anything but a Jesus band, offered several biblically inspired tunes between 1969 and 1975. "Shine a Light," "I Am Waiting," and even "Sympathy for the Devil" all tap into the Jesus thing somewhat.

Bob Dylan recorded numerous spiritual songs even before becoming a Christian in the late 1970s. Most notable may have been "Knockin' on Heaven's Door," which has been covered by many groups, including The Byrds and Guns N' Roses. Then there was "All along the Watchtower," "Blowin' in the Wind," and so on.

Argent's power rock tune "God Gave Rock and Roll to You" was a modest hit. In the mid-1970s, it was covered by Christian rock pioneers Petra and brought fully into the realm of Jesus music. Imagine the Christian kids' surprise when Kiss covered the song in the 1980s! Many thought they were covering a Petra song.

Leon Russell dove deeply into both Christian lyrics and a gospel sound in the early 1970s. "Stranger in a Strange Land," "Roll Away the Stone," and "Prince of Peace" all sounded like they were straight out of a tent meeting. Russell was not a believer, but he found the lyrics inspiring.

Roger McGuinn of The Byrds (who had a huge hit in 1967 with "Turn Turn Turn") turned in another Jesus song in 1969 for the *Easy Rider* album called "Jesus Is Just Alright." The Byrds' version was not a big hit, but when The Doobie Brothers covered it a few years later it was huge. (In the 1990s, Christian rappers/rockers DC Talk covered it again.)

Eric Clapton seemed to be fascinated with Christian symbolism as well. He named one of his bands Blind Faith and with it wrote and recorded the hit "In the Presence of the Lord." At the time, Clapton said that the song was about finding a quiet place in the country where the police couldn't catch him with his drug paraphernalia. A few years later, however, he recorded a solo album called *One in Every Crowd* that reflected a time when the guitar legend did embrace the Christian faith. His music has often touched on spiritual themes since then.

As long as Jesus wasn't taken too seriously in the 1960s, he was cool. Singing about him was one thing; however, if it became known that an artist really believed in him, dismissal by the rock and roll mainstream soon followed. In this way, the "free speech" element in the rock community practiced a type of social censorship. Other spiritual influences were assimilated into the rock vernacular, but rock stemming from a Judeo-

Christian worldview was quickly labeled (rarely by the artists themselves) as Jesus music, contemporary Christian music, gospel rock, or Christian rock. It became the only pop music variant labeled by its lyrical content.

At the same time, the church was far from accepting blue jeans, long hair, and electric guitars as legitimate tools for the expansion of the kingdom. Youth musicals and praise choruses were contemporary enough for it. Some evangelical leaders believed that Christian rock was even more dangerous than secular rock; others quoted obscure sources as proof that the beat of rock music was demonic. To many antirock activists in the church, Jesus music, especially the rockier type, was a more frightening enemy than any they had faced (perhaps because other societal ills, such as prostitution, drinking, and card playing, were kept safely out of the church). The Jesus rockers, ignorant of church politics and superstitions, couldn't understand why every church didn't open its doors for concerts and revivals.

Thus, by the end of the 1960s, purveyors of Jesus music found themselves fighting a two-front war. Christian rock was an infant in those days. One of its parents, pop culture, decided that it was irrelevant and old-fogeyish and kicked it to the curb. The other parent, the church, saw too much of "the world" in it and was frightened by it. The young musicians, wanting nothing more than to use their music to reach a hurting world, thus found themselves orphaned. They were left to be raised by wolves.

And they persisted, setting out to bring Jesus, if not traditional Christianity, into the discussions of the 1960s. As other spiritual searches proved to be fruitless, more and more people were willing to check this Jesus out. In the midst of the storm, a new movement was born that would shake both the tenets of the 1960s counterculture and the pillars of the traditional church.

A Movement Is Born

As the search for peace sent people in many directions, some found answers in a figure who'd been part of the American landscape all along. But when millions who had embraced the hippie counterculture turned to Jesus, they got the attention of everyone. The mainstream media chronicled the revival (about three years late) with great concern and speculation. Dubbing it the Jesus Movement (or the Jesus People Movement), media giants such as *Time*, *Life*, and *Look* magazines and the major television networks found the surface contradiction between Jesus and hippies fascinating. Unlike religious revivals of the past, this movement focused not on the external attributes of Christianity but on the personal

Phil Madeira is one of the most sought-after studio musicians and song writers in the business.

experience of getting saved. In fact, the Jesus freaks looked just like the peace freaks and the student radicals. With long hair, blue jeans, and guitar in hand, these young converts shattered the image of the buttoned-up, conservative Christian.

There are many theories about who started the Jesus Movement and about where it began, but close examination shows that, like other spiritual renewals before it, it had numerous streams that contributed to one major river. Although a simultaneous phenomenon across the country, the hippie movement largely originated in California, so the beginnings of the Jesus Movement are likely to be found there too. The movement was primarily sparked by established Christians who embraced Jesus' "great commission" (from Matthew 28.19–20) to "go and make disciples of all nations, baptizing them in the name of the Father and of the Son and of the Holy Spirit and teaching them to obey everything I have commanded you." These missionaries, instead of trekking to foreign lands, felt called to the communes, campuses, and farms of the counterculture movement. Many even joined some of the communal hives (or opened their own), offering the radical message of Jesus in a language that the hippies easily understood.

The Jesus Movement drew both unchurched members of the counterculture and churched youth who gravitated toward the movement because of its cultural hipness. The Roman Catholic Church was among the first of the Christian churches to use modern music in outreach. In the early 1960s, Catholic youth artist Ray Repp composed the first "Folk Mass." Shortly thereafter, "youth musicals" couched positive messages in almost hip ways. In England, some churches used and even recorded religious music set to what they called "the big beat." And as far back as the late 1940s Ralph Carmichael had tried to make the music of the church more contemporary. He began to compose some of the youth musicals and, along with several traveling "Up with People"-style musical troupes (e.g., Cam Floria's Continentals, The Spurrlows), was gradually warming the churches to the concept of going to the youth instead of waiting for them to come to church.

For the most part, though, the church shunned the real gritty music. Especially in evangelical circles, where the simple message of the Jesus Movement really came from, hostility toward rock and roll, and even toward the Jesus Movement itself, was vehement. The "straights" saw rock as the cause of drug abuse, violence, and general mayhem in America. They couldn't see that society was falling apart under its own weight and that the youth culture was merely the rotten fruit falling from a sick tree. Born suddenly were urban legends about witch doctors from the jungle hearing rock and saying that it sounded like their tribal attempts to call spirits out of the trees. There was talk about the droning beat hypnotizing youth to engage in unspeakable acts of violence and lasciviousness. And some concerned Christians looked for evidence of Beelzebub in satanic symbols and "backward masking" (messages supposedly heard when an album was played backward). So, to many churches and religious leaders, the Jesus Movement was a threat. As soon as the first few bands — All Saved Freak Band, Agape, and Love Song, along with solo artists such as Larry Norman and Randy Stonehill — hit the scene, preachers rose up to call them twisted. Rock, to them, was the devil's music, and most established churches refused to embrace the mix of rock and faith.

Bill Gothard, one popular fundamentalist teacher, actually preached that the syncopated 4/4 beat of rock and roll collided with the natural rhythm of the human heart and would therefore make listeners sick. Gothard also believed that, any time a song faded out instead of resolving itself naturally, it promoted ongoing anarchy. Minor keys, loud drums, and nonspecific lyrics were strictly of the evil one. Gothard's recipe for healthy music called for a dominant major-key melody. Harmony (only if absolutely necessary) was to be strictly in major-key formations and noticeably quieter than the melody. And the rhythm must be in 4/4 time, with the first and third beats emphasized slightly. Since his prescription rarely existed even among adult contemporary music, he was happy to offer his own recordings for sale.

Another famous evangelist, Jimmy Swaggart (the cousin of Jerry Lee Lewis), came down hard on Christian rock. He preached of its evil influences for years. Ironically, he had recorded several records that would have qualified as evil under his own definitions. Bob Larson, a Christian radio personality, spent the early years blasting Christian rock as an evil compromise with the world. In the 1980s, he would reverse his stance, and by the end of that decade he actually went on tour with the famously occultic metal band Slayer. And David Wilkerson, a significant part of the youth revival of the 1960s through Teen Challenge, had no love for modern Christian music. Throughout the 1970s, he went out of his way to attack it as a bad, even demonic, influence on young people. In 1980, he recanted his antirock sentiments in a booklet entitled *Confessions of a Rock Hater*. Unfortunately, a few years later, he would publish *Set the Trumpet to Thy Mouth*, which reinstituted his ban on Christian rock.

Often the antirock pastors and evangelists castigated specific artists. At one seminar, a clip of Glenn Kaiser from the hard rock Rez Band from a concept video that the band had made was presented as the band advocating a raucous rock lifestyle full of violence and money. The teacher didn't relate to the audience that the clip was taken out of context and that the band was part of a Christian commune and didn't even own a car or a house of their own. This type of attack was particularly problematic because negative rumors often travel much faster than the truth. The seminar reached about 20,000 people in one day, more than Rez Band would have played for in a year.

Early Christian rockers found solace in the stories of an earlier culture shaker for Jesus, Martin Luther, who faced the same kinds of attacks in his day. In fact, when Luther came under fire for adapting bar tunes into hymns, he asked, "Why should the devil have all the good tunes?"

The musicians also found comfort in Jesus himself. In his day, he was a sort of hippie, and, when presented as an antiestablishment radical who owned only the clothes on his back and preached about truth and love, he connected with the 1960s crowd. What could be more countercultural than suggesting that people "die to themselves, that they may live," or "consider others more worthy than yourself." The one-way sign (an index finger pointed upward with a cross beside it) and the icthus fish (actually an early church sign used to identify followers of Christ when Christianity was outlawed) easily supplanted the peace signs of two fingers and the crow's foot. The new converts fluently used hippie slang. When someone had an emotionally reaffirming time of worship, he or she was "high on Jesus." The Messiah was described as "the rock that doesn't roll." Stripped of the pomposity of formal religion, the message of Jesus made perfect sense to the seekers. A revival broke out, and soon converted hippies began to minister alongside (or in place of) the original missionaries.

In San Francisco (ground zero for the counterculture), several outreaches opened in quick succession. A church opened its Sunday school rooms, and for nine months a drop-in food-and-ministry center called The Soul Inn preached the gospel in the middle of the Haight-Ashbury scene. Shortly thereafter, Ted and Liz Wise, who'd founded one of the first hippie communes, grew tired of the drug scene and found their way to Jesus — Liz by way of her former church, Ted by a more radical intervention by God. (Ted believed God came to him during a drug trip and commanded him to stop what he was doing, go to church, and speak His words to everyone. His conversion was not altogether unlike St. Paul's conversion on the road to Damascus.) Along with three other couples with similarly empty experiences in the hippie culture, the Wises founded The Living Room, a coffeehouse ministry on Page Street, one block from the famous intersection of Haight and Ashbury. Originally, the young converts had sought to blend into the Baptist church that Liz had attended, but they had soon realized that they needed something different. With the support of the local Baptist church, The Living Room had an enormous impact at the core of the hippie movement.

Seeing the example of the early Christian church as recorded in the Acts of the Apostles in the New Testament, the group bought a house in nearby Novato and began a Christian commune later referred to as The House of Acts. The founders remember a young Robin Williams hanging out there as well as a few visits from the infamous Charles Manson. They also reached a young artist from Berkeley named Lonnie Frisbee. Frisbee eventually migrated south to the Los Angeles area and joined a tiny church called Calvary Chapel in Costa Mesa.

Southern California, and Orange County in particular, was in quite a conundrum at the time. On one hand, the area had deep conservative roots and a thriving middle class. On the other, it was increasingly populated (especially the beaches) with longhairs. One small nondenominational church in Costa Mesa had a pastor named Chuck Smith, who felt called to reach the new generation. Although Smith wasn't a longhair himself, and he didn't always "get it," he desperately wanted to bring the message of Jesus to the kids he saw all around his community. By recruiting Frisbee as an unofficial youth pastor, Smith's church exploded, eventually needing to erect circus tents for its services. Bible studies and midweek worship services became the norm, and Frisbee began bringing bands in for concerts. One band, called Love Song, was searching spiritually and was interested in Jesus. A hitchhiker told them about Calvary Chapel. They located the church, found Jesus there, and got baptized. In a recent video retrospective of those years, Chuck Girard, one of the band's members, reminisced that they knew very little theology then; in fact, they went out and got stoned to celebrate the baptisms. Love Song, with their hair long and their music straight from the folk-rock tradition, became a big part of the Calvary Chapel scene. Their music, along with that of other hippies for Jesus, became known as Jesus music.

Meanwhile, in Hollywood, a flamboyant evangelist named Arthur Blessit was claiming the Sunset Strip as his own. Blessit opened a 24-hour nightclub as a hostel for displaced youth seeking excitement on the strip. He brought in bands to play free concerts and even recorded some music of his own. His approach was a little over the top. Taking Paul's admonition to "become all things to all people so that some may be saved," Blessit decked himself out in full hippie regalia. His approach was simplistic, and he had a flair for the dramatic, but his impact was significant. He even convinced club owners and concert promoters to let him get up on stage and preach, leading several people to Jesus in the process. One such convert was folk superstar Barry McGuire, riding the wave of prosperity brought on by his runaway hit "Eve of Destruction." McGuire, after having left a successful career with the folk ensemble The New Christy Minstrels, scored big with his song, which is considered the epitome of 1960s protest music.

Also in Hollywood, Dr. Don Williams became the youth pastor of First Presbyterian Church. In an effort to connect to the kids, Williams opened the first music-based Christian coffeehouse in Hollywood. The Salt Company became a huge influence in the Jesus Movement of southern California. Many of the earliest bands and solo artists played at The Salt Company, and many of the youth who frequented the place went on to start similar ministries around the country. The neutral territory that a coffeehouse offered, even if it was located in a church, seemed to provide enough of a difference for hippies to feel comfortable. Such coffeehouses became a common feature of the Jesus Movement as hundreds, if not thousands, sprang up in church basements and storefronts all over the world.

Another common feature of the movement, perfected in many ways by Williams, was the invention of Jesus papers. Borrowing the idea from hippies, who did not trust mainstream media and had gravitated toward radical "rags" handed out at rallies and coffeehouses to get their news, Jesus freaks used the format to put their beliefs and passions in print. Many Jesus papers existed, usually only regional in scope. Williams used his intellectual background and doctorate to edit and publish the *Alternative*, geared toward college students more than street folks. Other papers targeted druggies, street bums, and flower children. One prominent Jesus paper published by the Jesus People USA community in Chicago still

Terry Scott Taylor debuted with his band Daniel Amos in 1974.

exists. Since 1984, in fact, *Cornerstone Magazine* has sponsored the largest and best Jesus rock festival in the country.

From its origins in California, the Jesus Movement spread out in many directions. In 1967, Scott Ross, a rock and roll DJ in New York, embraced the movement wholeheartedly (he also started a commune called Love Inn in a barn) and wanted to use his experience to reach people. After approaching Pat Robertson of the Christian Broadcasting Network (CBN), Ross was hired to specialize in reaching youth. Although facing serious protest from Christians who thought that even the folk music by Peter, Paul, and Mary was communist, Ross pressed on. His radio show, first broadcast on five stations in New York state and then syndicated nationwide on up to 175 stations, featured Jesus music and top secular hits with spiritual content. His show became the first Christian rock radio show (though the term "Christian rock" wouldn't be coined for some time). Since there were really no Jesus rock albums at the time (the bands playing the music focused on concerts and rarely had either time or money to record their music), Ross played Jesus-based pop songs that were increasingly on the charts.

In 1971, a sort of summit of Jesus People leaders occurred in the Pacific Northwest. From that meeting, Jim Palosaari and his wife, Sue, were sent on a scouting mission and landed in Milwaukee. Their initial group of seven swelled to over 150 full-time members. They bought a hospital building and set up Milwaukee Discipleship Training Center. Eventually, the group split into four smaller groups in order to proselytize better. The Palosaaris took the rock band that they had formed, Sheep, and answered a call to go to Europe. They toured through Scandinavia and eventually settled in London. A few years later, they returned to the Pacific Northwest. One of the other groups, headed by John Herrin Sr., began traveling by bus around the country and setting up concerts with their band, Charity (which later became Resurrection Band). They eventually landed in Chicago under the name Jesus People USA (JPUSA), where they exist to this day. The other groups eventually faded after a couple of years.

The movement continued to spread throughout the early 1970s. In California, Calvary Chapel launched Maranatha! Music as a record label and coordinated massive Jesus music concerts. The momentum on the East Coast created by CBN and Scott Ross led to large concerts at Madison Square Garden.

But the defining moment for the movement came in 1972 when Campus Crusade (a student outreach founded by Bill Bright in 1951 that was trusted much more by the established churches than the impetuous street ministries) held its World Student Congress on Evangelism in Dallas (also known as Explo '72). Seminars and classes filled area churches the week of June 17–22, but the whole crowd of about 80,000 people crammed into the Cotton Bowl each night for music and speaking by Billy Graham and other major names. Each night, various musical groups of all styles performed as well. The climax came the last day of the event

Resurrection Band combined the Gospel message with serious hard blues-rock.

at Woodall Rogers Parkway when 250,000 people showed up for a day of music. Performers included Larry Norman, Randy Matthews, Johnny Cash, Danny Lee and the Children of Truth, Barry McGuire, André Crouch and the Disciples, Kris Kristofferson, and many others. What had been at one time a loose network of Jesus music artists instantly gelled into an industry (for better or worse). It was a huge boon for the artists, many of whom developed international followings that day. Campus Crusade legitimized the Jesus Movement at Explo '72.

However, with the movement reaching the mainstream church as resoundingly as it did that week, Explo '72 marked the beginning of the end of the Jesus Movement. Churches started to accept the milder Jesus music, soon to be referred to as "contemporary Christian music," though the rockier stuff was still suspect. Gospel record labels and distributors made the music available across the nation. The hippie movement was over, and thus the streetier aspects of the Jesus Movement were no longer required. Many communes continued on into the 1980s, but the national fervor of the Jesus Movement soon passed.

How did the Jesus Movement fare across the Atlantic? Although initiated by some of the same people, the movement was different in the United Kingdom than in the United States. Perhaps it was because the British were already in such a post-Christian mind-set, but non-Christians were much more interested in the music and the goings-on of the Christians, and the Christians were far less worried about rock music and the like.

Palosaari's group ended up staying in Europe longer than they had expected. The plan had been to take their rock band and a musical called *Lonesome Stone* on tour through Europe. A rock opera in the tradition of *Hair* and *Tommy*, the musical was about one man's experience of coming to faith in Christ in the turbulent 1960s. *Lonesome Stone* was a big deal. With slide shows, pyrotechnics, dramatic lighting, and an emphasis on production, the simple message was driven home with punch. The group of longhairs seemed to be on to something.

After taking the show to Finland, Sweden, and Germany, the group ended up in England, where their ministry came to the attention of a wealthy Englishman who wanted to see young people in England impacted in the way that he had heard young people in the United States and across Europe had been. They set up the *Lonesome Stone* musical at the famous Rainbow Theatre and played on nights between shows by Eric Clapton, Paul McCartney, and Van Morrison. The production got great reviews in the secular press and drew significant crowds. Sheep recorded two soundtrack-type albums and developed a considerable following. At one outreach, a member of the cast of *Hair* became a Christian and then joined the cast for the musical.

An idea struck several members of the community. They would put together a Christian music and arts festival. With Woodstock still floating in their memories, they had a grand vision to present the rock opera alongside concerts by all of the Jesus music bands in the area. They called the event the Greenbelt Music and Arts Festival, and it was organized by members of the commune, including group member Henry Huang and a member of Sheep named Matt Spransy. The event was a huge success and began a run that continues to this day. Greenbelt became ground zero for artistic Christians in and around London.

Mere weeks after the first Greenbelt festival, the cast and crew of *Lonesome Stone* headed back to America to tour the states. Unfortunately, after only two months, the group was $20,000 in debt. They shut down the production and went their separate ways. Huang ended up at the Jesus People USA community in Chicago, where 10 years later he would head up the first Cornerstone festival.

Some estimates say that during the Jesus Movement over 800 communal-living experiments sprang up in North America. Estimates of changed lives reach three million. Hundreds of ministers took to street ministries, hip churches, musical outreaches, or communes. Several churches began then and exist to this day, many having become full-blown denominations. As the 1960s gave way to the 1970s, most Americans respected the movement as a legitimate expression of Christian faith. (Of course, a number of preachers, including the television variety, were thrilled to have something to whip up their congregations over, and Jesus freaks made a good target. It was also common for comedians or musicians to poke fun at the incongruous freaks.) Most mainstream evangelical churches now use music in their Sunday services that would have been unacceptable 30 years ago. Even the most conservative worship music these days is more aggressive than the most progressive church music was in the 1960s.

A whole industry designed to sell contemporary Christian music sprang from the embers of the Jesus Movement. But to many, it was the chemistry of rock and roll, complete with its dissonance, syncopation, and urgency, that most closely resembled their passion for Jesus. Although never achieving mainstream success, and rarely even achieving church-wide success, a few street-level Christian rockers managed to get the word out by playing free concerts in city parks, selling albums from the backs of station wagons, and finding fellowship wherever they could.

The Three Waves of Christian Rock

The development of Christian rock can easily be divided into three waves. The first wave spans from the Jesus Movement to the end of the

1970s. The era was characterized by a lack of support from both the mainstream music scene and the established church.

The first wave began with a bang. With the turmoil of the 1960s sending people looking for answers, and the vigor of a younger-faced church that believed the end was near, the chemistry was just right. Within a few years of its inception, Jesus music was drawing huge crowds at festivals, and recordings were circulating worldwide. The explosive growth of the early days was directly related to the Jesus Movement. The music outpaced the ability of either the established church or the music industry to control it. As the fervor of the movement wound down after 1973, the nascent Christian music industry took root.

Since Christian rock was almost certain to preclude one from fame, prosperity, or even respect within the community of believers, it did not attract poseurs. The unsophisticated Christian artists of the 1960s and 1970s believed that they had no choice but to communicate the message of Christ in the language that was most natural to them. The early artists had a passion for what they were doing that is unrivaled to this day. Knowing that they were likely to be chastised by the church, and certain to be ignored (at best) by the mainstream music business, these young musicians went underground, and their "ministries" were as spontaneous as their music, often with little or no superstructure around them. With a few notable exceptions (Jesus People USA or Resurrection Band), they wandered the country, selling low-budget recordings at their concerts. They certainly weren't in it for the money; in fact, many considered selling their music inappropriate and instead asked for donations. And they weren't in it for fame or power. They were just mixing lyrics that reflected their worldview with music that they enjoyed. Rock and faith: it was a blend that made sense to them if not to others.

The second wave roughly spans the 1980s. By the first few years of the decade, several of the youth pastors of the Jesus Movement had become head pastors of growing churches in southern California. In other parts of the country, too, head pastors began to notice that, when they allowed rock bands to play in their churches, many young people showed up. Since the music proved to be useful, the church began to welcome Christian rockers into its midst. Yet the "wolf factor" began to appear, for it takes a certain amount of ego for anyone to go on stage and rock out. Mixing rockers' egos with the values and expectations of the church was not always successful, and that dynamic made the 1980s an interesting time in the development of Christian rock.

The third wave spans the next decade. By 1991, Nirvana had bumped Michael Jackson from Billboard's top spot, and "alternative" music had officially become mainstream, much to the dismay of many parents. Scores of bands explored new wave, postmodern, and alternative musical styles and were called up for service. The mainstream church's reluctance to embrace rock and roll as a valid tool was relegated to its extremely conservative members. Retail distribution opened up a bit as mainstream companies such as EMI and Warner Brothers started buying Christian record companies. Hundreds of new bands were introduced, and everything from punk to ska to rave was booming out of youth rooms and Christian college dorms like never before.

The third wave brought about the fastest growth in the history of Christian rock, which is now a multimillion-dollar industry. Some bands had record deals before their members were old enough to vote. As the decade came to a close, Sixpence None the Richer, a longtime favorite of the thinking Christian music fan, hit it big with a simple love song called "Kiss Me" that peaked at third spot on Billboard's Hot 100 chart and reached first spot on many other charts. Shortly after this success, another Christian band, San Diego's POD, also exploded. Meanwhile, in the mainstream industry, songs of faith and searching came from the classic rock band Creed and even from the snarling lips of shock-rocker Alice Cooper. It has taken 30 years, but Christian rock has finally come into its own.

Chapter 2

The First Wave (1966-79)

In the 1960s, rock and roll, especially the edgy and driving kind, was primarily a live experience. With recording costs high and quality low, bands preferred to play live. Records were more or less souvenirs. Increasing sonic quality brought albums into their golden age in the early 1970s, but prior to that rock was about concerts.

Accordingly, hundreds of bands in the 1960s, some with huge followings, never recorded their music. The dawn of Christian artists playing rock and roll is shrouded by this fact. Several bands and solo acts took to coffeehouses, parks, garages, and nightclubs with their guitars, amps, and Bibles, but we have no record of their music. A few managed to record some songs, though they were often fairly crude and no where near as impressive as their live cousins.

In the aftermath of Vatican II, when the Roman Catholic church "modernized" by allowing Mass to be said in languages other than Latin and by allowing music to be used to reach the unchurched community, a wave of folk and even rock Masses swept across the country. Although not often recorded (at least not very well), they were occurring as early as 1966 and are many people's earliest memories of modern music associated with the church.

Michael Roe came to prominence in 1983 as the front man for the new-rock band The Seventy Sevens.

In England, a few "gospel beat" albums were right in step with the "teen beat" sound before the first Jesus rock albums appeared in the United States. The first record of Christian rock came from a band called The Crusaders in 1966. The album jacket proclaimed that "Now, for the first time, God is praised in song through the most contemporary musical expression: The Beat." The title of the record was *Make a Joyful Noise with Drums and Guitars*, and that's exactly what The Crusaders did, in a campy 1960s pop way.

In 1968, Zondervan Records released the debut album by a Maryland-based pop rock band called Sons of Thunder. Then, in 1969, two more records appeared, Larry Norman's psychedelic gospel debut *Upon This Rock*, on the mainstream Capitol label, and John Fisher's streety folk-pop *Cold Cathedral*, released on a small Catholic label. But there were numerous underground bands and even some obscure home-spun recordings circulating.

Mike Johnson was a Chicago native whose bluesy guitar chops landed him a gig with the Mike Bloomsfield Blues Band (which included "Memphis" Charlie Musclewhite). Johnson recorded one record with that band for CBS. After a dramatic conversion to Christianity, he began to use his music as an outreach tool. He formed a new band called The Exkursions, who blended heavy blues-rock with fusion and psychedelic influences. They toured the country from 1968 to 1970 and released one independent album in that time. Johnson went on to record numerous mellower records, both as a solo act and with his wife, Karen, but The Exkursions ranks among the first Christian rock bands in the country.

Three-quarters of the way across America, Fred Caban was somewhat of a local guitar hero in Azusa, California. When he graduated from high school in 1968, his band, with a heavy blues style reminiscent of Hendrix and Cream, developed a following along the southern California coast. That year, he and his bandmates stumbled upon the Lightclub in Huntington Beach. After hearing of Jesus there, Caban and another member accepted him as their savior. They were baptized the next day.

A few months later, back home in Azusa, the band reformed under the name Agape (Greek for "God's love") and began playing their old haunts with a new passion. A number of young people soon came to faith in Christ through Caban's preaching and playing. The heaviest band on the scene, Agape wasn't even aware of the larger Jesus Movement happening around the country. They recorded two albums, *Gospel Hard Rock* in 1971 and *Victims of Tradition* in 1972. Both albums became classics of the genre. Good copies of either have sold for well over $150. When Agape saw the birth of the Christian music industry and the trend toward separating Christian bands from secular bands, they felt that their calling was over and unplugged their amps in 1974.

One of the strangest stories in the history of Christian rock involves the mysterious Ohio band All Saved Freak Band. Founded under the name Preacher and the Witness in 1968 by pastor Larry Hill, the band was popular in Cleveland and was close to the action during the Kent State Massacre that year. Hill, who started out as an Assembly of God pastor and antirock preacher, left the denomination and started his own church based on some visions he'd had regarding the end of the world.

Fellow Ohio native Glenn Schwartz had been the lead guitarist for The James Gang (replaced by Joe Walsh in 1968 after Schwartz quit) and had played and recorded with Pacific Gas and Electric on their smash hit "Are You Ready." Schwartz had been called one of the top five blues guitarists in the world. He had a radical conversion at Arthur Blessit's His Place nightclub in Hollywood. On returning home and being released from an insane asylum to which he'd been committed by his family, he joined Hill's "church" and began playing with the band. The band changed their name to All Saved Freak Band and developed a style that combined blues, folk, and Celtic strains. They recorded several albums independently before disbanding in the late 1970s.

Hill's church became increasingly isolated from the greater Christian community, and his teachings grew more intense about the coming end of the world. Hill purchased some land in rural Ohio and started stockpiling food, weapons, and survival gear. (He allegedly also began abusing his followers sexually and physically and fled the state to avoid prosecution.) In the late 1970s, the commune was scattered by exposure of the abuse, and the artistic significance of the band was lost in a haze of shame.

The group's second album, *For Christians, Elves, and Lovers*, ranks among the most valuable collector's items in all of Christian music. Their first album, *My Poor Generation*, was recently reissued on CD by Hidden Vision Records, a small label devoted to early independent Jesus rock. The music, especially Schwartz's guitar skills, was groundbreaking in both Christian and secular rock.

While California got press attention for both the Jesus Movement and the hippie scene, there were spontaneous expressions of faith and rock across the Midwest and on the East Coast. Unfortunately, most of the bands couldn't afford to record, so they are remembered only by the members and whoever saw them play live. Most dealt in the folky acoustic music popularized by secular bands such as Crosby, Stills, Nash, and Young, Joni Mitchell, and Jim Crocé. But lurking in Kansas was one of the weirdest and most imaginative bands in the annals of Christian music.

The Concrete Rubber Band was an experimental heavy rock/psychedelic band comprised of believers who'd started out playing Beatles songs. By incorporating 1960s-era analog synthesizers into their music, they assured themselves of cult status from the beginning. Being strict Baptists, they wouldn't play at dances; being so loud and bizarre sounding, they never found much of a following in the church.

The most distinguishing feature of the band (aside from the sci-fi sound) may be that they actually recorded some of their music. In 1969, they recorded an LP called *Risen Savior*, which they released on their own label. The record never saw much national distribution and remains one of the rarest finds of early Jesus music.

The band broke up before they had even sold all 500 of their records, and they were never heard from as a band again. Founder Duncan Long and his compatriots had no awareness of the Jesus music being made in California or even Chicago. As far as they knew, they were alone. Such was the case with most of the musical groups outside California.

From within California came one of the most influential figures in the history of Christian music in the twentieth century. André Crouch, a pastor's kid from southern California, never took a music lesson in his life, yet he wrote his first song at the age of nine. His influence would span the globe and reach different generations of artists and music fans.

Crouch's first album with his backing band The Disciples, *Take the Message Everywhere*, was released in 1968, but Crouch had been performing electrifying concerts since the early 1960s. Released on Ralph Carmichael's new Light Records label, his version of gospel music was youthful and engaging. He sprinkled his songs with secular R&B influences, including his own vocal performance, which contained a swagger and confidence that would put rappers to shame. As the Jesus Movement took off in the late 1960s, Crouch and his band were already a tight and experienced ensemble. They were assimilated into the mostly white Jesus music scene and even appeared at Explo '72.

Although Crouch's first three albums were successful only among his fans, his 1973 release *Live at Carnegie Hall* was a huge hit and may be the first gospel album on a Christian label to achieve success as a crossover into the general pop and R&B markets. It put Crouch on the map throughout the white church community on a level almost comparable to his celebrity within the black community. His tours included sold-out concerts in South Africa, Asia, Europe, and all over North and South America.

Crouch ruled the 1970s, playing for presidents, kings, queens, and throngs of adoring fans. He replaced The Disciples in 1972 with a new backing group called Sonlight. In addition to being recognized as a fantastic singer, he earned great respect as a songwriter. His songs were covered by Paul Simon, Elvis Presley, Barbara Mandrell, and many others. He also wrote for films, including *The Lion King*, *The Color Purple*, and many others. So far, he has released 14 albums that have sold millions of copies worldwide. He has earned nine Grammy Awards and one Oscar nomination and has produced vocal arrangements for Madonna, Michael Jackson, and many other mainstream acts.

In 1982, Crouch was arrested for drug possession but released after one night in prison due to a lack of evidence. He claimed that the white powder the police assumed was cocaine was really an artificial sweetener. Even though no charges were pressed, rumors of Crouch's run-in with the Marina Del Ray police traveled far and threatened to end his auspicious career. In fact, a subsequent album did not sell well due to persistent rumors. The onetime unstoppable touring musician and writer began what became a 10-year sabbatical in 1984.

In 1993, Crouch signed with Quincy Jones's Qwest Records and subsequently released two hugely successful and critically acclaimed albums, *Pray* and *Mercy*. He was also inducted into the Gospel Music Hall of Fame and was the subject of a major tribute album. Crouch is currently the head pastor of the New Christ Memorial Church of God in Christ in the San Fernando Valley, the church that his father and mother founded when he was a child. Although he remains busy as a touring musician and is every bit as incredible in concert, his main priority now is his church. He also continues to write music and produce the music of other artists and bands.

Back in Ohio, in Youngstown, in the late 1960s, a band emerged that almost became a major breakthrough. They went by the name of Glass Harp, and they had such an impact on rock and roll that they made it into the Rock and Roll Hall of Fame. Glass Harp was a progressive power trio in the tradition of Cream, The Jimi Hendrix Experience, and The James Gang. But Glass Harp's sound was unlike anything that had come before or that has come since. The rhythm section of John Sferra on drums and Daniel Pecchio on bass was a taught and impressive unit, but the hallmark of Glass Harp was a nine-fingered teenage guitarist named Phil Keaggy. His fluid yet muscular style was truly transcendent. News of his guitar skills spread the world over, and, shortly after forming, Glass Harp toured with bands such as Grand Funk Railroad, Yes, Traffic, and Humble Pie. The band broke up after recording three studio albums (and one live album that would end up being released in 1997), just as they were on the verge of a major breakthrough in popularity.

Keaggy, raised a Catholic, embraced the Christianity of the Jesus Movement wholeheartedly. In fact, Glass Harp became an instant favorite of the Jesus People scene. In 1977, Star Song released a compilation of Keaggy's Glass Harp compositions from the three albums in the Christian market.

Keaggy felt called to play his music in Christian environs, and the seedling Jesus music scene was happy to have him. So upon the dissolution

Ashley Cleveland's bluesy style, full of soul and muscle, has earned her a devoted following.

of Glass Harp, Keaggy and his wife started traveling the country. First they went to the Love Inn in New York, where they hooked up with that community and Keaggy recorded his first solo album, *What a Day*. He also traveled to California to play with Love Song after hearing their album. His talent was brought to bear on recordings by 2nd Chapter of Acts, Keith Green, Barry McGuire, Love Song, and many others. His sweet voice and incredible guitar chops made him a hero in the Christian community. Rumors spread that during an appearance on *The Tonight Show* (or a similar show) Eric Clapton or Jimi Hendrix had been asked what it felt like to be the best guitar player in the world and had answered, "I don't know, ask Phil Keaggy." In an interview with *True Tunes News* in 1993, Keaggy addressed the long-standing rumor as just that. Although those stars had likely heard him play, he had no proof that such a conversation had taken place. However, Ted Nugent had once reportedly said that Keaggy going into the Christian scene was a waste. If Keaggy isn't the best, he is certainly among the 10 best ever to pick up a six string.

In the 1970s, he crafted a smooth and slightly jazz-inflected style of pop, though he was known to let it rip occasionally. For instance, his 10-minute live version of "Time" from the live recording with 2nd Chapter of Acts and A Band Called David from the mid-1970s remains one of the great jams of rock. But on balance Keaggy was about connecting songs to his audience more than he was about constantly mesmerizing them with his speed or accuracy on the guitar. Because he is a prolific writer and recorder, his career is just as strong in 2000 as it was in 1970. In fact, he continues to get more and more attention from guitar aficionados such as the editors of *Fingerstyle Magazine* and *Guitar Player*. Keaggy recorded some of the most important music of the past three decades, and his awesome career will be revisited as this history unfolds.

Another major figure of the early Christian rock scene was Larry Norman, a lanky kid from San Jose with long blond hair and a love for rock and roll that went back to his childhood. Norman achieved some local success with his band People (cleverly named in response to bands with names such as The Beatles, The Animals, and The Byrds). The Bay Area of San Francisco, the hippie center of the known universe, provided a large audience for the band's hooky garage style. After playing the Bay Area for a couple of years, the band was signed by Capitol Records. Their debut record never accomplished much, but their second did. Their song "I Love You (But the Words Won't Come)" climbed all the way to 14th position on the pop charts. Although the song was a simple love ditty, the other material on the album dealt with the problems of the hippie generation and the emptiness that it faced. The album was turned in to Capitol under the title *We Need a Whole Lot More of Jesus and a Lot Less Rock and Roll* and featured a cover picture of the band jamming with

Jesus. The label had other plans and changed the title of the album to *I Love You* and put a picture of the band on the cover. Norman reportedly quit the band the day the album was released, saying that he'd rather not play than face that kind of censorship. The band went on, though, and released one more album before breaking up in the early 1970s.

Capitol resigned Norman in 1969 to record a solo album, *Upon This Rock*, now considered to be the first full-blown Christian rock album. The music was a blend of folk, psychedelic, and rock influences. Even the lyrics went beyond people's expectations. What little Christian music they'd heard was mostly upbeat and inspirational. *Upon This Rock*, however, was full of haunting, dark, and nightmarish songs that did little to make the listener feel happy. Norman was far more concerned with being truthful than inspirational. Although the album was never a secular hit, it made history in the church and remains a highly valued collector's item.

Norman followed *Upon This Rock* with two independent releases in the next year. *Bootleg* and *Street Level* were low budget, gritty, more than a little strange, and hugely important. By 1970, Norman was featured in *Time* and other national media outlets. As the spokesman for the Jesus Movement, and probably its most engaging personality, he had become Christianity's first rock star.

Norman's songs "I Wish We'd All Been Ready," "Sweet Sweet Song of Salvation," and "One Way" became international anthems for the hippie church. The first was covered numerous times, including some hysterically bad versions. The song told of believers being taken to heaven suddenly, leaving others behind. This wasn't a new theological concept, but many Jesus People were obsessed with the idea that the "rapture" was just a day or two away. Norman captured the chemistry of the counterculture and the Jesus Movement perfectly in his music, and he quickly developed a devoted following.

1972's *Only Visiting This Planet* assured all concerned that Norman was no one-hit wonder. Released originally on MGM/Verve and somehow "arranged" by George Martin, producer for The Beatles, the album received widespread critical acclaim. In fact, *CCM* magazine, in its 20th-anniversary issue of 1998, called *Only Visiting This Planet* the top Christian album of all time. It's hard to argue with that assessment. The album featured numerous soon-to-be classics. With his liner notes, lyrics, and album art, Norman began to create a mystique that went way beyond the music. In future liner notes, he would mention numerous secular artists who claimed to have been heavily influenced by the album, including U2's Bono, Edge, and Larry Mullen Jr., Frank Black (who covered "Six Sixty Six" on a solo album in the late 1990s), John Mellancamp, and others. He would also claim that an unreleased rock opera that he composed was the inspiration for The Who's *Tommy*.

The album was packaged as the first part of a trilogy, which continued with *So Long Ago the Garden* (MGM/Verve, 1973). The cover featured a seminude Norman with a photo of a lion superimposed on his skin. The symbolism (an Old Testament prophecy referred to the Messiah as "the lion of the tribe of Judah," and C.S. Lewis's Narnia series made a Christ-like figure out of a lion named Aslan), as well as the obvious insinuation of Adam in the Garden of Eden, flew over the heads of many people, who focused on a patch of grass covering Larry's nether parts. Lyrically, as the title suggests, the album reflects on the darkness of the human condition. The songs deal with characters (no one but Norman knows which are autobiographical and which aren't) knee deep in the madness of life without God. "Nightmare #71" had Norman playing the stream-of-consciousness prophet, rattling off historical and present-day fears and doomsday scenarios. Even on the 20th-anniversary reissue, when he attempted to explain the song, it just became more confusing. By consistently writing dark, bizarre, and inexplicable lyrics, Norman inspired countless other artists. He established, convincingly, that a Christian needn't be limited to feel-good-isms and shallow sentimentality. MGM pulled a few of the more spiritual tunes off the record, ostensibly looking for hits. When faced with censorship again, Norman got out of his contract and planned to start his own label. He retitled the album *Almost . . . So Long Ago the Garden.*

Norman recorded songs with secular record companies (Capitol, MGM/Verve) or on his own imprints (Street Level, Solid Rock, Phydeaux), but only once (and not until the 1980s) did he record with a Christian label. Christian labels weren't comfortable with songs that dealt with suicide, drugs, sex, venereal disease, politics, and a healthy scorn for religion. Frequently, his records were trimmed, edited, or simply changed and then licensed for release by Christian labels. But he made it clear that his mission had little to do with pleasing the church.

Several Christian labels existed by the time that Norman finished his deal with MGM/Verve, but selling a long-haired rocker along with the more streamlined "pop" artists wasn't going to work. So, in the absence of alternatives, and possibly inspired by the Apple imprint of The Beatles, Norman started his own label. Solid Rock Records had a distribution deal with Word music, which meant the mixed blessing of some advance money and some accountability. Word seemingly wanted the music but couldn't put its name on music that progressive. Norman quickly signed up his friends (Mark Heard, Randy Stonehill, Pantano-Salsbury, and Tom Howard) and released a couple of albums of his own. He also licensed Daniel Amos's *Horrendous Disc* from Word, which had purchased it from Maranatha! Music.

In 1978, Norman recorded one of the roughest, bluesiest, and best rock and roll albums of his career or the whole industry. Called *Something New under the Son,* it was a sort of blues-rock concept record. On a song called "Watch What You're Doin'," he rattled off the lines "Momma killed the chicken, thought it was a duck, put it on the table with its legs stickin' up. Pappa broke his glasses when he fell down drunk — tried to drown the kitty cat turned out to be a skunk, you gotta watch what your doin'." Such lines endeared him to the growing but still minuscule underground of Christian rock fans, but they assured him of outsider status in the industry.

Solid Rock became an important moment in the history of Christian rock music since it was the first truly artist-driven label. By 1970, Norman had the most recognized name (and face) in the Jesus Movement and the Christian music scene, and the label banked a little too much on his celebrity. Although a hero among his fans, his persistent envelope pushing kept him at odds with the mainstream and Christian music industries. He produced almost all the albums, which featured the line "Larry Norman Presents" before the band name. He sang backing vocals and even contributed songs. By releasing high-quality music by the best bands, Norman doomed his label to certain financial ruin. He was simply way ahead of the curve with Solid Rock. Strange business dealings, grumblings, and broken friendships marked the end of the label. The blow sent Norman off to Europe and Australia in the 1980s. Almost all of the Solid Rock artists went on to long and significant careers in and around the Christian music scene.

Although Norman had always been a lightning rod of controversy, the late 1970s was a particularly dark time for him. His marriage ended, as did his long friendship and musical partnership with Randy Stonehill. His label went under, and even some of his die-hard fans grew impatient with him as several albums recorded in 1977 and 1978 took until 1980 and 1981 to be released. Norman became a musical hermit, ceasing relationships with record companies and focusing on selling his music directly to his fans through the mail. Years later, he claimed that he'd actually suffered brain damage during a flight when some baggage fell on him. To this day, Norman remains a revered part of Christian music's past and a shadowy part of its present. Recent gestures on his part seem to be bringing him out of his shell and back into the family.

Norman wasn't the first Christian to record rock and roll, but he was the best in the 1960s and 1970s. His songs were more palatable than many of the earlier recordings due largely to access to better studios and producers. The songs were simple but thought provoking. In that respect, he followed the folk tradition, but his music was also full-on rock, not unlike Neil Young's blend of folk and rock. Despite the controversy, hype, and low points, Norman's impact on Christian music cannot be overstated.

As a songwriter, Norman crystallized the heart of the Jesus Movement; as an artist, he pushed the creative envelope well beyond what had been considered appropriate; as a producer, he brought to prominence some of the most significant artists in Christian music; and, as a businessman (undoubtedly his weak suit), he ran a label that brought some of the most important albums into the world. He has also modeled a successful independent recording career as an alternative to working for a label. Larry Norman continues to record music and perform live, and he was one of the first artists to set up shop on the Internet (www.larrynorman.com).

After the release of *Upon This Rock*, the newly anointed father of Christian rock proceeded directly to the streets. Although never far from the spotlight, Norman had a passion for the pavement. He took his signature voice and his beat-up nylon-string guitar to festivals, coffeeshops, and major theaters. Along the way, he ran into Randy Stonehill, who was also from San Jose and had been hugely influenced by the cultural climate of nearby San Francisco. Both adept guitarists and aspiring songwriters, they found a sense of kinship in their worldviews and artistic sensibilities. Shortly after meeting Randy, Larry led him to faith in Jesus (the conversion is immortalized in Stonehill's song "Norman's Kitchen"), and soon Stonehill became involved in the Jesus music scene.

The first step was making a record. The two hippie disciples had heard that the wealthy pop maven Pat Boone was supportive of the Jesus Movement. They went to his house and asked for some money to start a little label called Street Level Records. Boone gave the pair about $2,000. They found a cheap studio and rented some gear. With the money, Larry recorded two albums of his own and one of Randy's. *Street Level* and *Bootleg* etched Norman as the prophet laureate of the Jesus Movement, and Stonehill's classic *Born Twice* was the introduction to this amazing young talent. *Born Twice* (depending on the version) features Randy with guitar and Randy with full band. Despite the album's meager $800 recording budget, Stonehill emerged as a major presence.

His next effort was a secular project for the British Phonogram label called *Get Me Out of Hollywood*. Unfortunately, the record was never officially released and has thus been heard by few people (in 2000, Norman rereleased it). On returning to California, Stonehill hooked up with Norman again for 1976's *Welcome to Paradise*, one of the most important albums in all of Christian music. *Welcome to Paradise* legitimized both Stonehill as a songwriter and singer and Norman as a producer. The record contains scorching rock and roll alongside brilliant ballads. In many ways, it was the best album of Jesus rock since Norman's *Upon This Rock*.

Stonehill began a heavy touring schedule that often saw him sharing the stage with Norman or other Solid Rock acts such as Daniel Amos, Mark Heard, or Tom Howard. His live show became one of the treasures of the Christian music underground. A fan could take anyone to a Stonehill show knowing that it would be great. From his songs to the hilarious stories between them, he delivered.

Another band that delivered was Love Song, perhaps second in importance only to Norman as founders of Jesus music. Comprised of Chuck Girard, Jay Truax, John Mehler, and Tommy Coomes, the band played together before any of them became a Christian. Girard even had a mainstream record deal with his first band, The Castells, on Mercury Records, and he had a top-20 hit with the ironically titled "Sacred" before he was even out of high school. Opening for Roy Orbison and Jerry Lee Lewis and living the rock and roll dream comprised his agenda. He spent much of the 1960s writing surf hits, and he hit the jackpot as the lead vocalist on the top-10 hit "Little Honda" with his band The Hondelles.

Girard developed a serious alcohol problem and then moved on to pot and LSD. His band at the time, Six the Hard Way, was playing a lounge in Las Vegas called the Pussy Cat a Go Go with another band called 5th Cavalry. Denny Correll, a member of that band, got the musicians together one night on a break and told them that they needed to find Jesus. Correll's passion and conviction made an impact on Girard, and when the band went back to Los Angeles they began reading the Bible and looking for God. Drugs were still a big part of their lives since they thought that the enlightenment would help them find the answers.

After being told about a church in the Costa Mesa area called Calvary Chapel, a number of the band members headed south to see what it was about. They found a full-blown Christian commune living out of a hotel on Newport Beach called the Blue Top, and they searched there for answers to some nagging spiritual questions. They found themselves in the middle of the burgeoning Jesus Movement and were invited to Calvary Chapel that night for church. Overcoming their nervousness about anything called Christian, they went and checked it out. They would never be the same. The casual and gentle spirit of Pastor Chuck Smith reached them, and soon some of them became Christians. A few weeks later, they got baptized and started Love Song.

Love Song formed just as the Jesus Movement was gaining speed. The band's skills had been sharpened by years of professional gigging and recording, so Love Song was primed and ready. With Denny Correll involved for a short time, the members of Love Song began writing heartfelt lyrics that reflected their recent experiences. They were typical Jesus freaks, hippies who'd looked to drugs and sex trying to find peace and who'd ended up at the feet of Jesus.

Due to their musical skills and the attention of media suddenly fascinated by the goings-on of this Jesus Movement, Love Song quickly rose to international acclaim. They recorded two studio albums, both of

Bassist Tim Chandler has played with Daniel Amos, The Choir, and Phil Keaggy's band.

which remain classics. The self-titled *Love Song* was released in 1972 and the follow-up *Final Touch* in 1974. The band then broke up, and each member went on to work with other bands or pursue a solo career. In 1976, they reunited for a special live album called *Feel the Love*. Chuck Girard recorded several influential rock albums that culled everything from his surf-rock background to the California sound popularized by The Eagles and Jackson Browne. Tommy Coomes eventually helped to run Maranatha! Music, a Calvary label that would greatly shape the Jesus music scene. Drummer John Mehler and bassist Jay Truax added their skills to many a record in the 1970s. Correll played in various other bands and released one amazing solo album in 1979.

Love Song's impact was enormous. While Larry Norman was more representative of the rock side of the counterculture movement, Love Song's mellow style was even more popular at the time, and the band's music resonated the world over.

Another young singer-songwriter in search of spiritual answers was Paul Clark. In 1970, the 18 year old was in a cabin in the Rocky Mountains when a box of books from his grandmother arrived. He picked one, and read it from cover to cover. At the end of the book was a prayer to follow Jesus as his disciple. He had found what he was looking for — he would soon be caught up in a movement about which he knew nothing.

Clark began performing the new folk songs he'd written about his discovery of faith at a Denver coffeehouse. He then began to record the songs. His debut album, *Songs from the Savior*, was picked up by the Creative Sound label and featured mostly Clark and his guitar, with some pedal steel and upright piano. The record became a favorite of the Jesus People and brought Clark to the attention of people around the world. His follow-up, *Songs from the Savior Volume 2*, featured more of the same acoustic style, with a heavier emphasis on the rural flavor. His simple singing style and rootsy sound further endeared him to the hippie crowd and won the attention of some of the biggest names in the scene.

For his third and fourth records, Clark enlisted the help of some major names: Jay Truax and John Mehler (of Love Song) on bass and drums, Bill Speer on piano, and Phil Keaggy on lead guitar. The results were incredible. With an organic sound like the *Harvest* era of Neil Young, *Come into His Presence* and *Good to Be Home* rank as highlights in the history of Christian music.

Clark started his own label, Seed, for *Good to Be Home*, and his independent streak continued with his startlingly contemporary-sounding *Hand to the Plow* album. Although it had its share of mellow material, the album moved boldly into the current day with the addition of jazz players Harlan Rogers and Hadley Hockensmith. Keyboards, piano, layered backing vocals, and electric guitar took over and gave *Hand to the Plow* an almost Steely Dan feel.

The year 1970 was also important for Canadian Bruce Cockburn (pronounced koe-burn). Since his debut that year, he has been building a devoted following on both sides of the border. Cockburn has defined a folk-based pop rock that, while drawing on the same influences as his contemporaries (e.g., Jackson Browne, Paul Simon, and Bob Dylan), has a sound all its own. His amazing talent on acoustic and electric guitar (rhythmic strumming, fingerstyle picking, and soulful lead playing) is complemented by his expressive baritone voice and percussive tastes in accompaniment. He has not been afraid to experiment with technology, instrumentation, or production.

Cockburn became a Christian in 1974 after being heavily influenced by the writings of C.S. Lewis and George MacDonald. He grew up in an agnostic home, in a country where evangelicalism hadn't permeated society to the extent that it had in the United States. His interesting worldview has been played out artfully over the span of his 26 albums. His is a more liberal perspective, both spiritually and politically, than that of most of the Christian music crafted south of the border. That unique perspective has been debated by both his Christian and his non-Christian fans since the mid-1970s. But unlike many other artists whose fans refused to listen to their expressions of faith (Bob Dylan, Richie Furay, Dan Peek, and so on), Cockburn has had fans who've always come back for more.

Cockburn is an anomaly to be sure. He is known publicly as a Christian, he has criticized the governments of the United States and Canada (and those of many other countries) for what he sees as hypocrisy and evil in the area of human rights, and he has peppered his songs of faith and righteous indignation with strong language. He has been letting it fly, whether "it" happens to be a song celebrating his faith ("Lord of the Starfield," "Wondering Where the Lions Are," "Nothing but a Burning Light") or a song attacking the economic-political machinations of war and oppression ("Call It Democracy," "Mighty Trucks of Midnight," "If I Had a Rocket Launcher"). Yet he has retained respectability among fans on both sides of the faith issue, and in the 1970s he quietly influenced a generation of believing artists who would come to light in the 1980s.

Cockburn's UK counterpart may have been the activist troubadour Garth Hewitt. His folk style sounded easy at first, but he wasn't afraid to tackle unpopular issues such as politics and the environment. Hewitt quietly released album after album from the 1970s to the 1990s and beyond.

Liberation Suite was also popular in the United Kingdom. Formed in Texas, and unaware of the Jesus Movement as it raged in California, the band existed both before and after its members became Christians. Ironically, they hooked up with a traveling ministry group as the house band and then made their way to the United Kingdom, where they recorded their debut album, *Liberation Suite*, in 1974. Their sound was basically pop rock with horns, à la Chicago. By the standards of the day, they were quite edgy, and their production was up to mainstream standards. They went on to release two more records in the 1980s, but *Liberation Suite* stands as their definitive statement. Although their albums would eventually all be distributed in the United States, this group of Texans found their largest following overseas.

More aware of the Jesus Movement was Barry McGuire, who first rose to national prominence as a member of the folk group The New Christy Minstrels. But it was in 1965 that he became a superstar with his megahit "Eve of Destruction." Not finding any sense of peace or fulfillment, McGuire was a searcher. Intrigued by press coverage of the Jesus Movement, McGuire decided to check it out. He encountered a member of Arthur Blessit's outreach in Hollywood and shortly thereafter became a Christian. He was baptized on Father's Day in 1971.

McGuire had a supporting role in Jesus music at first. As a high-profile pop artist, he could give credibility to the fledgling scene. Thus, he played the role of sponsor, mentor, and inspirer for many Jesus music artists. In 1973, he signed with Myrrh Records and released his first Christian album, *Seeds*. With help from a then unknown sibling trio called 2nd Chapter of Acts on backing vocals, Mike Deasy on guitar, Michael Omartian on keyboards, and Buck Herring as producer, McGuire put together an album accessible to the church crowd and relatable to his folk pedigree. It was an instant favorite in the Jesus music scene, but it never managed to get beyond the Christian subculture to the world beyond.

McGuire was very active throughout the 1970s in helping to develop Christian music. He released seven albums, but he also collaborated with other artists on their work. He was an advocate of quality children's music as well, lending his skills to several projects. McGuire's song "Bullfrogs and Butterflies" became the centerpiece of one of the most successful Christian albums of all time. *Bullfrogs and Butterflies* (produced by Mike Deasy) was part of the Agapeland series and was the first Christian album to be certified platinum (one million copies sold) by the RIAA. It was also significant in its quiet subversiveness.

Although most of the Christian pop music created in the late 1970s was tame and safe, *Bullfrogs and Butterflies* was produced like a real rock record. The drums were upfront and well recorded, the bass and guitar were fresh and tight, and the overall sound was rootsy and classic. The only thing that made it a children's record was the chorus of child singers, the lyrics, and the cartoon packaging. No doubt this record, in addition to an earlier, slightly more animated-sounding Agapeland record called *The Music Machine*, developed a taste for basic rock instrumentation in children and parents alike. It was a far shorter jump from *Bullfrogs and Butterflies* to, say, Petra or DeGarmo and Key than it would have been if kids were listening to their parents' Jimmy Swaggart or Praise records.

Producer Deasy had a long pedigree in rock and roll. As a legendary "guitar hero," he had played with Eddie Cochrane, The Coasters, Elvis Presley, The Beach Boys, Billy Joel, The Monkees, and many others. He also worked on film soundtracks such as that for *Dirty Harry*. Deasy became a Christian at a Billy Graham crusade and quickly found his way to the Jesus music scene, where someone with his amazing chops was badly needed. His guitar playing and studio savvy came to the aid of 2nd Chapter of Acts, Keith Green, Larry Norman, André Crouch, John Michael Talbot, and many others. He was part of a core of studio musicians — including Richard Souther (later of the Souther, Hillman, Furay band), Hadley Hockensmith, Billy Batstone, Buck Herring, and Alex MacDougal (among many others) — who'd all had been, and continued to be, major players in the secular rock scene. These players often gave the instrumental credibility to early Christian music that set it apart from the campfire sound of the religious music of the 1950s and 1960s. McGuire consistently used Deasy and the others throughout his career.

McGuire scored a major Christian radio hit at the tail end of the 1970s with "Cosmic Cowboy" (cowritten with Deasy), from the album of the same name. It was an interesting metaphor for Jesus seemingly influenced by "trucker/country" songs such as "Convoy." He spent the

1980s in New Zealand and returned to America in 1990. He would eventually hook up with Terry Talbot, and sometimes John Michael Talbot, and tour more extensively than he had since the early days.

Before the Jesus music craze really took off, young folk singer Randy Matthews was signed to Word Records. Word president Billy Ray Hearn had heard a passion and importance in his voice. Matthews's 1971 debut, *Wish We'd All Been Ready* (the title song was one of Larry Norman's most popular compositions), was a safe and well-produced entrance into the acoustic-dominated Jesus music scene. His follow-up in 1972, *All I Am Is What You See*, was released on the Word imprint Myrrh, which had really been established for Matthews. But it was his third album, 1973's *Son of Dust*, that defined the latent power in his voice and writing. Raw and gripping, *Son of Dust* thrilled the Jesus People, who were looking for something along the lines of Neil Young's grittier style.

Matthews continued to write and record during the rest of the 1970s, and he would appear occasionally in the 1980s and 1990s. As Christian music became more sanitized, he lost interest in it and opted out, an unfortunate loss for listeners.

Before Matthews became a name in the Christian rock scene, Mason Profit was one of many regionally successful country-rock bands of the late 1960s. With a major-label deal and several albums to its credit, Mason Profit was on the verge of genuine stardom, opening for heavy hitters such as Janis Joplin and riding the same stylistic wave that would soon make the members of The Eagles millionaires. The band's founder was a young man named Terry Talbot. His teen-aged brother John joined the band early on. With a style that married traditional folk and country to the newer folk-rock style coming from California bands such as Buffalo Springfield, Mason Profit was all potential in the late 1960s.

John Talbot became a Christian in 1971 and eventually felt led to leave the rock world. Shortly thereafter, his brother shut down the band and also came to faith in Christ. In 1974, the duo recorded an ambitious album together as The Talbot Brothers that was released on Warner Brothers Records that year. The album contained both clear and vague references to the brothers' newfound faith. Musically, it delivered a much more polished version of what Mason Profit had always hinted at.

Two years later, the brothers signed separate record deals with Hearn's new Sparrow label. John had grown his hair and beard to generous hippie lengths. His self-titled solo debut was a fully realized folk-pop album, from his gently picked guitar to his crystal-clear voice. He rocked a bit too, the kind of rock that Neil Young was perfecting. On *John Michael Talbot* and 1977's *The New Earth*, the younger brother crafted some of the best acoustic rock in the early Christian music scene. The following year, he converted to Roman Catholicism and took his music in a totally new direction. Beginning with 1979's hauntingly beautiful *The Lord's Supper* and continuing through more than 37 records recorded between 1980 and 1999, John crafted a contemplative style of music that focused on his classical guitar and voice, with occasional orchestral embellishments. He became a Franciscan monk in 1979 and was the first, and one of the few, Catholic artists in the contemporary Christian music industry. He took profits from his music sales and began a hermitage and retreat center in northern Arkansas called The Little Portion Hermitage.

Terry Talbot also debuted with his first solo album, *No Longer Alone*, on Sparrow in 1976. While his kid brother had opted for the James Taylor style, Terry wanted to keep rocking. His debut was right in step with the country-pop of The Eagles. He followed it with two more mellow albums: 1977's *Cradle of Love* and 1978's *A Time to Laugh a Time to Sing*. He continued into the 1980s with a more contemporary adult style and a charismatic evangelical lyrical style, in counterpoint to his brother's contemplative Catholic music. One of their greatest musical moments would come in 1980 when they joined forces on the classic acoustic album *The Painter*.

Zanier than the Talbots was Gary S. Paxton, who'd been the lead singer in the band The Hollywood Argyles on their hit "Alley Oop." He brought his unique sense of humor and tacky Nashville fashion to gospel music and took the Best Gospel Grammy Award in 1977 for *The Astonishing, Outrageous, Amazing, Incredible, Unbelievable, Different World of Gary S. Paxton*. His wild humor and Elvis Presley-like rock and roll found many fans of different ages.

Also with a warped sense of humor was Ian Smale, a Brit who hit the music scene a decade or so too early. His first musical offering, *Ready Salted* in 1973, introduced his weird humor and deft touch with a tune. That album was under the artistic name of Ishmael and Andy (with Andy Piercy, who'd go on to form After the Fire later in the decade). Smale went solo in 1975 with the amazingly progressive and hilarious *Charge of the Light Brigade*. In the early 1980s, he'd launch two other projects: Ishmael United and Rev. Counta and the Speedoze.

One of the most respected guitarists in the music business in the late 1960s and 1970s was James Vincent, a native of the south side of Chicago immersed in the blues of B.B. King and Johnny Smith. He formed a band called The Exceptions with Peter Cetera, who would go on to fame with the band Chicago. Vincent ended up building a successful career as a studio musician at Chess Records, the label that would serve as ground zero for the blues scene in America.

Vincent met rock business legend Bill Graham and was recruited to join a new band called H.P. Lovecraft that he was managing. As a result of moving to San Francisco for that job, Vincent hooked up with Jerry Garcia of The Grateful Dead and toured with Garcia's Hooter Roll band for a

Michael Knott joined the early Christian punk band The Lifesavers in the late '70s.

while. He was then influenced by the fusion style of John McGlaughlin, an innovative guitarist in Majavishnu Orchestra, which opened for Hooter Roll.

Vincent released a couple of mainstream records before becoming a Christian in the late 1970s. Although still on the secular Columbia/Caribou label, his 1978 record *Waiting for the Rain* was miles beyond any Christian record in terms of production and playing. His music was later rereleased into the Christian market, where he found a small but devoted group of fans. Vincent is still an active session player and has recently released a new instrumental jazz album called *Second Wind*.

Fans of Christian jazz had little to call their own, but one incredible group was Seawind. Although they released only two albums, they became a favorite of the cutting-edge crowd and are now sought by collectors.

Another short-lived but influential group was Fireworks. A young Marty McCall, who ended up in the AC group First Call in the 1980s, started out in Fireworks, one of the more adventurous rock bands of the 1970s. The band evolved from slick studio cats playing mostly mellow church music to firebrand rockers.

Anyone with a résumé that included playing in a major secular pop group got instant hype in the Christian market. The fans and the industry, desperate for respectability, looked to secular-to-Christian crossovers as manna from heaven. Thus, when Dan Peek, a founding member of the hugely successful pop group America, became a Christian and announced the release of a Christian solo album, fans of Jesus music were elated. His résumé actually got him further than his music did. His 1979 solo debut, *All Things Are Possible*, scored a relatively successful pop hit with the title track. Peek recorded a few more solo records in the 1980s and then formed an independent acoustic group called Peace in the 1990s.

Songwriter Richie Furay also had great credibility in the early 1970s. As a member of the seminal Buffalo Springfield with Stephen Stills, Neil Young, and later Jim Messina, among others, Furay went down in history (and in the Rock and Roll Hall of Fame) as part of one of the most important bands in rock music. Buffalo Springfield debuted when pop music was dominated by British-invasion bands and American bands that were far too influenced by the British bands. Buffalo Springfield crafted a truly American sound that combined folk, country, and blues with rock and roll. Not only did the band influence hundreds of upcoming artists (including many from overseas) to embrace the sounds of North America, but it also spawned many of the best bands in the history of American rock. When the band broke up in 1968, Crosby and Stills formed Crosby, Stills, and Nash; Young began a genre-shaping solo career; and Furay and Messina started Poco with Rusty Young and George Grantham.

Furay recorded six albums with Poco before leaving to start the Souther Hillman Furay band with former Byrd Chris Hillman and J.D. Souther, who'd penned several songs for The Eagles. With the assistance of David Geffen, the band scored a gold album and a moderate radio hit with "Fallin' in Love." In the midst of their rise, Furay was led to faith in Christ by band member Al Perkins.

After the release of Souther Hillman Furay's second album, *Trouble in Paradise*, Furay went solo and released *I've Got a Reason* in 1976. His band consisted of Jay Truax and John Mehler, formerly of Love Song, and Tom Stipe, with production by the amazing and ubiquitous Michael Omartian. *I've Got a Reason* was a musical triumph and a commercial failure. Furay's songs connected with the growing Christian music underground but not with the mainstream audience — at least not at the level necessary for a major label. Nonetheless, Elektra/Asylum released two more solo Furay albums, 1978's *Dance a Little Light* and 1979's *I Still Have Dreams*, both solid but tragically obscure examples of thoughtful music created by a Christian in the general market. In 1981, Myrrh rereleased *I've Got a Reason*, officially launching Furay into the Christian music realm. In 1983, Furay became the pastor of a church in Denver. He hooked up with Poco for a reunion album, *Legacy*, in 1989. He also continued his career as a solo artist with the 1997 release *In My Father's House*.

Across the Atlantic, in England, Bryn Haworth was respected as a master guitarist before the close of the 1960s. He played with several regionally successful bands before moving to California to play with The Jackie Lomax Band and Wolfgang. With the management of Bill Graham behind them, they toured with heavyweights such as Jefferson Airplane, Taj Mahal, and The Moody Blues. In 1973, Haworth returned to England and signed a solo record deal with Island Records, with which he'd eventually record two albums, *Let the Day Go By* (1974) and *Sunny Side of the Street* (1976). In 1974, Haworth and his wife became Christians. Throughout his relationship with Island Records and then A&M (*Grand Arrival* in 1978 and *Keep the Ball Rolling* in 1979), Haworth carefully and tastefully wove his faith into his smooth blues-flavored rock.

In 1980, he hooked up with Dave Markee and Henry Spinetti, Eric Clapton's rhythm section, and recorded *The Gap*, a classic of Christian rock. *The Gap* was a tasteful blend of folk-rock, blues, and gospel, with excellent production courtesy of Markee and Haworth's eloquent bottleneck slide-style guitar all over the place. The professionalism of the playing, singing, and writing was much higher than fans of Christian music were accustomed to. Although it wasn't an official Larry Norman production, it did have "Larry Norman Presents" along the top of the front cover, which hurt neither Haworth's nor Norman's credibility. Haworth recorded many other albums in the 1980s and 1990s, mostly in the praise-and-worship vein.

A name familiar to fans of Christian music is 2nd Chapter of Acts, a band that connected immediately with fans. Perhaps it was the air-tight sibling harmonies of the trio of Matthew Ward and his sisters, Nelly Ward and Annie Herring. Perhaps it was the adventurous writing and arranging. Likely it was all that along with a sense of "heart."

By the age of 12, Matthew had lost his mother to a brain tumor and his father to leukemia. He and his 14-year-old sister Nelly moved to Los Angeles to live with their 24-year-old sister Annie and her husband, Buck Herring. Shortly after the relocation, the trio began to make music, in no small part as therapy to help them deal with their grief. Buck, a producer and music industry insider, realized that they had something special. With the help of Pat Boone and Billy Ray Hearn, 2nd Chapter of Acts took its unique sound and ministry to millions around the world. For 17 years, they would be a mainstay in Christian music.

Although the band's music was far from the brash sound of Resurrection Band or the edginess of Larry Norman, it had a freshness that wasn't completely beyond the pop music performed by Elton John or America. There were several serious rock moments throughout the trio's first few records. Their third album, *Roar of Love*, pays homage to C.S. Lewis's Narnia books with a rich conceptual thread and some intricate and artistic music. Their first album, *With Footnotes*, is considered by many to be among the best Christian albums of all time.

Matthew Ward also had a solo career in which he cut loose more than he did with his sisters. On his solo debut, *Toward Eternity* in 1979, he teamed up with Phil Keaggy and a host of other major talents. The result was an impressive classic rock record reminiscent of Styx. Ward continued with other solo records in the 1980s and 1990s. In 1994, he was diagnosed with cancer. He endured years of painful treatment, but finally the cancer went into remission, and he recorded the inspirational CD *My Redeemer*.

2nd Chapter of Acts had major hits with their hymns records from the mid-1980s. After *Far Away Places*, the band decided to call it quits. Annie Herring recorded several solo contemporary adult records, and Matthew Ward released *My Redeemer*, but rumor has it that there's something else in store for the trio.

The Jesus music craze was not a specifically American phenomenon, though it seemed to be at the time. The duo of Malcolm Wild and Alwyn Wall from Liverpool, England, debuted in the United States in 1973 on Myrrh Records with *Fool's Wisdom*. Their tight vocals and progressive acoustic instrumentation made them a favorite among audiophiles and fans of Simon and Garfunkle and The Beatles. The duo released one more record, the amped-up *Wildwall* in 1974. After touring America six times, the duo split to pursue individual careers. Wall put together the Alwyn Wall band, which continued the top-notch production of Malcolm and Alwyn but pushed firmly into rock and roll territory. The band recorded two records, 1977's self-titled album and 1982's *Invisible Warfare*.

Back in the mid-1960s, Keith Green was yet another young hippie musician searching the LA scene for fame and fortune. He was signed as a child to a major-label deal, and plans were made for him to be a superstar. Although he grew up Jewish, he read the New Testament and ended up caught in the balance somewhat. Searching for peace and meaning, Green tried drugs, fame, sex, and spiritualism. In 1975, at the age of 21, Green accepted Christ and his teachings as true, and he found the peace that he'd been looking for. His young wife, Melody, was also converted to Christianity.

Green had been a prolific writer and a pianist since childhood. Once the peace of Christ came into his heart, the songs exploded from his mind like dynamite. First he was a writer and pianist for the band Good News, which included Bob Carlisle (who'd go on to form the Christian rock band Allies and later score a top pop hit with his ballad "Butterfly Kisses"), Bill Batstone (who played in the Richie Furay Band), David Diggs (keyboardist for Irene Cara, Quincy Jones, and many others), and John Hernandez (who went on to join Oingo Boingo in the 1980s). Green recorded on that band's second album. His song "Run to the End of the Highway" was a relative hit for the group, and it became one of his most loved songs down the road.

Green signed with Billy Ray Hearn's Sparrow label for his debut in 1977, *For Him Who Has Ears to Hear*. His percussive piano style and passionate tenor voice earned him an instant and enormous audience. He went from playing coffeehouses for 50 people to stadiums of 15,000 in a few short years. The album was even more intense lyrically than it was musically. Green became a sort of John the Baptist figure, vehemently calling for Christians to get serious about their faith. He railed against casual or social Christianity and declared that it wouldn't have taken him so long to see the truth of the gospel if Christians had acted like true followers of Christ. He was an evangelist and a prophet who, though he mellowed a bit with maturity, never lost the desire for Godliness.

Green's follow-up album, 1978's *No Compromise*, was an even bolder statement, and his ministry grew exponentially. His songs, though considerably more modern sounding than most Christian music, were well received on Christian radio, and Green became a big name in Christian music. Ironically, the more popular he got, the more vociferously he rejected the trappings of success and pride.

In a controversial move, Green asked to be released from his contract with Sparrow because he believed that it was wrong to charge people for his music or concert tickets. Hearn supported him in his decision. Green recorded his third album, *So You Wanna Go Back to Egypt*, on his own Pretty Good Records label and offered it to the public at concerts and through the mail for whatever people could afford to pay. His ministry, Last Days Ministries, shipped over 100,000 copies of the album, including many to unscrupulous concert promoters and retailers who took armfuls for free and then resold them. The move was shocking to some but inspired some artists to follow suit. Eventually, Green relented and had Sparrow distribute the albums to Christian retailers at a discounted price, though he still refused to charge for his concerts.

Beginning with *So You Wanna Go Back to Egypt* and continuing through the rest of his work, Green allowed his gentler and even humorous side to shine through more on his songs. Doing so further endeared him to his audiences and made his concerts major events. One more studio album, *Songs from the Shepherd*, and a best-of collection came out in 1981 and 1982. Green continued to tour and to lead a discipleship training group of up to 70 believers at a time who went to the Last Days Ministries center in Texas for teaching and Bible study. Fortunately, several of his concerts were recorded.

Green, along with his three-year-old son Josiah and his two-year-old daughter Bethany, died in a small-plane crash on July 28, 1982. His wife was home with their newborn daughter Rebekah and was six weeks pregnant with their fourth child, Rachel. Green was only 28.

In seven short years, he recorded over 75 songs and performed for

Derri Daughtery of The Choir (with Tim Chandler on the right).

hundreds of thousands of people. Sometimes his youthful passion carried him too far. At one point, he published a booklet that drew attention to what he thought was wrong with Roman Catholicism. He presented his views a little too vehemently and alienated many Catholics and mainline Christians. Unfortunately, his apologies never seemed to travel as fast or as far as what he had to apologize for. But overall his impact was like a clarion call to basic faith without compromise. His influence would resound through the years, and his music continues to impact people today. Several tribute albums, cover versions of his songs, and books have been released. Green not only brought the piano to Christian music as a rock instrument, and crafted some of the best produced and performed pop rock music of the day, but he also set a lyrical standard that would influence countless later artists. Several taped concerts and videos were culled together for posthumous release, and in 1987 Sparrow put all of his recorded output into *The Ministry Years Volumes 1 and 2*.

Representing Jesus music from the southeast was an exceptional songwriter named Pat Terry and his three-piece Pat Terry Group, with partners Randy Bugg and Sonny Lallerstedt. The band's style of laid-back acoustic and country was somewhat akin to that of Daniel Amos. They released an independent LP simply called *The Pat Terry Group* in 1974 and then signed with Myrrh Records.

The band recorded three other albums in the 1970s: *Songs of the South*, *Sweet Music*, and *Heaven Ain't All There Is*. Hailing from the Georgia countryside put them in close contact with Mark Heard, who produced some records for Terry in the 1980s. After *Heaven Ain't All There Is*, the band split up, and Terry migrated to a rockier sound. His solo records included the incredible *Film at Eleven* and *Humanity Gangsters*. He may be the most forgotten member of the Jesus music movement. Even though his solo records were excellent, and were distributed by Word, it's been so long since Terry released new work that a whole generation of music fans has never heard of him or his band, from which bands such as Vigilantes of Love and Third Day were loosely descended.

Any discussion of Christian rock has to mention the group Petra. They weren't the first, and they've seen their share of struggles, but they are credited with defining the "Christian rock band."

Although the lineup has changed numerous times, including three lead vocalists (currently, and since 1986, former Head East vocalist John Schlitt), the roots of Petra go back to 1972 and a man named Bob Hartman. Petra played as the house band at Adam's Rib coffeehouse in South Bend, Indiana. In 1974, they released their self-titled debut record on Myrrh Records. It was recorded on a measly $900 budget over a few days, and it showed. Although it was more aggressive than most Jesus music of the day, especially the song "Backslidin' Blues," it failed to sell up to label expectations. With guitarist and band leader Bob Hartman singing lead vocals (a mistake that they wouldn't repeat, at least not for a whole record), the band churned out legitimate stripped-down rock and roll with a country twist.

By the time they recorded their second album, *Come and Join Us* in 1974, they had secured the rock-ready vocals of Greg X. Volz, an impressive tenor who'd been a member of A Band Called E, also from Indiana. Although Volz sang lead on only two songs and backing vocals on the rest, listeners got a chance to hear the next lead singer of Petra. *Come and Join Us* was a paramount achievement in Christian music history. It was recorded for Myrrh, a division of Word, and was marketed through the Christian bookstore network, and it was one of the first well-produced and decently distributed Christian rock records. With a classic rock sound somewhat like the emerging arena style of Journey, The Rolling Stones, and Queen, Petra took to the road and developed one of the most talked-about live shows in the emerging Jesus rock scene.

Myrrh dropped Petra after *Come and Join Us* failed to sell well. After several years of touring full time without a record deal, the band was picked up by the progressive Star Song label from Texas. Their third album, *Washes Whiter Than*, featured their first Christian radio "hit" "Why Should the Father Bother?" and a much softer rock sound.

The 1970s showed Petra how to tour, record, and promote, which the group would do with a vengeance throughout the next two decades. Although most of their post-1970s music was riddled with stylistic identity crises (most secular rock bands faced the same problem in the 1980s), they were extremely influential for many younger bands growing up with Christian music. They'd emerge in the 1980s as one of the first huge Christian rock bands, the answer to the arena rock of Def Leppard and Boston, and they'd go on to become the best-selling band in Christian rock, selling over six million records and earning multiple Grammies, Doves, and other awards.

Another group that should be mentioned is DeGarmo and Key. In 1974, two friends in Memphis started playing rock and roll. One of them, Eddie DeGarmo, accepted Christ and shared the news with his partner, Dana Key. They began creating serious southern rock à la The Allman Brothers. They called their band The DeGarmo and Key Band, and soon they recorded their debut album, *This Time Through*, for Pat Boone's Lamb and Lion label. The album, though produced slightly mellower than the band's scorching live show, was a new high point in Christian music.

But the follow-up, *Straight On*, was a serious shot in the arm to the blooming Christian rock scene. Key's soulful vocals and seasoned guitar chops coupled with DeGarmo's deft touch with a Hammond B-3 created an album full of legitimate rock. *Straight On* became an instant classic in the rock underground and fueled the band's growing popularity on the touring circuit. The band's third album, *Stella This Aint Hollywood*, was a deep record lyrically, and it wasn't devoid of rock and roll, but it was decidedly more laid back than *Straight On*.

DeGarmo and Key released a live album in 1982 that brilliantly captured the best of their southern rock and the worst of their emerging fixation with synthesizers. DeGarmo left his Hammond B-3 behind and donned a keyboard that could be held on with a strap. Much like ZZ Top did, the band left their rootsy sound for the processed sound of arena pop in the 1980s.

Also heavily synthesized was Michael Omartian's *White Horse*. Omartian was a professional writer, keyboardist, and producer in the pop world who wrote and recorded "Theme from S.W.A.T.," a surprise hit. His personal musicianship, however, first became clear on *White Horse*, a solo record for ABC Dunhill later licensed by Myrrh for rerelease. Production on the album was amazing; featuring synthesizers and jazzy progressive rock, Omartian crafted a masterpiece. Another classic of the early days was his *Adam Again*, a more mainstream affair. The two records were huge influences on many young musicians.

Omartian continued to produce records, becoming one of the most sought-after helmsmen in both the Christian field, where he produced Amy Grant and many others, and in the secular field, where he worked with Rod Stewart, Peter Cetera, and others. One young Californian who cited Omartian as a major influence was Sweet Comfort Band's Bryan Duncan. The band's Maranatha! debut ran along pop/R&B lines, but by their second release they'd grown into one of the slickest Christian rock bands. With the best production of the lot, and a stable full of amazingly talented musicians, Sweet Comfort Band quickly became the lead horse in the race. Fronted by the spunky vocals of Duncan, the band released several important albums, including *Hold on Tight* and *Breaking the Ice*. Once they signed with Light, they released a few great albums before breaking up in 1984.

Sweet Comfort Band mounted several major tours and became the benchmark in Christian rock. Although too slick for some hard rock fans, their music nailed the emerging arena rock sound of Boston, Styx, and Journey, with slightly jazzy instrumentation added. On breakup, most of the members went on to considerable success in contemporary Christian music, notably Duncan, whose solo career began with high-energy pop music and evolved into a more mature blue-eyed soul sound.

Another well-known name in early Christian music is Mark Heard, considered by many to be the best songwriter in the genre and a prodigious talent on many levels. As far back as 1970, while still in high school,

Heard was involved in modern Christian music. His band, Infinity Plus Three, released one independent album of folk-rock, which included a cover of Clapton's "Presence of the Lord." In 1976, he released his self-titled debut solo album on the Airborn label. That record was rereleased two years later with a new album cover and a new title, *On Turning to Dust*. To the few who discovered Heard at this early stage of his career, it was obvious that he could write complex songs. With an earthy acoustic sound and a classic warble to his voice, he showed great promise.

In 1979, Heard released an album that turned many heads. *Appalachian Melody*, released on Larry Norman's Solid Rock label, was sweet, stark, and at times haunting. Norman's production was delicate and airy, and Heard's songs sailed. Fans of James Taylor and Carly Simon finally had a full-blown troubadour to call their own. Heard entered the 1980s as a respected artist, thinker, producer, and writer. His fingerprints are all over the second and third waves of Christian rock, and he remains one of the strongest voices in Christian music even though he died from a heart attack in 1992.

During the heyday of the Jesus Movement, a sizable group of Christians created a commune in Milwaukee called Jesus People USA. After a time of growth, the group split into three parts. One group traveled to Europe, one joined a more mainstream evangelist, and the leftovers headed to Florida for the winter.

That third group, retaining the basic Jesus People title, traveled the south looking for any opportunity to minister and evangelize. As had been the case in Wisconsin, music was one of their most effective tools. Their in-house band was comprised of a young pastor named Glenn Kaiser and his soon-to-be-wife, Wendi, along with Stu Heiss, Jim Denton, and the son of the group's head pastor. That young man, John Herrin, hadn't even known how to play drums before joining the band. But a lack of experience didn't hold these young radicals back. Herrin learned quickly, and before long the band had developed a distinctive blues-based, mid-Western, hard rock and roll style. They adopted the name Resurrection Band, and in 1974 they made their first recording, *Music to Raise the Dead*.

Eventually, they found their way to Texas-based Star Song records, where they released their first nationally distributed album, *Awaiting Your Reply*, in 1978. The album shocked most listeners. From the elaborate album cover to the cutting-edge music, it was a world-class rock effort, on par with era albums by Aerosmith or Blue Oyster Cult. Even die-hard rockers had a hard time reconciling their hard blues rock with Christianity. The band faced more than their fair share of criticism, but they were undergirded by their community and pressed on.

Awaiting Your Reply was followed by an even stronger musical and lyrical statement, 1979's *Rainbow's End*, which combined textured and thematic hard rock with more intense subject matter. In fact, Resurrection Band may have been the first rock group to challenge apartheid in South Africa. Front man Glenn Kaiser had such a passion for ministry that often at concerts much time was dedicated to evangelism. The band constantly tackled sticky social issues such as respect for the elderly and the need for fellowship and community.

Kaiser may have been the front man, but he had much more than four bandmates behind him. Jesus People USA was one of the few Christian communes that outlasted the counterculture movement. As the larger body of individuals set up shop on the north side of Chicago, feeding the hungry and sheltering the homeless, the musical outreach set up concerts in parks, on beaches, and in schools. They took their music and its message around the world. Their strength was that they were an extension of a family that was growing larger each year.

Two bands called Servant emerged in the late 1970s. Although they were completely separate, they did have something in common. The earlier one was formed in Joliet, Illinois, in 1977. The lineup included Matt Spransy, who'd been a member of Sheep, which had gone to England in 1971. He'd also been involved in launching the Greenbelt Festival. Also in the Joliet version of Servant was a bass player named Doug Pinnick, who'd later rise to national and international fame as the front man for King's X. That Servant was an aggressive and progressive rock band along the lines of Emerson, Lake, and Palmer or Yes. They developed a considerable following among musicians, both Christian and not, and were widely thought to be the best Christian band of the day in terms of musical skill. Unfortunately, the band never managed to take off, and after three years they decided to call it quits.

It turned out that Owen and Sandy Brock, fellow members of the Lonesome Stone troupe that went to Europe with Spransy, had started a rock band called Servant based in Oregon. When they came through Chicago, Spransy went to see them and noticed that they didn't have a keyboardist. He donated all the gear that the Joliet Servant had accumulated, including their PA, a truck, and keyboards. He was then asked to join the band.

If you went to see DeGarmo and Key or Resurrection Band in the late 1970s, you might have seen Servant with them. Servant sprang out of a communal living situation that followed the end of the Lonesome Stone run. The location and lineup changed, but core members Owen and Sandy Brock, Bruce Wright, Matt Spransy, and Bob Hardy formed a band that pushed the envelope. Sandy's powerful voice was reminiscent of Heart or Jefferson Airplane, and the band toured constantly. Along the way, they released some excellent albums as well.

The band's debut, *Shallow Water*, was released on the Canadian

Tunesmith label. From the beginning, Servant made two things clear: their music was pure ministry, and they were a rock band. There were a few mellow cuts, but the band generally rocked. Their debut was followed by another Tunesmith release called *Rockin' Revival*, which featured "I'm Gonna Live," a kitschy tune (cowritten by Pinnick) that became a favorite for years on the few Christian rock radio shows that existed. In the 1980s, the band migrated to Rooftop Records (distributed by Benson Records, meaning that they were widely available for the first time). *World of Sand* combined Servant's muscular rock with a serious recording budget and major-league production. The Jesus rock, apologetic "Jungle Music" appeared on that album, complete with references to nearly all of the other Christian rock bands on the scene. The song poked fun at the frail critique still being lobbed by antirock preachers. The chorus chanted, "Jungle music, can God really use it?" Their answer was a resounding yes.

In the 1980s, the band evolved into a synthesized pop band behind Spransy's considerable talent and scored a major Christian radio hit with "We Are the Light" from their Myrrh release *Light Maneuvers*. With production by Bob Rock (Motley Crue, Skid Row, Cher, Bon Jovi, Veruca Salt, Mettalica, The Cult), the album was their best sounding and most accessible to date. After one more album, *Swimming in a Human Ocean*, all the members of Servant except the Brocks quit. They tried to keep the band going for a while by enlisting three young men from their hometown. After a short time, the band dissolved, and the three young men, Linford Detwiler, Rich Hordinski, and Brian Kelly, hooked up with a singer named Karin Bergquist and started a band called Over the Rhine.

The hallmark of Servant was a dedication to the full-on rock experience (they were famous for elaborate concerts complete with laser light shows, pyrotechnics, and wild costumes), all the way down to their album packaging. Servant's slick arena rock represented a tidal change as the rock fringe gained credibility within the larger contemporary Christian scene. Along with bands such as Sweet Comfort Band, DeGarmo and Key, and the even heavier Barnabas, Servant perfected the rock concert-as-evangelism as invented by Petra and Resurrection Band.

In the early days of the Jesus Movement, strumming acoustic guitars and singing stacks of vocal harmonies were considered controversial. The association between Beatniks, marijuana, social unrest, hippies, and folk music seemed to obscure reason for conservative churchgoers who thought groups such as Love Song were too aggressive. Even Larry Norman's debut, though bordering on psychedelic, wasn't a true rock and roll record. There was the hard rock of Agape, but for the most part early Jesus music was folk based. To be fair, so was Neil Young, The Band, and Country Joe and the Fish.

In the 1970s, though, raucous music came from the Jesus music

Linford Detwiler led his band Over The Rhine to a position of high honor in the Christian underground and eventually to a record deal with Backporch/Virgin Records.

camp. Resurrection Band was the widest known, and arguably the most influential, but they weren't necessarily the hardest rocking. The doors that Rez kicked open were then demolished by the early metal bands.

Hailing from Sweden, heavy rockers Jerusalem recorded music that rivaled the energy of secular groups such as Ted Nugent, Rainbow, Deep Purple, and AC/DC. Founded in 1975, and considered the first Christian hard rock band (Resurrection Band formed in 1974 but didn't release an album until 1978), the band toured Sweden extensively. In 1978, their self-titled debut rocked the Swedish church. With music fully associated with Satanism and drugs, the band's up-front Christian message could barely be heard, at least by the critics. Resurrection Band's Glenn Kaiser heard a copy of the debut (in Swedish) brought to the United States by a fan who'd seen Jerusalem at the Greenbelt Festival in England. Kaiser forwarded the record to Pat Boone, of all people, who loved it and distributed the first three Jerusalem albums in America on his Lamb and Lion label. The first two albums, *Jerusalem* and *Jerusalem Volume 2*, were classic driving rock albums. Due to the language barrier, front man Ulf Christiansen struggled to make the lyrics deep. But by the third album, *Warrior*, the band was in stride.

Warrior stands as one of the finest Christian hard rock albums ever. The production was thick, the lyrics challenging, and the vocal and guitar work devastating. Not afraid to make the lyrics as intense as the music, Christiansen bellowed out the lines "Sodom is Sweden, Sodom is Europe, Sodom is America. . . ." *Warrior* pulled no punches.

Jerusalem began to tour the United States with artists such as Larry Norman and Resurrection Band. They'd continue well into the 1980s and usher in the era of Christian heavy metal. Christiansen took a cue from Kaiser in on-stage ministry. Bold preaching, urgent pleas, and altar calls marked every Jerusalem show. The band recorded all through the 1980s and 1990s, but their albums have been hard to find in America since their 1994 release *Prophet*.

Bob Dylan needs little introduction. He represents the best of the singer-songwriter ethic. He owned the 1960s and has been one of the most influential artists in Western cultural history. His fans don't just enjoy his music; they also follow him. He is an icon, a living legend, and at one time he was a Christian rocker with the highest profile.

Although Dylan, born Robert Zimmerman in Loves Park, Minnesota, was raised in an observant Jewish home, his agnosticism was well documented in his early days. In the halcyon days of the folk revival, belief in systems or organizations was a waste of mental energy. In the documentary *Don't Look Back*, Dylan can be heard questioning the existence of anything that he couldn't see with his own eyes. But what he said wasn't always literally what he believed. He enjoyed toying with the minds of both his mates and his adversaries.

Dylan was a spiritual seeker for many years, especially after his near-fatal motorcycle accident and the breakup of his marriage in the mid-1970s. Many of the most thoughtful songwriters of the 1960s and 1970s eventually turned to Christianity, and Dylan often said that he loved reading the Bible, which he found fascinating. In 1979, Dylan sought spiritual counsel from a few pastors in the Los Angeles area. One of those pastors was Larry Myers, who relates that in early 1979 he and another pastor, Paul Emond, met with Dylan at his request and went through the meaning of the entire Bible, starting in Genesis and working their way through to Revelation. On his own and in private, Dylan came to believe that Jesus was the Messiah as depicted in the Bible, and he ultimately accepted Christ as his savior. He then joined a three-and-a-half-month-long "School of Discipleship" under pastor Ken Gullickson and was privately baptized. There was an undeniable change in Dylan from that point forward.

The first manifestation of Dylan's newfound faith came in the form of his favorite means of communication: a record. On August 20 of that year, he released *Slow Train Coming*, arguably his finest work ever and certainly his most controversial. It featured Dylan singing in his most accessible voice, songs that were literal statements of faith. The opening song, "I Believe in You," laid his agenda bare. Then, song by song, it became clear that something had happened to Dylan. At first evasive during press inquiries, he eventually granted several interviews in which he testified that he'd come to believe in Jesus. Public response was less than enthusiastic. In fact, critics lampooned the album, and journalists seemed to incite the fans to revolt. Dylan's lyrics came back as prophetic: "everybody must get stoned."

At an infamous series of 14 concerts outside San Francisco, Dylan did little to comfort the fans who wanted to hear "Tangled Up in Blue." At a previous long stint in Los Angeles, he refused to play any material from before his conversion, even though the pastors at the Vineyard church that he was attending had supposedly told him he should play the old songs. When Bill Graham booked him for 14 nights, he wanted to make sure that Dylan would please the crowd. Graham got a confirmation from Dylan that he'd play some familiar songs, and he did, though barely. But he spent most of his time on stage singing his new gospel songs and talking about the end of the world and the New Jerusalem. The crowd booed incessantly. This scene was repeated as Dylan and his gospel band traveled the United States. At one point, he said, "I told you the times were a changin,' and they did. I told you the answer was blowing in the wind, and it was. Now I'm telling you that Jesus is coming back, and he is, and there is no other way of salvation." But the critics would hear none of it. Some speculated that he'd lost his mind, but many Christians started to notice the heat that he was taking without backing down.

Dylan befriended Keith and Melody Green for a time and surrounded himself with other believers. He even played harmonica on a song on one of Green's records. The Christian community was quick to embrace Dylan as one of their own, though a struggle broke out among Christian fans in the LA area who wanted to claim that Dylan went to their church. Ironically, despite the backlash, *Slow Train Coming* earned Dylan his first Grammy Award.

He recorded two more blatantly Christian albums, 1980's *Saved* and 1981's *Shot of Love*. Both were incredible artistically, especially *Shot of Love*, which at least tied *Slow Train Coming* in technical merit. After *Shot of Love*, Dylan clammed up about his personal beliefs. He spent some time studying with the Lubavitch Jews in New York, and some of his Jewish fans celebrated his return to their faith. Traces of New Testament theology, especially of the apocalyptic sort, still appeared on his records, though.

Whether or not Dylan is currently a Christian is a fascinating question that may say more about the bias of the fan than about the beliefs of the singer. Regardless, his music remains as intense and important as ever, and his gospel records stand as three of the most important in the annals of Christian rock. Dylan brought Christian rock to millions, whether they liked it or not.

Also spreading the word through music was Terry Scott Taylor, raised in Dana Point, California, by his grandparents, both old-time believers. Although he'd been raised around the church, music was his passion. By the time he was a sophomore at Los Gatos High School in San Jose, he'd already formed his first band, Scarlet Staircase, with a few other students who'd be involved in his life and career for years to come.

Taylor left Scarlet Staircase to join The Cardboard Scheme (one of the members was rhythm guitarist Tim Warner), a cover band that played British-invasion music and eventually some of the more adventurous American bands such as Buffalo Springfield. The Cardboard Scheme opened for Van Morrison in 1966. The band lasted only about a year.

Shortly after its breakup, Taylor became involved peripherally with some members of his old band Scarlet Staircase in a new group called Copperplate Window. The new band sported two lead singers, inspired by another local up-and-coming band called People (Larry Norman was one of the two vocalists for that group). Scarlet Staircase had opened for the very popular People in 1968. In 1969, after graduating from high school, Taylor was invited to join a new band called Pecos Bill, which sometimes went by the name Down Home. It was in that band that Taylor began to gravitate toward the new "California country" sound of bands such as The Flying Burrito Brothers and Poco.

In 1971, during the height of the Jesus Movement, his friend Tim Warner phoned him to say that he'd rededicated his life to Christ. Taylor had also committed his life to Christ. The two instantly began looking for ways to create music that reflected their newly revitalized faith. The result was a trio called Good Shepherd, and the group (an acoustic band at that point) played many concerts all over northern California at parks, beaches, Bible studies, and wherever else the new Jesus freaks congregated. They were featured in the 1971 film about the Jesus Movement called *The Sonworshippers*, along with Larry Norman and Love Song. They were about to record an album when Warner left the band for personal reasons.

Taylor then formed another Bay Area band called Judge Rainbow and the Prophetic Trumpets before hitting the right combination with Steve Baxter, Kenny Paxton, and Chuck Starnes in a band called Jubal's Last Band. Then in 1973 Taylor opened for Love Song, at that time the premier Christian band in the country. The same night, before Love Song played, Taylor was coerced into playing his song "Ain't Gonna Fight It" for Chuck Girard and the members of Love Song (at that time including Phil Keaggy). The response from Love Song was warm, and that was enough encouragement to get Taylor and the rest of Jubal's Last Band to move to Orange County and get involved in the Maranatha! scene.

Shortly after arriving at Calvary Chapel in Costa Mesa, Steve Baxter bumped into Marty Diekmeyer, who'd been playing bass and piano in various bands around the southern California scene. Various musicians coalesced over the coming weeks. Kenny Paxton quit, and Terry Taylor, Marty Diekmeyer, Steve Baxter, and another newcomer from Calvary named Jerry Chamberlain formed a new band, temporarily called Jubal. After playing coffeehouses and churches for half a year, the band worked up the nerve to go to a Maranatha! music meeting. All the bands got together to share what they were doing, swap stories, and hear from head pastor Chuck Smith. When asked to sign in under their band name, which they'd been planning to change, they found out that Darrell Mansfield's band was also called Jubal. In a rush, the band members huddled together to come up with a new name. Diekmeyer then signed the band up as Daniel Amos, named after two Old Testament prophets (and sounding intentionally like some old farmer type), and Mansfield signed his band up as Gentle Faith.

Shortly thereafter, Daniel Amos auditioned for Tom Stipe, the pastor in charge of booking bands to play at Calvary Chapel, a venue that Taylor described as "The Carnegie Hall of Christian Venues." The band played on a Saturday night and brought the house down. Taylor's mellow coun-

Terry Scott Taylor of Daniel Amos has released several solo albums, including 2000's *Avocado Faultline*.

try song "Ain't Gonna Fight It" was a huge hit, and it ended up being the first song that the band recorded at the Maranatha! studio. They signed with Maranatha! Music in 1975, and the song was released on the album *Maranatha 5* later that year. Daniel Amos was now an official part of the Jesus music scene. "Ain't Gonna Fight It" used Michael Omartian's skill on a Fender Rhodes and as a string arranger and one Alex MacDougal on percussion, and it was stunningly beautiful with its lush layers of vocal harmonies.

In 1976, the band recorded their first album for Maranatha! Simply titled *Daniel Amos*, the album featured a full-tilt country sound with more imagination, humor, and artistic vision than almost any album released to that point. Although at first they were referred to as "that country band," Daniel Amos soon proved to be one of the best bands ever to create Christian music. *Daniel Amos* was a resounding hit across the country, and the band became the biggest thing since Love Song, who'd broken up by that time.

In 1977, the band recorded their follow-up to *Daniel Amos*. Wanting to expand the country sound with various rock elements and somewhat psychedelic references and to tackle the formidable Book of Revelation as their subject, the band produced the epic *Shotgun Angel*. Alex MacDougal (who'd toured as a member of the Richie Furay Band with Loggins and Messina, Leon Russell, and The Beach Boys) returned to add percussion to the songs and actually cried when he heard the tracks. He described them as "overwhelming," as did keyboardist Bill Hoppe of Aslan, who added sound effects. The production by Jonathan David Brown was textured, crystal clear, and massive. Although still full of country elements such as steel guitar and lyrical references to trucks and posses, the subject of the end of the world was artfully woven through the tracks with both menace and hope. The instruments added color to the literary lyrics, and the result was breathtaking. *Shotgun Angel* was a huge success for the band and a crucial moment in the development of Christian rock. The 1977 lineup, which included Ed McTaggart (formerly of The Road Home) on drums and Mark Cook on keyboards, played numerous high-profile concerts around the California scene and toured across the country. During the tour, the band wrote new material that promised to take the creative spark from *Shotgun Angel* and fan it into a full flame.

Just as Daniel Amos became more popular, Maranatha! Music decided to focus on its Praise series of records and on its children's projects and to divest itself of Daniel Amos as well as Sweet Comfort Band, Mustard Seed Faith, Gentle Faith, and all the other bands on the roster. Daniel Amos left Maranatha! on good terms, with their third album ready to be released. They called it *Horrendous Disc*, and on it their transformation from country band to modern rock and roll ensemble was completed. Maranatha! sold the album to Word music (which had distributed Maranatha! records to Christian bookstores), and Word in turn licensed it to Larry Norman's Solid Rock label. The band was also signed to Norman's Street Level Artists Agency for booking and management, meaning that their career was completely under the control of Norman. The album was ready to go, but Norman decided that the artwork Taylor had concocted was too controversial for the Christian market and that at least two songs needed to be replaced. The new songs were recorded, and then the waiting began.

In what became a very public struggle, the release of *Horrendous Disc* was delayed for three years. During this time, albums by Randy Stonehill, Mark Heard, and Tom Howard, and even Norman himself, were also delayed. Norman explained that the delay had to do with issues at Word and a one-year moratorium that he placed on all artists with whom he worked, in order to shore up performances and spiritual issues. In a recent rerelease of *Horrendous Disc* on CD, Norman went into great detail about the persecution that he believed the artists had received at the hands of Word Records, persecution that he'd sheltered the artists from at the time. A series of articles, letters to the editor, and reader mail ensued in *CCM* magazine about the nonrelease of *Horrendous Disc*.

The long delay forced Alex MacDougal and Mark Cook to take their leave. MacDougal went to work for Calvary's Ministry Resource Center (MRC), which would become an integral part of the modernization of Christian music in the 1980s. Cook became a youth pastor first in San Diego and then in Virginia. Prior to their departure, Steve Baxter left the band to play country music in Colorado. Thus, as the 1980s dawned, Terry Taylor, Jerry Chamberlain, Marty Diekmeyer, and Ed McTaggart waited as what should have been the best album of the first decade of Jesus music languished. It was finally released on April 10, 1981, just weeks before the band's new album, *Alarma!*

With *Horrendous Disc*, the first wave of Christian music hit the shore, and the rules changed. As it was finally being shipped to Bible bookstores around the country, new young bands began to rock in garages around Orange County, itching for their chance to step on stage. *CCM* magazine began to coalesce thousands of fans of Christian music, and churches finally began to understand that the rock beat wasn't necessarily a hypnotic rhythm of Satan.

An Industry Is Born

The Jesus Movement was a spontaneous cultural phenomenon. Such phenomena are difficult to package and market for commercial gain, but the music that sprang from the Jesus Movement was a different story.

In 1969, the music industry was only about 30 years old, but it had been a major moneymaker only since the late 1940s. Some of the first music to be recorded and sold on 78-RPM records had been gospel. Thus, gospel music labels had been in existence for years by the time the music of the Jesus Movement found its way to wax. Companies such as Word Records and Benson Records had been cranking out various strains of sacred music since the beginning of the music business, but the new music was a tough fit for the straight-laced gospel labels.

General-market labels did their best to capitalize on the Jesus craze. Although Larry Norman's first major deal was with the pop band People, his first solo album was promoted as "Jesus music" by Capitol Records. *Upon This Rock* was a commercial flop, but Norman got another shot with 1972's *Only Visiting This Planet* before moving to MGM/Verve for 1973's *So Long Ago the Garden*. Although none of his albums was successful by mainstream standards, they were hugely influential among believers. Danny Lee and the Children of Truth recorded and were propelled by the Norman composition "One Way," a sort of anthem of the Jesus People. Mylon LeFevre (who used only his first name), a member of the successful LeFevre Family gospel group, struck out on his own in 1970 with a self-titled album for Word. It was even more gritty and rock based than *Upôn This Rock*, and Word balked. LeFevre sold the album to mainstream Cotillion Records, where it was eventually released. While it remains a favorite among collectors, and was dearly loved by a handful of cutting-edge Jesus freaks back in 1970, the record failed to bring gospel rock into the mainstream of either Christian or secular music. Since the early Jesus music releases failed to see widespread commercial success, by the early 1970s general-market labels had given up on Jesus music as the next big thing.

Executives at some of the major gospel labels wanted to distribute the new music through their networks, but they were afraid of backlash from the southern gospel fans and the traditionalists. A new retail phenomenon was emerging as well. Christian bookstores, often evolving from book tables at churches, became clearinghouses for Christian books, jewelry, art, and music. As pop and rock music exploded, mainstream record stores, short of shelf space, became increasingly reluctant to stock the new gospel music, and Christian bookstores became the only national network that would sell Jesus music. However, unlike their secular counterparts, Christian bookstores considered themselves to be gatekeepers, and they often determined the ministerial viability of a given book or record before selling it. Certain Christian records were thus "banned," and, once retailers refused to stock a contemporary album, labels took note. Eventually, the renegade spirit of the Jesus Movement was stripped out of "contemporary" Christian music, leaving a tepid version of gospel music in its place.

However, many, including people at the highest levels, believed that the more aggressive music was a valid expression of faith and a potentially powerful evangelistic tool. To support the fringe music, which became more rock based as the years moved on, they had to come up with creative strategies. It didn't take a marketing genius at Explo '72 to see 250,000 youth going crazy over the new bands and recognize a business opportunity. Some churches at the center of the movement and the music started businesses of their own. Chuck Smith's Calvary Chapel in Costa Mesa started Maranatha! Music (*maranatha* is Greek for "Come Lord Jesus") and released several of the first successful contemporary Christian music albums. Maranatha! often took several bands, recorded a few songs from each, and created "compilation" albums to sell at concerts and churches or by mail order. Groups such as Love Song and JC Power Outlet had their first exposure on compilations such as *Everlastin' Music Jesus Concert* and *Jesus Power*. Some of the early concerts brought thousands of new fans who wanted to take the music home with them.

Probably the earliest actual Jesus music label was a California imprint called Creative Sound. Owned by Bob Cotterell, it released some of the earliest progressive Christian music and distributed various independent records. Creative Sound's roster included early albums by Larry Norman, Randy Stonehill, Mark Heard, Agape, Maranatha! (the first three Maranatha! projects were distributed by Creative Sound), Agape Force, Armageddon Experience, Children of the Day, and many others. Once the major gospel labels became involved, Creative Sound was eventually shut down. But its role in spreading the earliest Christian rock can't be overstated.

In 1971, a year before Explo '72, Maranatha! Music released its first album. By 1975, though Maranatha! had given several rock bands excellent national exposure on compilation albums, the label had steered toward inspirational and adult-oriented music. The term "praise music" replaced the old "gospel" moniker, and the music became a huge success in the Christian bookstore networks. Maranatha!'s early records were simply called *Maranatha! One*, *Maranatha! Two*, and so on, until the company released its first praise album, called, not surprisingly, *Maranatha! Praise*. It spawned almost 20 sequels and many copycats. With full orchestral accompaniment, and a chorus of vocalists, Maranatha! music was unlike anything prior to it. It was definitely "contemporary" compared with the organ-based music of the church, but it wasn't rock and roll. Thus, the softer side of contemporary Christian music gained prominence, while the harder side was pushed farther into the shadows.

But somehow, amid the welter of *Maranatha! Praise* albums and children's recordings, one band was formed at Calvary Chapel and became one of the most important bands of the Jesus Movement. Daniel Amos blended country-rock music with humorous and thought-provoking lyrics and became a huge hit in southern California. In 1975, the band released their debut self-titled album on Maranatha! Music, and Christian music would never be the same.

Another rock band from the Maranatha! fold was Mustard Seed Faith, which released a progressive art-rock album. Sweet Comfort, fronted by Bryan Duncan, brought some rhythm-and-blues inflected boogie-pop to the roster in the late 1970s. Other bands included Gentle Faith (featuring future blues-rock master Darrell Mansfield) and JC Power Outlet. However, by the time Daniel Amos left Maranatha!, so had the other rock bands. Maranatha! then became synonymous with praise music. Sweet Comfort became Sweet Comfort Band and signed with Light Records, where they recorded some of the first full-on rock albums with mainstream production values. Oden Fong (of Mustard Seed Faith) would record one solo album in the 1980s and would join the leadership of Calvary Chapel (which by then had spread across the United States).

Maranatha!'s modern worship songs would become some of the most popular church music in the world and would influence a flood of other contemporary worship music from around the globe. But even though by 1980 Maranatha! was known for its contemporary adult praise music, its involvement in rock music was far from over.

Also involved in the modernization of Christian music was Billy Ray Hearn, a player since 1965. He penned one of the first folk teen musicals, an "Up with People"-style production called *Good News*. Within the confines of the ever-conservative Baptist Assembly, he and Ralph Carmichael (who'd recently recorded a relatively contemporary soundtrack to the Billy Graham film *The Restless Ones*) staged the musical for the Southern Baptist Convention in 1968. Hearn went on staff at Word Records in Waco, Texas to promote the musical full time. He also helped to pen various follow-ups inspired by the medium's ability to reach across generational lines.

By the late 1960s, Word had become the largest distributor of gospel music in the world. Carmichael's Light Records (then a division of Word) and Hearn's projects at Word achieved significant progress in the field of contemporary Christian music. In the early 1970s, Word formed Myrrh, an in-house label for its more contemporary artists, with Hearn at the helm. Mark Joseph, in his 1999 book *The Rock and Roll Rebellion*, aptly pointed out that choosing the word *myrrh*, which many non-Christians could neither pronounce nor understand, was a telling moment in the early evolution of the Christian music industry.

Derri Daughtery, Dan Michaels, Tim Chandler, and Steve Hindalong of The Choir.

Myrrh flourished under Hearn's guidance, bringing out records by Randy Matthews, B.J. Thomas, Honeytree, David Meece, Michael Omartian, the Pat Terry Group, and many others. Myrrh also acted as a distributor for other labels, such as Larry Norman's Solid Rock Records, Good News (Love Song), New Song (Phil Keaggy), Lamb and Lion, New Pax, and others. By the late 1970s, the Myrrh-Word family had become the undisputed leader in contemporary Christian music by adding Maranatha! Music to its roster.

In 1975, Hearn left Word to start his own label. Several of Myrrh's top artists, including 2nd Chapter of Acts, went with him. Sparrow Records made its mark early with major signings and a renewed ministry sensibility. Artists such as The Talbot Brothers, Keith Green, 2nd Chapter of Acts, Barry McGuire, and Scott Wesley Brown characterized the community feeling of the Sparrow label. Sparrow also distributed records from other labels, as Word had done. Affiliation with Birdwing brought Sparrow groundbreaking music by Candle, whose Agapeland children's series was a great success and would influence a new generation of Christians.

Sparrow and Word would rise to new levels of success and influence in the 1980s. Sparrow would introduce Steve Taylor to the world, the explosive career of Phil Keaggy, Steve Camp, and the monastic contemplation of John Michael Talbot, while Word would make Amy Grant a superstar, transform Petra into a near-household name, and sign heavy metal bands Guardian and Holy Soldier. Sparrow and Word remain two of the major players in the contemporary Christian music business. Hearn's legacy is now carried on by his son Bill, who took the reins when his father retired in the early 1990s.

Another visionary label was Star Song Records of Pasadena, Texas. It signed some of the heaviest and most progressive Christian music bands ever. The first official records by Resurrection Band (later shortened to Rez Band and then just Rez) were among Star Song's first releases. The label then went on a rock-and-roll tear, releasing the medieval folk and progressive rock of Kemper Crabb and his band Arkangel and eventually the most successful arena rock of Petra. In the 1980s, Star Song would have some contemporary adult success with signings such as Twila Paris, but its subversive roots could be seen in releases by Canada's Quickflight and the hyperactive synthetic rock of The Newsboys. By the mid-1990s, Star Song would be purchased by EMI Music (which also acquired Sparrow and Eddie DeGarmo's Forefront), but in the early 1970s it was among the most respected propagators of edgy rock.

In one of the great paradoxes in the history of Jesus music, one of the few other labels to promote heavy rock and roll was Pat Boone's Lamb and Lion Records. His label first brought the European heavy metal of Swedish band Jerusalem, whose 1978 debut rocked even harder than the music of Resurrection Band. Lamb and Lion also introduced DeGarmo and Key to the world. Boone, who could never shake the image of his clean-cut pop music and his white buck-skin shoes, was not only a believer in the viability of Christian rock but also a fan of it.

Getting the Word Out

With no significant radio play, Christian musicians needed a national voice. *Rolling Stone* kept the secular rock scene together, and Christian music needed similar press.

The first publication to achieve a national readership, other than the scattershot early Jesus Movement rags, was *Harmony Magazine*. It featured interviews with artists, reviews of records, and information about tours. It was well received but couldn't make it financially and folded after 14 months. From its ashes rose a second attempt.

A Christian bookstore called Maranatha Village in southern California published a tabloid called *Contemporary Christian Acts*. It hired local DJ John Styll to edit the music section since he had contact with the bands and experience in the scene. Eventually, the music section was spun off, and *Contemporary Christian Music* magazine was born. Not only was the new magazine the national voice that Christian music needed, but also it defined the music from that point forward. Instead of gospel music,

Christian music, or Christian pop, it would all be called contemporary Christian music or CCM for short.

CCM would grow in the 1980s and become one of the largest Christian magazines in the world. CCM Communications currently produces radio shows, books, other magazines, and the widest-read magazine in Christian music. *CCM*, though not focused on rock, gives rock bands good coverage and, since the beginning, has helped even the fringiest bands to get exposure. An early cover featured Daniel Amos with the caption "Angry Young Men." The magazine got some mail, but the band got a lot of attention. Considering how many conservative readers have to be accommodated, its coverage of extreme music has been impressive.

Other publications in the first wave included *Cornerstone Magazine*, *Strait Magazine* from England (published by the Greenbelt Festival), and a few other smaller ones. In the 1980s, a whole crop of aggressive and critical magazines would appear.

By the late 1970s, contemporary adult music had become the mainstay of Christian music. Rock artists were still vilified by antirock preachers and kept off the shelves by conservative bookstore managers, but they enjoyed the enthusiasm of their largely underground fans. Southern gospel quartets still had a lock on the industry, and a decade would pass before rock artists were fully welcomed into the Christian music scene without castigation.

Chapter 3

The Second Wave (1980–89)

The earliest Jesus music, though often acoustic based and folk oriented, was far more edgy and street level than what became mainstream Christian music of the late 1970s. A hybrid — "contemporary Christian music" — developed and eventually found purchase among conservative evangelicals. While Roman Catholics stuck to their folk and guitar masses well into the 1980s, evangelicals constantly evolved. The praise-and-worship music popularized by Calvary Chapel's Maranatha! label was much more palatable to the Midwestern churches than the rock and roll of Larry Norman or Daniel Amos. Artists such as Dallas Holm and The Imperials took slightly contemporary stylings and blended them with traditional trim to create a unique musical style. It wasn't southern gospel, and it wasn't rock and roll. In fact, it may be easier to describe what it wasn't than what it was. Since it bore no resemblance to any secular music of the day, it can hardly be called contemporary, yet, compared with gospel music in the 1950s and 1960s, it was revolutionary. By the time the rag-tag labels managed to coalesce into an "industry," the concerns of marketing and money had come to the fore. As they softened their sounds to accommodate conservative churches (and their own aging personal tastes), and learned to run themselves as businesses, the spirit of the Jesus Movement

Michael Roe, Terry Taylor, and Derri Daughtery of The Lost Dogs.

was seen more clearly in the ministry and music of the underground rockers.

They thrived in relative obscurity. The persistent touring of bands such as Daniel Amos, Petra, and Resurrection Band developed a devoted underground in which Dallas Holm just didn't cut it. A network of coffeehouses and a handful of regional concert promoters brought rock bands and solo acoustic artists into most areas of the Midwest and to the East and West Coasts. Many albums were actually banned from retail for one reason or another, but they still made their way into a few progressive stores and mail-order outfits. Selling music at concerts was still a major method of distribution. The safer, Christian middle-of-the-road music was easier to find and far less controversial, but for some the quality, attitude, and verve of the rockers were worth the search.

Another key distinction between the slick contemporary Christian music and the rock underground was aesthetic quality. Even though many rock bands had to work with minuscule recording budgets, they tended to have finer ears for production values. In the early stages of the second wave, many rock albums actually sounded much better than the adult contemporary efforts. Bands such as The Seventy Sevens held out hope that their music would be heard by the world at large, and they created it accordingly. By the mid-1980s, the Christian pop scene had become a machine that could sell a certain amount of anything, regardless of quality. The folks who grew up on traditional music didn't even know the difference between good and bad production. The result was waves of awful Christian pop records that still sold well enough to make many people wealthy. Meanwhile, a handful of rock and roll gems sold barely enough to justify the efforts.

Many of the established Christian rock bands of the late 1970s became the foundation of what was to come in the 1980s. Servant, Sweet Comfort Band, Jerusalem, DeGarmo and Key, Resurrection Band, Daniel Band, Barnabas, Petra, and others toured, recorded, and aggressively pushed the limits of what rock mixed with faith could accomplish. For the most part, the music was overtly evangelistic. Most concerts featured presentations of the gospel, invitations to accept Christ as savior, and, in many cases, follow-up with local church leaders. Some concerts were held in churches, but more often the bands performed in schools, civic centers, and parks. Fans were encouraged to bring friends, and the shows became evangelistic tools for individuals who wanted to share their faith. In the spirit of the outdoor concerts of the Jesus Movement, it was all about spreading the word.

In California, some of the former kids of the Calvary Chapel scene were becoming youth leaders. They'd grown up with contemporary Christian music and weren't prepackaged with the mistrust of rock and roll of their parents. As early as 1979, the raucous sound of punk rock could be heard in some sanctuaries in Orange County. Both Undercover and The Lifesavors took the relevant music of the day and incorporated a simple — and sometimes simplistic — gospel message into it. The churches completely supported the bands, and the result was like a mini Jesus Movement. As new wave and punk rock took root on the radio stations and college campuses of the southern California scene, Calvary Chapel prepared to shake things up all over again.

Shortly thereafter, youth leaders around the country went to their jobs with stacks of records by DeGarmo and Key, Rez Band, and Servant. They introduced the next generation to underground Christian rock music with great enthusiasm, sometimes to the detriment of their careers. Many elders and deacons hadn't quite come to terms with long hair and blue jeans, let alone heavy metal.

In the 1980s, the children of those affected by the Jesus Movement started to seek out music for themselves. Many had been weaned on *Music Machine*, *Bullfrogs and Butterflies*, or *Kid's Praise*, all of which had been closer to "contemporary" music than most of what their parents had listened to. So, as they discovered Petra or the local Christian radio station, their parents weren't nearly as distressed as they would have been a generation before. They'd heard the "devil's music" rhetoric and knew that listening to different tempos or beats hadn't turned them into tree-worshipping pagans or bloodthirsty Satanists. Odds were good that their kids would be fine. Thus, the new permissiveness began in the home and spread from there. In fact, by the mid-1980s, there was far less resistance to full-on rock, metal, punk, or even dance music in homes than there was among retailers ("gatekeepers").

So, with Ronald Reagan in the White House, thin ties back in fashion, and an all-music TV channel hoping to change the way that people listened to music, Christian rockers were still moving, shaking, and causing no end of controversy.

Faith-Rock in the Mainstream

For some time, T-Bone Burnett has been lurking in the shadows of Christian music, leaving his mark on it without ever "officially" participating in it. His roots in rock and roll precede Christian rock, and Burnett has shaped some of the best music in the world since his first gigs as a producer in the early 1970s.

Born Joseph Henry Burnett in 1945, T-Bone Burnett has had a love for rootsy music, including folk, blues, and country, since childhood. He moved to Los Angeles in the early 1970s and produced albums for Delbert McClinton and Glen Clark. He released his own solo debut in 1972, *The*

B-52 Band and the Fabulous Skylarks, under the name J. Henry Burnett. The record wasn't a commercial success, but Burnett was becoming more and more appreciated as a guitarist and producer with a sound well beyond his years. He toured with the blues band Delaney Bramlett and became acquainted with Bob Neuwirth, who'd been associated with Bob Dylan for many years and was featured in the classic documentary on Dylan's 1965 tour called *Don't Look Back*. Through Neuwirth, Burnett hooked up with Dylan, who asked him to join his Rolling Thunder Review tour in 1975. During that tour, many of the players in the band either came to Christ for the first time or returned to the faith.

When that tour ended, Burnett hooked up with two other members of the review, Stephen Soles and David Mansfield, and bassist David Miner, who'd played with Leon Russell and Bread, and formed The Alpha Band. Although all the members of the band (and Neuwirth and eventually Dylan) were Christians, they never considered making music in the Christian market and were never blatant about their faith. Yet their worldview affected their esteem of celebrity, materialism, and the overall culture of the world (their second album was the deeply sarcastic *The Statuemakers of Hollywood*). The Alpha Band didn't take off, and the members split to pursue other ventures. Years later, Soles produced Christian albums and even recorded two of his own in the early 1980s. His talent, like that of too many others, was off the charts for Christian music in the early 1980s. Mansfield also played later on some Christian albums and on dozens of mainstream ones. But it was Burnett who had the most profound impact on gospel music.

In 1980, his now classic *Truth Decay* album was released. On it, Burnett further defined his unique style of progressive roots music with scathingly satirical and critical lyrics that, while informed by his Christian faith, skewered hypocrisy in politics, religion, and even his own heart. He was brutally honest. His skills as a writer and musician were so consummate that his faith was not only tolerated but also celebrated by his musical contemporaries. He'd occasionally be chided as "preachy" by critics, but in general his spiritual commentary was so self-deprecating and sincere that he got away with it. He represented the maturing Christian of the 1960s crowd. A little jaded, yet a little romantic, Burnett defined himself and his art on his own terms.

In 1982, he continued to develop his sound with the release of a punchy and far more accessible EP on the Warner Brothers label called *Trap Door*. His cult status continued to grow. The next year saw the release of a more commercial and catchy solo album. *Proof through the Night* featured guest appearances by Pete Townsend, Richard Thompson, and blues man Ry Cooder. It was critically lauded as a masterpiece but sold very poorly.

While music consumers weren't enamored of his brilliance, rock's elite were. Burnett found himself in the company of legends on a regular basis. He produced albums for Marshall Crenshaw, The BoDeans, Los Lobos, and Elvis Costello in the mid-1980s. He produced the 1989 concert film and all-star tribute to Roy Orbison, *Black and White Night*, in which he shared the stage with Bruce Springsteen, Jackson Browne, Bonnie Raitt, Tom Waits, Glen Hardin, k.d. lang, J.D. Souther, Mike Utley, and, of course, Orbison himself. The live concert was filmed for HBO, and the soundtrack, called the most important and best Orbison concert ever recorded, is still considered one of the high points in the history of rock and roll. Although Burnett released one other solo record in the 1980s, the incredible *Talking Animals* album of 1988 (which included contributions by Bono, Tonio K., Peter Case, Mitchell Froom, and others), he was becoming more widely known as an ace producer, songwriter, and discoverer of new talent.

One talent he "discovered" was Christian singer Leslie Phillips. She'd released three albums in the Christian market that had been fairly well received. Although tame compared with later in her career, she represented the radical left wing of Christian pop in the early to mid-1980s. Her work only hinted at her latent talent, which she thought the Christian industry didn't understand and wouldn't allow her to explore. Thus, when looking for the right producer for her 1987 Christian market swan song *The Turning*, Phillips hired T-Bone Burnett. The resulting album is now considered by many to be among the finest ever made by a Christian artist. *The Turning* was startling and unsettling in its simplicity and candor. Many of the basic tracks had been recorded as simple demos in her apartment. Painfully honest songs such as "Answers Don't Come Easy" and "The Turning" were tempered with moments of sober hope such as "Love Is Not Lost" and "Libera Me." The record went on to be her best selling and most loved.

Burnett's production and guitar work were masterful. He pitched the newly available artist to Virgin Records and got her signed. Her 1987 album *The Indescribable Wow* was released under her nickname, Sam Phillips, as have all of her subsequent albums. Burnett and Phillips were married in 1991 prior to the release of her sophomore album as Sam, *Cruel Inventions*.

T-Bone released one more solo record in 1992, *The Criminal under My Own Hat*, and has been teasing audiences with rumors of a new record since 1995. However, his lack of recorded output is no indication that he has suddenly become a slacker. In the 1990s, he produced albums for Los Lobos, Bruce Cockburn, Elvis Costello, The Wallflowers, Counting Crows, Jackson Browne, and others as well as soundtracks for *The Big Lebowski* and *Clay Pigeons*.

Charlie Peacock brought uncompromising artistry and integrity to Christian music when he debuted in 1983.

In 1980, Burnett told *LA Weekly*, "If Jesus is the Light of the world there are two kinds of songs you can write. You can write songs about the Light, or you can write songs about what you can see from the Light." That simple sentiment took root among Christian artists and is often cited on the subject of faith and music.

Also about 1980, a central figure in one of the biggest rock bands in the world became a Christian. Kerry Livgren had written some of the best "searching" songs in the history of rock with "Dust in the Wind," "Carry on Wayward Son," and "Point of Know Return." As a founder of and the main writer for Kansas, Livgren had explored many spiritual paths. He finally realized that the peace he was seeking all along could be found in Christ.

The first indication of his conversion came in the song "Hold On" from the band's 1980 album *Audio Visions*. The hit single was a song written to his wife, who hadn't yet accepted Christ. Other songs, including "Relentless," referred tacitly to Livgren's new faith. The articulation of his Christian beliefs upset some members of the band, notably Steve Walsh. Livgren found the backlash surprising since he'd been writing spiritual lyrics all along.

He also recorded his first solo album in 1980. *Seeds of Change*, recorded for Kirshner Records, enlisted the vocal services of Ronnie James Dio, David Pack (Ambrosia), Mylon LeFevre, as well as Steve Walsh. The songs were more obvious in their messages, and the album was designed to be an outreach to both Livgren's artistic friends and his fans. Ronnie James Dio sang "Masque of the Great Deceiver," a song about the deceptive nature of Satan. LeFevre sang "Whiskey Seed," an admonition to avoid alcohol. Eventually, David Pack and Mylon LeFevre either got saved for the first time or recommitted their lives to God. The division between Livgren and Walsh grew and eventually led Walsh to quit the band.

Other members of Kansas had become Christians as well, creating a house divided. The band found a new vocalist, John Elefante, and had another Christian in their midst. This was good news for Christian fans and bad news for the non-Christian members of Kansas, who were becoming increasingly outnumbered. Their 1982 album *Vinyl Confessions* was their most blatantly Christian. Although the lead track was the band's first top-20 single in four years, *Vinyl Confessions* was the first record not to go gold.

The band, with Elefante remaining as vocalist, released a follow-up, 1983's *Drastic Measures*. It was a heavier album dominated by songs written by Elefante and his brother Dino. The record was a commercial flop and precipitated Livgren's cessation of all things Kansas for a while.

Meanwhile, he started a band called Kerry Livgren AD with Kansas bassist Dave Hope and two other musicians. The first AD record, *Timeline*, was released by CBS in 1984. Livgren premiered his new Christian band at Cornerstone '84. He was a superstar within the church, as were most secular-Christian converts. Livgren and his band left CBS and then recorded two excellent follow-up records, *Art of the State* and *Reconstructions* (Kerygma/Sparrow), as well as several other projects.

In 1999, the original Kansas band, including Livgren, recorded a new album for release in the general marketplace in mid-2000. Livgren remains an independent artist, making music in his house.

After the Fire was a band originally formed in 1972 in England by Peter Banks. It disbanded after a few years and was rebuilt by Banks with new members Andy Piercy (who'd played with a British songwriter known as Ishmael), bassist Nick Battle, and drummer Ivor (Iva) Twidell. Although all the members were Christians, their progressive art rock style generated a significant buzz among the general market in London. They released the self-produced album *Signs of Change* in 1978 and soon signed a mainstream deal with CBS.

Their major-label debut, *Laser Love,* featured a sound that split the difference between their keyboard-driven progressive rock of the 1970s and the emerging new wave sound from Germany and France. The single "One Rule for You" (produced by Rupert Hine), a wonderful treatment of the apparent censorship placed on Christians who want to speak their minds in the art world, managed to hit the top 40 in the United Kingdom.

After the Fire's third album, *80-F*, was released in the United States but accomplished little there. Their fourth album, *Batteries Not Included*, fared even poorer and led to some restlessness among the band members. They toured America with ELO, Van Halen, and Queen in 1982, doing 51 shows in 99 days. CBS reps heard some demos and asked the band to do some more recording. Later in 1982, with half the band wanting to move in a rock direction and half in a pop direction, they announced that they were breaking up. Subsequent to their dissolution, CBS released their cover of Falco's "Der Kommissar" as a single, and it flew up the charts, making the top 10 worldwide. CBS asked the band to reform, but they refused. Piercy remixed some works in progress, and the label released *ATF* in an attempt to cash in on the hit single. "Der Kommissar" is still remembered as a seminal 1980s tune, and it was featured in the hit Adam Sandler movie *The Wedding Singer.* Ivor Twidell released a few solo albums in the Christian market, and Andy Piercy remains involved in it as a producer and songwriter.

Originally formed under the name Feedback while the members were still attending Dublin's Mount Temple High School (the only nondenominational school in Dublin), the members of U2 knew, as the saying goes, just enough to be dangerous. They set out to combine the passion of punk with an inspirational message of hope and truth. Unlike the throngs of doom-and-gloom UK bands arising from the wreckage of the punk experience, U2 had not only questions but also answers.

It all started when drummer Larry Mullen posted a note on the bulletin board of his high school looking for musicians. Paul Hewson, Dave Evans, and Adam Clayton all responded, as did a few others. After an impromptu jam in Mullen's kitchen, the band was born. Although they weren't exceptional musicians, the Dublin punk scene in 1978 did not list "skill" as a prerequisite. What they didn't know beforehand they learned while they were playing. Under the names Feedback and briefly The Hype, they played garages, basements, parties, and clubs. The four members clicked on a deep level, and their chemistry was inspiring to everyone around them.

The spiritual climate of Dublin is like that of no other city. In a country where religion equals politics and hatred goes back centuries, there is no such thing as being, simply, a Christian. Hewson grew up the son of a Catholic father and a Protestant mother. He has often cited the influence of both denominations on his worldview. The pageantry of Catholic services impacted him, as did the passion of Protestant services. Somewhere in between, the simple faith of his parents had the biggest influence on him. His mother died when he was a child, a tragedy that led him to deeper sources for peace and comfort.

Hewson, Evans, and Mullen joined a charismatic Bible study called

Shalom, and it ended up having a profound impact on their lives. They skirted the Catholic/Protestant question by considering a third option. The Shalom folks encouraged them to integrate their faith into everything they did, including their music, without being preachy about it. Although a believer, Clayton wasn't part of the Shalom group; he was just not comfortable with that style of worship. He has always been much more guarded in the articulation of his beliefs than the others.

For the first few years of their professional career, the band, at least the three Shalom members, wrestled with the music business as it related to their faith. From the release of their 1979 debut EP *U23* on CBS Records, the band was divided. Hewson (who'd adopted the pseudonym, Bono Vox, that his friends had given him), Evans (The Edge), and Mullen would have Bible studies on the tour bus and in hotel rooms while Clayton would hang out with the band's manager, Paul McGuinness. The division almost led Bono and The Edge to break up the band early on. Fortunately, that didn't happen, and, as the feverish passion of their early faith settled into something more mature and less acerbic (some Christian fans would later call it compromise), the band regelled.

Through interviews and comments on stage, their faith was confirmed for both Christians and non-Christians alike. But it was in their music that it came up in the first place. One of their first college hits in the United States was "Gloria," which obviously expressed the band's desire to honor God. Similarly, songs such as "I Will Follow," "Pride (in the Name of Love)," "Rejoice," and "40" all made no effort to hide the inspiration behind U2. From the beginning, their songs generously reflected their faith. They were certainly the first hit band since Elvis Presley that was not only comprised of Christians but also incorporated their faith into their music. At a time when many Christian musicians were holed up in their subculture in both the United States and Europe, U2 blasted into rock and roll with their faith blazing. Many musicians, especially Christian musicians who felt unduly sentenced to a life of obscurity in a community that didn't understand or appreciate their art, looked with hope and fascination as U2 climbed from one level to the next.

The band's third album, *War*, with the assistance of a live MTV concert and regular video rotation, hit the United States hard. "Sunday Bloody Sunday," which many misunderstood lyrically, was an instant hit on college and AOR radio. Their concert at Red Rocks in 1983, the one MTV broadcast, was released as a video and live CD, and the fire spread. In 1985, *Rolling Stone*, from the incredible buzz of the band's US tour and *Wide Awake in America* EP, dubbed U2 "The Band of the 1980s." The magazine was absolutely right.

That a band of Christians had so infiltrated mainstream pop was astounding to many Christian artists, and U2 represented their hopes and

U2 became the most successful rock band of the '80s, despite the fact that their songs were based on their Christian faith and worldview.

dreams. Not only did U2 influence how some American bands, such as The Seventy Sevens, Charlie Peacock, and In 3D, approached the promotion of their music, but they also influenced almost every band in terms of how they articulated their faith and played their music.

1987's *Joshua Tree* was the band's first dominant release worldwide. No longer in the realm of college radio and theater tours, U2 released an album that accomplished something rare in rock and roll history. Not only was it one of the most critically acclaimed and influential albums in the history of rock, but it was also one of the most successful. *Joshua Tree* sold over one million copies in the first 24 hours of its release and went on to top 15 million copies sold. The band toured sold-out arenas all over the world. The success of *Joshua Tree* also signaled the beginning of the end of the "empty" pop of the 1980s. U2's purposeful music made the vacuous drivel of artists such as Madonna, Bon Jovi, and Whitesnake particularly pointless. Within five years, the pop landscape would shift toward "deeper" lyrics.

Unfortunately, the band that opened the doors was brutalized for its efforts. The elation of critics and fans as they watched the underdogs climb the charts, somehow vindicating all fans of music that sought meaning and depth, turned to cynicism because of the overexposure factor. Whereas in 1986 it was a thrill to hear a U2 song on the radio, and phones around the country would start ringing when an obscure video of "I Will Follow" or "New Year's Day" showed up on MTV, by 1988 the band was everywhere.

Attempting to provide an honest look at the band's *Joshua Tree* tour and their exploration of Americana along the way, U2 released a full-length feature film and double album called *Rattle and Hum*. Including clips of the band visiting Graceland, sound checking with B.B. King, and rehearsing in a cavernous Dublin warehouse, *Rattle and Hum* was classic rock on an arena scale. It was beautifully filmed, tastefully edited, and intrinsically successful in allowing fans to see what made the band tick, but a community overdosed on Bono's altruism and idealism turned on the band, the album, and the film. Critics lampooned the band's heart-on-sleeve approach. Even the white flag waving from the Red Rocks concert that had been so inspiring just a few years earlier was reimaged as a holier-than-thou and naïve belief that somehow Bono could save the world. Even the band seemed to be embarrassed and made various excuses for what they called a lapse in judgment.

On New Year's Eve 1989, at a concert in Dublin that wrapped up U2's Love Town tour, Bono said, "We've had a lot of fun over the last few months, just getting to know some of the music which we didn't know so much about — and still don't know very much about, but it was fun! . . . This is just the end of something for U2. And that's why we're playing these concerts — and we're throwing a party for ourselves and you. It's no big deal, it's just — we have to go away and . . . and dream it all up again." Rumors of a breakup spread, and in the following year that almost happened. U2 seemingly realized that their run as wide-eyed rock idealists had ended. It was time to reinvent U2 or pack it in.

The band members spent 1990 and 1991 writing, raising kids, and trying to figure out whether they had a place in the pop music of the 1990s. Already the desire for depth, coupled with the emptiness at the core of Western civilization, had turned music darker, more jaded and hopeless than ever. There was no way that the inspirational U2 could enter a post-Nirvana rock culture that had collectively crucified any references to absolute truth or hope. When the band nearly reached the point of no return, a single song came to them and gave them a sense of what their future could be. The song, "One," looked at the isolation, fear, and pain that had the world by the throat by distilling them down to a relationship between a father and his son dying of AIDS. The metaphors were rich, and the message was inspiring, but it was articulated in a way that resonated with the postmodern worldview of the 1990s. The band took off on a songwriting tear that would see them dig even deeper into their souls.

The next step was to record an album. Seeking inspiration, the band converged on Berlin as its inhabitants celebrated the tearing down of the

Berlin Wall. Along with producers Brian Eno and Daniel Lanois, they began to compose and record *Achtung Baby*. The grueling process took months and strained the band's famously tight friendships. *Achtung Baby* explored some of the deepest territory into which the band had ever dared to venture. The band reinvented itself musically as well. Leaving the influences of Memphis rock and roll, rhythm and blues, and gospel behind, U2 embraced the sounds of Europe. Their palette was covered with heavily effected guitars, synthetic loops and samples, electronic drums, and cold industrial sound effects. The 1991 version of U2 bore little musical resemblance to the band that had ruled the 1980s. The lyrics were more dark, oblique, and full of double entendre than any that Bono had crafted to date. The result was a sort of postmodern melee that seemed to doubt everything and to embrace the shallowest surface pleasures of life.

But the lyrical juxtapositions on the album were nothing compared to the ensuing Zoo TV tour. Bono, seemingly having learned that pop music didn't take to sincerity as well as it did to grandiosity, developed a strategy for the all-important live presentation of *Achtung Baby*. The Zoo TV tour was a larger-than-life send-up of technology in the infotainment age. With hundreds of televisions, cars in the rafters, cell phone calls to the White House, and live satellite feeds, the band attempted to roast what had become the technological revolution.

Instead of avoiding the conflicts between the message of Christ as read in the Bible and the trappings of the late twentieth century, U2 dove into those conflicts with abandon. Many fans, both Christian and not, assumed that the band had turned from their faith. For their part, the band let the charges go unanswered. Bono wouldn't even do any interviews unless he could don the shades and vinyl clothes of his pop-star alter ego The Fly. As The Fly, he answered questions in riddles, trying to trip up as many people as possible, and it worked. Although *Achtung Baby* and two world tours were huge successes for U2, allowing the band back into the good graces of an obviously fickle public, most Christians were distraught at best. What had happened to the band that at one moment would wave a white flag and chant "no war" and the next would have thousands of people singing the words to Psalm 40 like a choir? Years later, Bono and The Edge would assert that they had never abandoned their faith. Citing the scriptural admonition "Mock the devil, and he will flee from thee," they attempted to explain their choices. Off-stage problems such as the end of The Edge's marriage, Clayton's tryst with supermodel Naomi Campbell, and Bono's continuous antics (e.g., stripping naked in a public restaurant in London during an interview) all served to convince most people that U2 had abandoned the vigorous faith of its halcyon years.

Despite U2's struggle to live in, but not of, the world, to dismiss the band's relevance to the overall role of Christianity in modern culture is to miss an important point. U2 is one of the biggest bands in the history of rock and roll, and there are really two eras with respect to Christians in pop music: before U2, and after U2. The band proved that Christians could speak to the masses, and how U2 came to prominence has been the subject of much study and attempted replication throughout both the Christian and the secular industries. The lesson seems to be that executives of record labels don't listen very closely to music; hence, as long as a band isn't tagged as Christian before they "make it," they'll be let through the gates, especially if they are a hit. Thus, after U2, many Christian musicians used stealth. If they could keep their faith cloaked long enough to be a hit, while still telegraphing it to their established Christian fans, they could articulate it with impunity thereafter. In fact, many bands gained increased popularity in the post-U2 climate, and it turned out that many artists in the pop scene were believers. Although many never claimed in public to be Christian, there was a marked increase in music, especially in the alternative scene, that dealt with Christ, faith, or at least a deeper Judeo-Christian worldview. Many of the artists had been inspired by Bono's lyrical style, and no doubt his lyrics are some of the best Christian poetry of the century.

Comparisons have been drawn between the political activism of U2 and that of Midnight Oil. Formed in 1976, and releasing their self-titled debut album only in their native Australia, Midnight Oil, from the beginning, was a band with an agenda. Their breakthrough in the United States came with 1987's *Diesel and Dust* and its hit single "Beds Are Burning." Front man Peter Garrett's tall, lanky form, striking bald head, and even more striking voice captured the attention of the world.

The band's small cult of fans was quick to point out that Midnight Oil had been releasing albums for over a decade and that their passions were well documented and understood. Their advocacy of returning land to Aboriginal tribes was famous, and Garrett was outspoken in favor of strict environmental protection and basic human rights. He also happened to be a committed Christian who attended church and made no bones about it.

Garrett always claimed that his political activism was inspired by his worldview, which was in turn inspired by his understanding of the Bible. His consistency and determination earned him an enormous fan base in Australia. At one point, he was nearly elected to the country's senate even though he hadn't sought political power. He simply told Australians that they knew what he thought and that if they elected him he would serve them. In the end, though, Garrett remained on the political fringe and used music as his medium of information.

Christians, due to special coverage of Midnight Oil in magazines such as *Harvest Rock Syndicate* and *True Tunes News*, embraced the band as one of their own. When the band dropped back to the more obscure (but still successful) level before *Diesel and Dust*, they'd added many Christian fans to their list. Midnight Oil, though never willing to don the "Christian band" tag, did play the Greenbelt Festival and granted interviews to Christian publications such as Australia's *On Being*. Their approach to the integration of faith and art was influential for many Christian artists. In the lull after *Joshua Tree* and as U2 seemed to be wandering from their earlier convictions, Midnight Oil provided a welcome dose of real-world commitment and relevance.

The Call formed in 1980 in California and released their debut album on Mercury. Led by the gripping voice, muscular bass, and inspirational lyrics of front man Michael Been, The Call became a serious buzz band early on. Their second album, *Modern Romans*, yielded a minor college radio hit, "The Walls Came Down," in 1983. The song referred to the Old Testament story of the Israelites and Joshua and their challenge of the city of Jericho. It wouldn't be the last time that Been mined the Bible for inspiration.

The Call came onto the US college scene about the time that U2 came into prominence there. The bands played together, and the members developed a friendship since they had much in common spiritually and musically. Both bands crafted modern rock on an epic scale, often going to dizzying heights as opposed to sinking to societal depths, which seemed to fascinate most postpunk bands. Both bands found inspiration in the story of Christ and his teachings. And both bands wanted to fly below society's radar, not wanting to cheapen their faith by turning it into a marketing ploy.

The Call remained with Mercury through 1984 and for their third album, *Scene Beyond Dreams*. But in 1986 the band released *Reconciled*, their first for Elektra. *Reconciled* featured stunning production, sweeping lyrics inspired by southern authors such as Flannery O'Connor, and more hooks than a meat locker. Peter Gabriel made a guest appearance, as did Robbie Robertson. Although every song packed a wallop, the most prominent of the batch was "I Still Believe," a driving anthem of determination and faith that instantly gripped AOR and college radio as well as the attention of fans of Christian music. The song has remained one of the transcendent moments of faith in art for many fans. Russ Taff covered the tune on his self-titled album in 1988, and a version of it was prominently featured in the movie *The Lost Boys*. Other songs on the album, such as "Oklahoma" and "Everywhere I Go," were also relatively successful singles, but "I Still Believe" went down as *the song* from *Reconciled* and is still the most requested song at concerts by The Call.

Tom Ferrier, Michael Been, and Scott Musick of The Call.

The band followed *Reconciled* with the darker but equally intense *Into the Woods*. By 1987, the band had become one of the hippest in the world. Their live concerts, Been's writing and singing, and their recordings had earned them many top-drawer fans, including Martin Scorsese. Following the tour supporting *Into the Woods*, Been flew to north Africa to play John the Apostle in Scorsese's *The Last Temptation of Christ*. The experience would be documented in the song "For Love," released in 1989 on *Let the Day Begin*.

That album featured another small-scale hit with the title track, as did the 1990 album *Red Moon*. However, despite rave reviews, endorsements by some of the biggest names in entertainment, and constant world touring, The Call couldn't eke out a presence large enough to sustain its members. In 1991, the band went on a long hiatus that saw Been record a solo soundtrack to the movie *Light Sleeper* (starring Willem Dafoe, who'd played Jesus in *The Last Temptation of Christ*) and release a solo album in 1994 called *On the Verge of a Nervous Breakthrough*.

In 1997, The Call reunited to support the release of *The Best of the Call* and a new recording, *To Heaven and Back*. With Dan Russell (former manager for Mark Heard and Vigilantes of Love) on their team, the band toured and found that they had not been forgotten. Interestingly, although Been had been very vocal about his faith, the band hadn't had any official contact with the Christian music industry other than the enormous influence they'd had on many artists. The two 1997 albums were released in the Christian market as well as in the mainstream market, and in 1998 the band finally appeared at the Cornerstone Festival in Illinois. The tremendous audience response inspired the band to keep at it just a little longer, and the strength of *To Heaven and Back* indicates that they still have the goods.

Hailing from the Amish country of Lancaster, Pennsylvania, The Innocence Mission became a significant buzz band after the release of their self-titled A&M Records debut in 1989. The band was formed by Karen Peris, her husband, Don Peris, Mike Bitts, and Steve Brown in 1982 after the members met during a high school production of *Godspell*. From the beginning, the members' Catholic background held their ethereal music together. They came to the attention of Charlie Peacock early on and even appeared on a compilation album of independent Christian bands in the mid-1980s. However, it was finally A&M that signed them and set this amazing group of musicians loose on the world of pop music.

The hauntingly beautiful vocals of Karen Peris set The Innocence Mission apart from the testosterone-driven mainstream music of the late 1980s. But behind her voice were levels of compositional skill and musicality that made The Innocence Mission's music unexpectedly listenable. The lyrics, written predominantly by Karen, read like Victorian poetry. The music, also written by Karen, with contributions by Don, shimmered beneath the lyrics and Karen's breathy and vulnerable — almost child-like — voice.

Although the band never scored any major hits, they did develop a devoted following and were very influential for artists such as Sixpence None the Richer, Sarah McLaughlin, and Over the Rhine. They continue to release records, having recently signed with Kneeling Elephant Records. An independent CD of hymns and religious songs was released in 2000, with all of the profits going to Food for the Poor and local Lancaster food banks.

Like T-Bone Burnett, Daniel Lanois has received more recognition as an ace producer than he has as an artist. His atmospheric spacial relationships and otherworldly ambience have become near trademarks. In 1984, he was enlisted by Brian Eno to assist in the production of U2's *Unforgettable Fire*. His technique helped to propel the band to their greatest success to date. The sound got the attention of Peter Gabriel, who hired him to coproduce the soundtrack to the film *Birdy*. By that point, Lanois was on the A list of up-and-coming producers.

In 1989, Lanois finally released his debut solo record. Titled *Acadie*, the record delivered all the expected atmospherics along with a healthy dose of his deeply spiritual side. Raised in the French Catholic area of Hull, Quebec, Lanois relied heavily on his faith in his music, both in his original compositions and in his choice of cover tunes. He followed

Acadie in 1993 with *For the Beauty of Winona*, which featured the cuts "Messenger," "Unbreakable Chain," and other achingly beautiful songs of faith and love. His was a sensual articulation of faith, both vulnerable and visceral. Again Burnett-like, Lanois connected with artists if not with the general public. As a result, he found his dance card remarkably full throughout the 1990s. In addition to producing up-and-comers, Lanois found his niche as a resurrector and reinventor of legends. He reinvigorated Emmylou Harris's career with the stunning *Wrecking Ball*, Willie Nelson's career with *Teatro*, and Bob Dylan's career with *Time out of Mind*. Interestingly, each musician is also a Christian aiming to incorporate faith into music in tasteful ways.

David Schelzel, Bobby Mittan, Steve Lau, and Rob Minning were friends through their church in Pennsylvania in the 1980s. They began a band called The Ocean Blue that signed with Sire Records and released their self-titled debut in 1987. The band has since signed with various labels and released independent albums.

The Ocean Blue crafted dreamy pop songs with a distinctly British sound. Although never affiliated with the Christian market, and always refusing to be tagged as a Christian band, The Ocean Blue was one of the first examples of a band being influenced by the Christian rock underground and making it entirely in the pop realm. (They did give a nod to their influences by covering "Renaissance Man" by The Seventy Sevens both as a B side to one of their early singles and as a regular addition to their live set.) Their lyrics, mostly poetic tales of love, subtly reflected their faith more by what they did not contain than by what they did. The band tapped into a widespread underground of fans across the United States, many of whom were Christians who resonated with the music and lyrics and loved the fact that the group played clubs instead of churches. With the exception of original keyboardist Steve Lau, who left the band to work at Sire Records and produce albums, The Ocean Blue continues to create and record music.

Mr. Mister, formed by session musicians Richard Page and Steve Ferris in 1982, scored a rare one-two punch with back-to-back singles "Kyrie" and "Broken Wings" in 1985. The third single — "Is This Love?" — cracked the top 10, making Mr. Mister one of the biggest pop bands of 1985. Page's strong Christian faith and church upbringing informed his writing. Once kids asked their parents what "kyrie eleison" meant (any Catholic can tell you that it means "Lord Have Mercy"), Mr. Mister was outed as a "Christian" band. Page successfully steered the band away from the Christian market and made sure that the music, which he considered to be an honest reflection of his influences, wasn't miscast as gospel. "Broken Wings" continued with the biblical imagery, though it was more oblique.

But on the band's follow-up album, *Go On*, Page was much less cryptic. "Man of a Thousand Dances" and "Healing Waters" were obviously inspired by a Christian worldview. The single "Something Real" was a minor hit. And "Stand and Deliver" was used for the soundtrack of a movie by the same name, but the album never reached the dizzying heights of success enjoyed by its predecessor.

Mr. Mister took an interesting approach. Although they could write catchy hooks and pop tunes, for *Go On* they opted to go deeper as opposed to cashing in on their previous hits. The spiritual overtones were noticed (and mocked) by many critics, but the overall content of the album was harshly critical of the late-1980s consumer mind-set. Page and Ferris, along with the rest of the band, boldly challenged the very pop culture that had made them millions of dollars and hugely famous. Although they never achieved pop stardom again, they did earn the respect and admiration of fans of Christian music.

Another mid-1980s band that almost hit the big time was the California-based Lone Justice. Formed by a spitfire young singer named Maria McKee and guitarist Ryan Hedgecock in 1982, Lone Justice came to quick prominence in the LA club scene. The roster included Don Heffington (who'd played with Emmylou Harris) and Marvin Etzioni on bass. It was eventually the endorsement of Linda Ronstadt that got the band a deal with Geffen Records. Their first record featured a single penned by Tom Petty called "Ways to Be Wicked," but in the balance McKee's Christian background shined through, giving the band an unsought cultish Christian following.

With Lone Justice failing to sell well, all of the original members except McKee left. With the help of her manager, Jimmy Iovine, she reconstructed the band with new players (including guitarist Shane Fontayne and "Little Steven" Van Zandt as cowriter and producer) and recorded *Shelter*. Although the single "I Found Love" was modestly successful on college radio, Lone Justice wasn't clicking and was quickly broken up for good by McKee in favor of a solo career.

Geffen, showing rare commitment to an artist who was obviously more talented than her record sales indicated, continued to support McKee through most of the 1990s. Her debut and self-titled solo effort was released in 1989 to strong reviews and poor sales. Her follow-up, 1993's *You've Got to Sin to Get Saved*, wowed critics and fellow musicians alike. Her determination to redefine country music was becoming more appreciated as the Americana movement gained speed with publications such as *No Depression* magazine leading the way. McKee toured regularly, solidifying her standing among her fans but failing to click with a wider audience. In 1996, she released her final record for Geffen, the beautiful *Life Is Sweet*.

Although never taking off as an artist, McKee earned a well-deserved reputation in the music business as an excellent producer, vocal arranger, and even guitarist. She contributed to projects as diverse as the soundtrack to *Pulp Fiction* and albums by Bette Midler, Marvin Etzioni, Steve Earle, and many others.

McKee's faith has always informed her music, and McKee can count many Christians among her most ardent fans. Newer female artists such as Sixpence None the Richer's Leigh Nash, Beki Hemingway (of This Train and solo), and The Wayside's Michelle Thompson, as well as male artists such as Dimestore Prophets and Model Engine, all cite McKee as a major vocal, musical, and lyrical inspiration. She remains a figure that, while never associated with the Christian industry, made a serious impact on it by articulating her faith in new ways and through mainstream rootsy rock.

Claiming to have been influenced to start a band by seeing the passion and energy of a young U2, Mike Peters formed The Alarm in 1981 in his native Wales. Comparisons to U2 abounded based on the band's inspirational tone, high-energy live shows, and frequent spiritual overtones. Musically, the early Alarm, essentially acoustic-guitar-driven punk rock, was nowhere near the style of early U2, but to fans of Def Leppard and Van Halen it was all the same.

Peters, a Christian, articulated his faith with conviction and bravado. The band was known, first in the college scene, as a "kinda Christian band . . . you know, like U2!" as one college reviewer noted. Songs such as "The Stand," "Strength," and "Rain in the Summertime" reflected a fresh spiritual perspective that decried the nihilistic angst of the punk scene.

Although the only US chart action the band saw was their 1987 single "Presence of Love," they developed a rabid cult following and sold out clubs on their numerous US tours. With post-*Joshua Tree* comparisons to U2 unrelenting, the band decided to shed their anthemic style with 1989's *Change*. They tried again in 1991 with the bluesy *Raw*, but by 1992 the band had called it quits. Peters continued with a solo career that showed promise but left most fans reminiscing about the glory days of The Alarm.

The 1980s saw many other mainstream artists tackling spiritual concerns. Some were Christians, others were not. Some didn't know what they were. Van Morrison released the auspicious *Avalon Sunset* in 1989, which featured a duet with Cliff Richards called "Whenever God Shines a Light." The song actually charted on Christian radio. Van Morrison, rarely talkative in interviews, explored various Christian themes in his music from that point forward. 1991's two-CD set *Hymns to the Silence* was his definitive Christian statement, however.

Victoria Williams earned her fame as a singer-songwriter in the mainstream market.

Jim Kerr of The Simple Minds routinely mined scriptural material, though he never went so far as to call himself a Christian. Songs such as "Good News from the Next World," "Sanctify Yourself," and "I Wish You Were Here" resonated with Christians big time. Rumors that Kerr was a believer persisted, and, though he never confirmed or denied them, his music never lost its inspirational tone.

In the late 1980s, British dance pop band The Underworld released two alternative pop records with enough spiritual content to get the band quite an underground following among Christians. Their song "Pray for Me" was covered later by the Christian band Raspberry Jam. The Underworld toured with The Eurythmics for a few months in late 1989 and reportedly used a lot of Christian imagery, including a crucifix and scripture readings. The pop version of The Underworld failed to ignite, and the founders Karl Hyde and Rick Smith reinvented the band (again) as a techno-electronica outfit that came to prominence, sans the Christian content, in the early 1990s.

The Waterboys were formed in 1981 in London by Scottish writer and singer Mike Scott. For their sophomore effort in 1984, they were joined by Karl Wallinger and released the seminal album *A Pagan Place*. It expanded their significant fan base, including a growing contingent of fans in America. But 1995's *This Is the Sea* catapulted them onto the charts. The single "Whole of the Moon" was a minor hit that articulated Scott's persisting interest in Christian spirituality and mysticism. Upon the release of *This Is the Sea*, Wallinger left to create World Party (an excellent band in its own right with more than a few nods to Christian thinking), and Scott moved the band to Ireland for a reinvention. The result was 1988's critically acclaimed *Fisherman's Blues*, featuring a much more traditional Celtic flavor. Scott continued to work with The Waterboys until he moved to New York without his bandmates in 1991 and recorded *Dream Harder* with studio musicians. He then moved back to Scotland, joined a spiritual commune, and released his first solo album (if you don't count *Dream Harder*). On *Bring 'Em All In*, he dove further than ever into spirituality. Although his faith seemed to evolve into a more universalist vein, Scott did much to bring faith in God into the alternative vernacular in a positive way. Many Christian bands were big fans of The Waterboys.

One unlikely but consistent source of Christian thought in mainstream music came from Wisconsin's Violent Femmes. Although just as likely to offend some ears with songs about sex, the band's Gordon Gano was a believer who'd been raised in a strict Baptist home. Part of the group's appeal, no doubt, was tied to his nervous attempts to reconcile the geek-punk image that he'd constructed for the band with his deeply rooted Christian beliefs. Like Bono in the 1990s, Gano embraced the conflicts and laid them out for all to hear. The band's 1983 self-titled debut was largely devoid of spiritual content, but on 1984's *Hallowed Ground*, and even more on 1986's *The Blind Leading the Naked*, Gano was just as blatant about his faith as he'd been with his temper and libido before. The band never charted but was a massive hit with the underground. Songs such as "Blister in the Sun" would simply not die, showing up in movie soundtracks throughout the 1990s. As a result, the debut album eventually sold more than a million copies.

In 1987, the band took a break while Brian Ritchie set off on a solo career and Gano established an all-gospel band called The Mercy Seat. For their one and only album, Mercy Seat featured Zena Von Heppinstall on lead vocals, Gano on guitar, Patrice Moran on bass, and Fernando Menendez on drums. The song list was comprised of traditional gospel tunes such as "Let Me Ride" and "Let the Church Roll On" and some penned by Von Heppinstall. The Mercy Seat was well received by the pocket of fans whom it was intended for, but unfortunately the band never released another album.

A few rock legends reflected Christian beliefs on their records in the 1980s. Robbie Robertson, formerly of The Band, released his debut solo album in 1987 to critical acclaim and heavy AOR and college airplay. The first single, "Show Down at Big Sky," combined biblical imagery with Native American imagery. Bono, Peter Gabriel, and Maria McKee made guest appearances, and Daniel Lanois brought the songs together in a ghostly way. Robertson's follow-up, 1991's *Storyville*, was recorded in New Orleans with members of The Neville Brothers (many of whom were also Christians) and continued to mix biblical and carnal images into haunting songs that played like gothic minifilms.

Donna Summer became the queen of disco in the 1970s and is one of the most successful female artists of the past 30 years. But before the flash of disco, she was a rocker in a 1960s band called The Crow. Even her disco hits had more of a rock than an R&B feel, and several of her Grammy Awards and nominations were for Best Rock Vocal Performance ("Hot Stuff," "Cold Love"). In 1980, however, she began to have a change of heart. Beginning with the song "I Believe in Jesus" (Grammy nominated for Best Inspirational Performance) from *The Wanderer*, and driven home on the albums *She Works Hard for the Money* (a major hit) and *Cats Without Claws*, Summer took every opportunity to share her recently renewed faith in Christ. Her song "Forgive Me" was an enormous Christian radio hit and won her another Best Inspirational Performance Grammy. Critics blasted her for it, and she did see a drop in sales and popularity for several years, but as time went on her audience realized that this was no phase. Along with her expressions of faith, Summer was delivering some of the best music of her career. Her 1989 album *Another Place and Time* is an example. Summer was one of the rare "divas" who wrote many of her songs and stretched herself in many creative directions, including rock, pop, dance, R&B, and inspirational. Many pop artists from Madonna to Cyndi Lauper cited Summer as an influence on their music.

In the late 1990s, as boomers saw Y2K looming, many nostalgia trips turned into renewed careers. Summer, who'd sworn off her "secular" music through most of the 1980s and 1990s, finally dipped back into her bag of hits. Although she occasionally changed some lyrics and couldn't bring herself to sing a few songs, she connected with a throng of fans who'd lost track of her.

Although heavily influenced by the rock and psychedelia of the 1960s, David Hidalgo, Cesar Rosas, Louis Perez, and Conrad Lozano made their early living as a band that performed traditional Mexican and Spanish music at weddings and restaurants in east Los Angeles. Originally formed under the name Los Lobos del Este de Los Angeles (The Wolves of East Los Angeles), they jammed to heavy funk and experimental rock in private and studied the best of the roots music of Mexico as their day job. Eventually, they shortened the name to Los Lobos and added more of a rock base to their sound. In 1982, they signed with the Warner Brothers punk label Slash and released *. . . And a Time to Dance* in 1983. Their unique blend of traditional Latin music with LA punk influences has earned them one of the most respected reputations and most devoted followings in rock.

MC Hammer began as a gospel-based rapper before devolving into typical secular rap fare.

Main lyricist David Hidalgo has often referred to biblical stories as starting points for his songs. When asked about his persistent Christian overtones, he points out that the band members grew up in the Catholic Church and maintain their church connections dearly. The Mexican American community in east Los Angeles is not nearly as secularized as the white community, and the band just wrote about what they were going through, and their faith was a big part of that.

Los Lobos had their only major-charting single with their cover of Richie Valens's "La Bamba" for the movie of the same name in 1987. The bulk of the soundtrack was done by Los Lobos, and it went on to sell over two million copies. Unfortunately, that success pinned the band into a stylistic corner, out of which they spent the bulk of the 1990s trying to emerge.

Los Lobos, like U2 and Midnight Oil, earned the respect of the musical community overwhelmingly. Their inclusion of faith elements has never posed a problem for them, but they are still waiting for their first breakthrough single of their own.

Back in the Subculture

Randy Stonehill's classic 1976 album *Welcome to Paradise* was followed in 1980 by the two-year-late release of *The Sky Is Falling*, his last collaboration with Larry Norman. Upon the dissolution of Solid Rock Records, Stonehill moved to Myrrh Records, where he'd spend all of the 1980s and then some. His 1981 album *Between the Glory and the Flame* established his slightly darker and more earnest side, whereas 1983's *Equator* contained more of his trademark silliness than he'd ever dared to commit to vinyl. Songs such as "American Fast Food," "Cosmetic Fixation," and the hugely successful "Shut De Do" became concert staples.

Love beyond Reason and *Celebrate This Heartbeat* saw Stonehill heading into pop land more than ever. The title track to *Love beyond Reason* was a duet with Christian superstar Amy Grant, and it successfully increased his following among the CCM crowd.

But 1986's *The Wild Frontier* represented a major departure for Stonehill on several levels. Musically, it was his hardest-rocking and toughest-sounding album ever. Producer Dave Perkins got the artist in touch with his rock roots and helped him to collect songs about which he was passionate. The result excited his longtime fans but may have diluted some of the CCM crowd's enthusiasm. But the changes went beyond the music and the lyrics. *The Wild Frontier* was the first Stonehill album since *Get Me out of Hollywood* to be recorded for the general market. Through a distribution deal with A&M (Amy Grant's secular label), Myrrh was able to launch the album beyond the CCM ghetto. Unfortunately, though the album was excellent, A&M didn't make a major effort on Stonehill's behalf.

Stonehill didn't miss a beat, though, and in 1988 he balanced the scales with *Can't Buy a Miracle*, an album that rocked hard, experimented with electronica, and served up a few hits for Myrrh. Stonehill found that his home was in the CCM scene, and he entered it willingly.

The 1980s closed out for Stonehill with a stripped-down acoustic classic called *Return to Paradise*. On it, he returned lyrically and thematically to his landmark *Welcome to Paradise* album. A long-overdue live album followed as well as several "best of" collections.

Between 1980 and 1986, Daniel Amos (DA) released a remarkable series of four albums, the *Alarma! Chronicles*, now considered to be the band's magnum opus. While Larry Norman's Solid Rock Records delayed the release of *Horrendous Disc*, which basically was ready for release in 1978, Daniel Amos went on to record its next album in secret. The frustration that the band felt with Solid Rock, the politics of the Christian music industry, and the evangelical ghetto in which they seemed to be confined for life led main writer and vocalist Terry Scott Taylor and a few friends to start their own production company called Rebel Base Productions. Inspired by Luke Skywalker's intrepid Rebel Alliance in the *Star Wars* universe, Rebel Base Productions set out to create cutting-edge music. Its first salvo was *Alarma!*, a postpunk album labeled as the first volume of the four-part *Alarma! Chronicles*.

Alarma! was released in June 1980, mere weeks after *Horrendous Disc* finally saw the light of day in April 1980 (ironically, Norman had hurried to release *Horrendous Disc*, possibly fearing that the album would be obsolete on the release of *Alarma!*). *Alarma!* was released by NewPax records and distributed by The Benson Company. The one-two punch of *Horrendous Disc* and *Alarma!* was more than most Daniel Amos fans could handle at once, leading some to write letters of protest to the band and their labels. What should have been a gradual evolution had turned into an overnight change, and Christians aren't known for their ready acceptance of change.

Taylor's vision for the *Alarma! Chronicles* was vast. Perhaps sensing that their fans listened to music more closely than most fans of rock and roll, the band created an album that demanded repeated playing, referral to the lyrics sheet, and close examination of the album art. Then there was the story of the *Alarma! Chronicles*, a science fiction novella inspired by C.S. Lewis's celebrated sci-fi trilogy *Out of the Silent Planet*, *Perelandra*, and *That Hideous Strength*.

Alarma! was the perfect opening assault. The production (handled by the band and Thom Roy) matched or even exceeded the standards of the secular rock scene. Since Christian music was often satisfied with awful production, this alone was a surprise to some. The drums were crisp, the amps were crackling, and the vocals were mixed back in and weren't as disproportionately loud as in most Christian music. Taylor's lyrics were rapid fire and were hard enough to understand, but *Alarma!* was supposed to sound like a live album, and it does. With minimum overdubs and plenty of rough edges, the album achieved its goal and introduced Christian music to the brash, postpunk style of rock popularized by artists such as Elvis Costello, Blondie, and MC5. Unfortunately, the Christian community wouldn't be ready for real rock and roll for another decade or so. With the controversy surrounding the first installment, many — including members of the band — doubted that the project would see completion.

Yet 1983 saw the release of volume 2 of DA's *Alarma! Chronicles*. Establishing a pattern of using foreign words or phrases as titles, this release was called *Doppelgänger*, German for "double walker," "double goer," or "double man." The lyrics centered on the flesh/spirit conundrum established on *Alarma!* ("Shedding the Mortal Coil," "Ghost of the Heart") and took it to new extremes and sometimes to difficult conclusions. The album opens with the haunting "Hollow Men," a spoken poem written in the style of William Blake and the Book of Proverbs that sets the tone for the exploration of the duality of the human heart. The musical bed was the final track of *Alarma!* played backward, thus contributing to the sense that this was a continuation of the first album. Although the production style was similar (also handled by Taylor and Roy), *Doppelgänger* was a more aggressive and layered musical statement than its predecessor. A few songs ("Angels Tuck You In," "Distance and Direction," "Do Big Boys Cry?") were more melodic and mellow, harkening back to the band's early sound, but the lyrics were as strange as ever. On the rest of the album, the rock meter was pegged. Adding to the urgency were layers of overdubbed audio clips and razor-sharp vocals. No individual song on *Doppelgänger* could really be understood completely out of context, but a couple became favorites on the few Christian rock radio shows around the country, namely "Real Girls" and "New Car," humorous pokes at specific aspects of the Christian experience (dating and materialism). The packaging kept the theme going with its use of mannequins, masks, and Venetian blinds as metaphors for the plastic identities that we cloak ourselves in and our separation from all things true and real. *Doppelgänger* upped the ante for the *Alarma! Chronicles* and may have been the final straw that separated the "old" DA fans from the "new" DA fans.

Ever aware of the happenings in pop music, Taylor took a surprising turn for volume 3 of the *Alarma! Chronicles*. Originally to be titled *Vox Robotica* (Latin for "The Robot's Voice"), it was eventually titled *Vox Humana*

("The Human Voice") and featured some of the most accessible pop hooks and melodies that Taylor had ever penned, couched in synthesized pop. Everything, down to the programmed drums, was synthetic, an irony considering the album's title. Released on the ill-fated Refuge Records label, *Vox Humana* found a good number of new fans. The sarcastic anti-antidance tune "Dance Stop" became an instant classic, and "It's Sick" seemed to be inspired by the punk-rock revival in Orange County in the mid-1980s. But the real depth of *Vox Humana* came in the slower and more vulnerable tunes. "When Worlds Collide" is a moving love song of God's commitment to his children. "She's All Heart" explores the challenges of the spiritual connection between two humans in a love relationship. "The Incredible Shrinking Man" takes a prophetic look at the fallout from the feminist movement and the resulting confusion of roles and responsibilities. But possibly the most telling single is "William Blake," an ode to the British mystic-poet. As Taylor sang, in possibly his most heartfelt voice yet,

> You felt it so,
> You wrote it down.
> You lift my soul,
> You wear the Crown,

one major influence on his writing and worldview became clear. *Vox Humana*, despite its artificial instrumentation and its frequent and blistering sense of humor and wit, was his most human record to date.

Changing labels yet again and signing with Frontline Records (where the band would stay until the early 1990s), Daniel Amos released the final installment of the *Alarma! Chronicles* in 1986. *Fearful Symmetry* (taken from Blake's poem "The Tyger") represented the culmination of the series. The hypocrisy in the church from *Alarma!*, the duplicitous nature of the human heart from *Doppelgänger*, and the broken relationships and separations from *Vox Humana* were all seen from the perspective of a perfect designer God. Although still intent on skewering the faulty thinking of the church on various subjects, *Fearful Symmetry* was a worship album in that it celebrated the majesty and wonder of God. Musically, it included the raw guitars of *Alarma!*, the layered production and sound effects of *Doppelgänger*, and the keyboard presence of *Vox Humana*.

By the time of *Fearful Symmetry*, Daniel Amos had stopped touring and, with the exception of an occasional Cornerstone Festival show, had become a studio band. They'd still produce many more outstanding albums continuing various themes in the *Alarma! Chronicles*. However, despite amazing musicianship, standard-setting lyricism, and amazing live performances, Daniel Amos would never become a mainstay in Christian music, let alone in secular rock. They'd rarely sell more than 10,000 copies of an album, and they'd never be able to rely on the band as their main source of income. Yet they continue to make music.

The artistry on the *Alarma! Chronicles* wasn't fueled by fame, money, or even the ego-boosting of critical acclaim. Terry Taylor, Marty Diekmeyer, Tim Chandler, Jerry Chamberlain, and Ed McTaggart were driven by a desire for excellence and a faith that wouldn't let them quit. The albums remain as four of the most important in the history of Christian music, and they are an example of what can be achieved by the intelligent blending of faith and art. That they exist in obscurity 20 years later despite the rampant success of Christian rock over those two decades is perplexing. In those 20 years, few records topped the urgency and passion of *Alarma!* Even the "alternative" music that found favor in the mid- to late 1990s pales in comparison to early Daniel Amos. Nonetheless, the records remain hidden from a younger generation who would likely find them as exciting now as the fans of the late 1970s and early 1980s did. (Fortunately, the entire trilogy was re-released in 2000 as a limited edition boxed set, and may see wider release in the near future.)

No doubt influenced by the innovation of Daniel Amos, which had sprung from the Calvary Chapel movement in the early to mid-1970s, a host of young bands emerged from southern California in the early 1980s with revolution on their minds. They embraced "personal relationships" with Jesus and the most cutting-edge music around, and they were remarkably similar in spirit, if not attire, to the Jesus freaks of 10 years earlier. Unfortunately, with a few exceptions, many of the same folks who'd changed the church in the 1960s and 1970s had become disconcertingly reminiscent of their forebears. Young punk bands were shunned by the very churches that had shaken the system earlier by bringing in drums and long-hairs. Calvary Chapel, which had evolved into a sort of denomination with churches all over California and some across the country, had become the "mainstream." In the late 1970s, in fact, it had divested itself of most of the bands on its roster so that it could focus on its praise series and kids' music. "Contemporary Christian music" was finally becoming mainstream, but real rock and roll, be it new wave, punk rock, or heavy metal, was still on the outside looking in. Some brave churches put on rock shows, but in many cases the artists at the edge were suspect.

Around that time, Calvary Chapel faced its first major split. One of the pastors, John Wimber, was heavily involved in the charismatic "signs and wonders" movement. Charismatic Christians looked for outward signs such as "speaking in tongues" or spontaneous and radical healings as indications of God's presence via the Holy Spirit. A dispute over the gifts of the spirit divided Wimber and his church from Chuck Smith and the rest of the Calvary crowd. As a result, Wimber formed Vineyard Christian Fellowship, which grew exponentially in the late 1970s and early

Ed McTaggart, Greg Flesch, Tim Chandler, Phil Madeira, and Terry Taylor of the influential band Daniel Amos.

1980s. It is now one of the larger evangelical denominations (though it doesn't claim to be a denomination) in the world.

As far back as 1978, right in step with the advent of punk rock in England and New York, several cutting-edge, punk-influenced bands emerged from the Orange County area. Bands such as JC Rose and Boaz cranked out music that made Larry Norman and Love Song look like antiques. Some of them even considered the members of Daniel Amos to be geezers. Members of bands changed around, and it wasn't until 1981 or so that any of them recorded anything significant.

One of the first, and arguably the best, of the early Christian punk bands was called The Lifesavors. Formed by members of Boaz and JC Rose, The Lifesavors played respectable British-style punk with a serious dose of California beach pop. Their concerts, mainly in secular clubs such as the famous Cuckoo's Nest and Radio City, were famous for being raucous, energetic, and controversial. One of the members was Chris Wimber, son of John Wimber, head pastor of the Vineyard Christian Fellowship. Both Undercover, another young punk-pop band comprised of other members of Boaz and JC Rose, and The Lifesavors played at Calvary churches until the controversy broke out. Their fans, many of whom were high school kids from area schools and not Christians, were into dancing at concerts. Calvary, though progressive by the standards of the 1960s, drew a line at dancing. No dancing of any kind was allowed at

Calvary concerts. When the bands failed to discourage dancing, they found themselves unwelcome at Calvary churches.

Wimber Sr. advised the young musicians that the kind of revival they sought always occurred outside the church and that they should take their music to the streets in order to make a difference. The bands thus began to book themselves in Catholic halls, roller-skating rinks, and clubs for dances. Soon they were drawing significant crowds.

Perhaps sensing that it was outside the new movement of kids clamoring for The Lifesavors and Undercover, Calvary Chapel established a special arm of the church to work with the young bands, providing training, discipleship, and bookings. It was called the Ministry Resource Center (MRC). The MRC had several functions. It was predominantly a networking group designed to help bands get shows and to get bands to come to Calvary Chapel. It also became a sort of "farm league" for the Maranatha! label. Since Maranatha! was now synonymous with praise music and children's projects, the label (in some way directly connected to Calvary) created a sublabel called Broken Records. About the same time, it also launched A&S Records. Although there was no official connection between the church-based MRC and either of the Maranatha!-owned labels, it was an unspoken rule that one led to the other. Both Broken and A&S had national distribution through Word via the Maranatha! relationship.

Darrell Mansfield, who'd released one album on Maranatha! with his band Gentle Faith and then moved on to Polydor for his classic *Get Ready* album, released a live album on the MRC label and then signed with Broken for his epic barnstormer *Revelation* in 1985. Mansfield, though affiliated with Calvary Chapel for years, was still from the previous generation of artists. And John Mehler, the accomplished drummer for Love Song, released an excellent classic rock record called *Bow and Arrow* on A&S.

But in 1981 it was the new Orange County bands that had everyone talking. Fronted by Mark Krischak and featuring Chris Wimber, Kevin Annis/Lee, and Michael Knott, The Lifesavors recorded their debut album, *Us Kids*, for the MRC in 1981. Then Knott's showmanship got the band in trouble with the Catholic churches. At the same time, Wimber encouraged the band to tour the country and help to plant Vineyard churches. Knott hadn't planned on church planting, and in frustration he quit right before the band signed with Refuge Records for the release of *Dream Life*.

His name was nonetheless all over *Dream Life* because he'd written or cowritten many of the songs, played most of the guitars, and even recorded vocals, which had later been replaced. *Dream Life* was a pleasant alternative-pop record along the lines of Modern English or Duran Duran but definitely not the punk sound of the band's debut. Refuge struggled to launch the band on a national level, but *Dream Life* was the first Lifesavors record to get major distribution. Christian rock radio played the song "Fourteen" frequently.

Within a year, the remaining members decided to quit. Knott had formed a performance art band called Idle Lovell that really pushed the limits of what could be done with rock. Their semigothic music and theater-driven performances earned them a following in the LA scene. They recorded one independent record. After a couple of years, Knott noticed that nothing was happening with The Lifesavors. He called former Lifesavor Kevin Lee and Idle Lovell member Brian Doige and launched The Lifesavors again (though he spelled it Lifesavers). This time the band had a more modern rock edge à la The Psychedelic Firs. They were quickly signed to Frontline Records, which released *A Kiss of Life* in 1985. The album was well received by critics, and the latest version of The Lifesavers was a hit.

However, Knott's passion wasn't for the lighthearted California pop of The Lifesavers. For the band's second album with Frontline, Knott adopted a decidedly darker tone. He changed the name of the band again, this time to Lifesavers Underground (LSU), and the album, *Shaded Pain*, was a thorough exploration of loneliness, depravity, violence, and hopelessness. Sounding like a gothic rock version of the Book of Lamentations, *Shaded Pain* simultaneously thrilled many fans of underground music by Bauhaus, Joy Division, or Public Image Limited and alienated many Christian rock fans who liked easy answers, catchy choruses, and simple lyrics. The catchiest song of the album was "Die Baby Die," which dealt with the concept of "dying to self and being made alive in Christ" as discussed by the Apostle Paul.

Shaded Pain would later be celebrated as one of the most important records in all of Christian rock, but in 1987 it was largely ignored. In fact, if not for a feature article published in *Harvest Rock Syndicate* some two years after its release, it may have been forever forgotten. The record was only released on cassette (though about 100 vinyl copies were pressed and are extremely collectible now), but it was rereleased in 1993 by Metro One Music.

With the disappointing reaction to *Shaded Pain*, which Knott felt good about, he decided to rethink Lifesavers Underground for a while. He started a mainstream band called Bomb Bay Babies that came close to signing with a secular label and received enthusiastic radio play at colleges. When the band was booked to play at Cornerstone '89, Knott became active and recorded an independent release called *Wakin' Up the Dead*. Although not as dark as *Shaded Pain*, it was still consistent with LSU's basic sound. Propelled by an excellent show at Cornerstone and an energized fan base, Knott got busy and prepared to launch his own label called

Blonde Vinyl. He'd become a key figure in the third wave of Christian rock in the 1990s.

Undercover, formed by Joseph (Ojo) Taylor and some friends from other bands, made sunny California punk pop much less street sounding than the music of The Lifesavors but much more usable by youth pastors. The band played in bowling alleys, at youth groups, at high schools, and literally in garages. They quickly became one of the most influential of the early southern California Christian bands. Their self-titled debut album was an independent MRC release barely available outside southern California until it was rereleased by Broken Records later in the decade.

But the band's sophomore album was a different story. *God Rules* wrapped up the new youth-oriented Christian rock better than any previous record. The lyrics were as bold, confrontational, and simple as those of any punk songs, and the songs presented the gospel as a fire-and-brimstone Pentecostal preacher would, with plenty of references to hell. The music ranged from anthemic pop to scorchingly heavy punk rock. And through the distribution deal with Word Records, it found its way to the record shelves of Christian bookstores across the country. *God Rules* would soon be emblazoned on the backs of many leather jackets. Undercover had struck a nerve.

In 1984, the band followed *God Rules* with the groundbreaking, and at times breathtaking, *Boys and Girls Renounce the World*. They had taken the rebellious nature of *God Rules*, tempered it with more self-examination and better songwriting, and created a captivating album of anthems for the new generation of believers. The cover sported a striking black-and-white photo of three children with defiant yet innocent faces holding a sword. The album advocated rebellion against the societal ills of consumerism, materialism, and hate and various cancers within the church, such as denominationalism, judgmentalism, and fear. *Boys and Girls Renounce the World* was released on the new Broken Records label alongside albums by Crumbacher, Youth Choir, and The Altar Boys.

Shortly after the release of the album, life got very complicated for the members of Undercover. Various personal struggles such as divorces challenged the simple faith espoused by the band's previous records. Broken/Maranatha! let the band go and let Taylor go as label director. Adversity had struck, and the cheery tone of Undercover was gone for good.

Many fans think that Undercover's magnum opus was 1986's Blue Collar Records release *Branded*. The cover was a closeup of Taylor's "three crosses" tattoo, and the album was a gothic masterpiece. Through with the sloganism of their first three albums and embracing a more sober self-examining theme, Taylor and company crafted an album that had no equal in the annals of Christian music and few elsewhere. Sim

Mike Stand brought youthful energy and the spirit of punk rock to Christian music with his band The Altar Boys.

Wilson sounded on the verge of tears as he lamented his own sins as well as the dismal human condition in general. It was hard music with keyboards, which was rare. *Branded* remains a pivotal release in the history of Christian rock, but unfortunately it is out of print and very hard to find. Blue Collar Records was unable to place *Branded* successfully in either the Christian or the secular market. After *Branded*, Undercover called it quits for a while.

Broken Records had been abandoned by Maranatha! around 1985. Taylor and Gene Eugene from another Blue Collar Records band called Adam Again snatched up the name and launched their own label using it. A 1987 live concert by Undercover and Adam Again's second record were released before Maranatha! informed them that it wanted the name back. Taylor and Eugene changed the name to Brainstorm Artists International, which became a very significant label in the late 1980s and into the 1990s.

Taylor pulled a new version of Undercover back together. The band's guitarist, Gym Nicholson, and vocalist Sim Wilson had formed an excellent band called Boy's Club that had tried fruitlessly to get a mainstream deal. Nicholson was influenced by some darker alternative bands during that phase, and when Undercover got back together they were totally retooled for the 1990s. The result was a hard rock style along the lines of The Cult or Guns N' Roses. In 1990, Undercover would emerge from their years of relative silence with a stunning album. *Balance of Power* rocked hard and maintained the dark tone while leaving the 1980s-sounding keys far behind. The band would release two more albums, 1992's *Devotion* and 1994's *Forum*, before calling it quits for good. Undercover was invited to perform a reunion show at Cornerstone Festival 2000.

The Altar Boys took the joy of three-chord punk and married it to a frenetic and boisterous fist-in-the-air faith. Their lyrics were rallying cries for kids to become "rebels for Jesus," fully co-opting the trappings of punk rock — from the clothes to the antiestablishment sentiments — and adding a Jesus spin.

Founder and front man Mike Stand, who'd watched his brother, Kevin Lee, drum for The Lifesavors, was primed and ready. The band's debut, also a local MRC release, featured the soon-to-be-classics "I'm into God" and "Oh Oh Nancy." Their appearance at the first Cornerstone Festival in 1984 made them the buzz band of the year. But before that they were the new hot band in the Orange County scene, often sharing the stage with Undercover and The Lifesavors.

The band landed on the Maranatha! version of Broken Records for their first national release, the stellar *When You're a Rebel* (1985). Before Broken Records was dismantled, one of the Calvary Chapel pastors, Jim Kempner, signed the bulk of the bands to personal service contracts.

Then Kempner started a new label called Frontline Records. One of its first releases was *Gut Level Music* by The Altar Boys in 1986 — arguably the band's high point.

Stand had developed a stage presence that rivaled anything ever seen. His fervor for post-punk rock was matched by his desire to relate the gospel in a way that made sense to punkers. Like the Jesus freaks of the 1970s, he questioned religiosity, materialism, moral relativism, and complacency.

Youth pastors loved the band. Although the music was loud, it was basically pop music on adrenaline. And even though the band members had big hair and ripped jeans, their lyrics were clear, passionate, and 100% about God. They were the first of the MRC bands to tour nationally, and they won fans wherever they played. Because of their touring, The Altar Boys became one of the biggest of the southern California bands of the early 1980s.

As the 1980s wound down, the band tempered their sound a bit. 1987's *Against the Grain* added more texture and sophistication to the basic power-pop sound. 1989's *Forever Mercy* was their high point musically and lyrically as they managed to combine the three-chord drive from GLM with acoustic guitars, more melodic vocals, and lyrics that gave listeners something to chew on. The lyrics, easy to understand, were designed to reinforce the biblical injunction to be "in the world but not of the world."

When the band announced that they were taking an indefinite hiatus in 1992, some fans actually wept. Fortunately, front man, writer, and vocalist Mike Stand was far from finished with music. He recorded two solo albums as he pursued his college degree. Then, in 1993, after receiving his degree, he launched Clash of Symbols, an excellent alternative band that released two records. Stand currently teaches music at an elementary school full time and plays worship music with his brother Kevin Lee every Wednesday and Sunday for a youth group, bringing his career full circle.

Also part of the Calvary Chapel scene, though more removed, was Derri Daughtery, who grew up a fan of Daniel Amos and other Jesus music bands in the 1970s, many of which he saw at the church that his father pastored. He started his career as a roadie and then studio hand for Daniel Amos. In 1981, when Daughtery was helping the band record *Alarma!*, he accidentally erased all but the bass tracks on a song that was to be on the album.

Daughtery formed a band called The Youth Choir with drummer Steve Hindalong and later added bassist Mike Sauerbrey. Obviously inspired by bands such as The Police and U2, The Youth Choir combined early new wave/alternative music with Daughtery's sweet voice to great success. The band released their debut, *Voices in Shadows*, on Broken Records in 1985.

Later that year, the band signed a deal with Shadow Records, a label that few people knew much about. Shadow managed to get The Youth Choir to tour with Steve Taylor for his 1985 *On the Fritz* tour. The band rushed to get a new five-song EP done in time to sell on the road. They eventually got out of the deal with Shadow and in 1986 signed with Myrrh as The Choir. As such, and with Charlie Peacock at the production helm, they recorded *Diamonds and Rain*, a beautiful album that, though only hinting at the talent to come, did put The Choir on the map nationally.

1987 was the big year for the band. Daughtery built his own studio called Neverland, and the band, which had grown to include the sax and lyricon skills of Buckeye Dan Michaels and the bass groove of Robin Spurrs, spent 20 weeks recording their first self-produced album. *Chase the Kangaroo* stunned fringe music fans. Deep rhythms, layered guitars, haunting vocals, and intensely poetic lyrics came together in a sublime way. The best elements of U2, Daniel Lanois, Echo and the Bunnymen, and The Police could be heard, but the sound was also entirely new. Rock and alternative fans called it the album of the year, and many called it the album of the decade. The Choir had officially graduated to the head of the class. In 1987, they were filling the role that Daniel Amos had filled 10 years earlier.

The Choir closed the decade with two more brilliant works. 1989's *Wide Eyed Wonder* brought increased romance and vulnerability to the band's style. Having made several national tours, The Choir was really becoming popular. *Wide Eyed Wonder* also featured one of the first video companion pieces. 1990's *Circle Slide* stands as one of the best Christian albums ever made. Taking the formula that they began with on *Chase the Kangaroo*, but achieving a much more live feel, the band simply soared. *Circle Slide* was also simultaneously released on Epic Records through a deal with Word. It was The Choir's first shot at the "real world," and it didn't go so well. Some college stations spun the tunes, but despite the obvious brilliance of the record a breakthrough didn't occur.

The Choir entered the 1990s as leaders of the expanding alternative Christian music scene. In 1992, they launched their own label, Glasshouse Records, from which they released some of the best records of the 1990s. Daughtery and Hindalong were tapped for production chores on many new bands, and Michaels became an industry leader as an A&R man for several labels.

Arguably the first electronic-techno band in Christian music was Crumbacher, named after front man Stephen Crumbacher. Their Broken Records debut, *Incandescent*, followed their appearance on the *What's*

Shakin' compilation and launched a brief but storied career over which they released seven albums. The band flourished in the 1980s but then faded in the 1990s. Nonetheless, their keyboard-driven music ushered in a number of techno bands throughout the 1980s and 1990s, many of whom still cite Crumbacher as a major influence.

In 1999, Crumbacher, now a resident of Nashville, released a CD of demos recorded between 1992 and 1999. Entitled *Reinvention*, it was sold in MP3 format on the Internet and was one of the first Christian albums available that way.

In the early 1970s, Maranatha! had discovered that one of the most effective ways to build hype for new bands was through compilation records. That trend continued in the 1980s. Since radio stations wouldn't play the music, compilations such as *What's Shakin'*, a low-budget record short on professionalism and long on spirit, were the only publicity some new bands got. *What's Shakin'* is a slice of history in its own way. As one of the first MRC releases to make it outside California, it served as the opening salvo of what would be a steady flow of fresh rock from behind the "Orange Curtain."

Most notable among the contributions is probably The Youth Choir's "It's So Wonderful," two minutes of the sweetest pop music ever. This recording predates the band's debut by over a year. Also of interest to many fans was the first appearance of The Altar Boys with the song "Go for You," a punk-pop tune with kitschy charm similar to The Youth Choir tune. As Mike Stand sings "Gonna gonna gonna go for you — ooh," it's impossible not to grin. Undercover's "One of These Days" was also clever and catchy. The only other artist represented who continued with a career beyond the MRC was Stephen Crumbacher. Sharon McCall's "From the Grave" was noteworthy since it featured the members of Daniel Amos as her band (McCall handled vocals, rhythm guitars, and B3) along with Randy Stonehill on backing vocals. The song was a muscular Joan Jett-type rocker that left many fans waiting for a full-length album that never materialized. The Proclaimers (not the Scottish band with the hit in the late 1980s), The Lifters, Omega Band, Malcolm and the Mirrors (featuring Malcolm Wild of Malcolm and Alwyn fame), and CIA rounded out the lineup. The transplanted Brit, Wild, did release one excellent and obscure album with his band called *Red Alert* through the MRC even though he was a seasoned artist from the early days of Jesus music.

Other bands showed promise but faded prematurely. CIA included a young drummer named Chuck Cummings, who'd go on to play for most of the California bands at one point and end up launching his own label after a stint as an A&R guy for one of the major Christian labels. Cummings had also played in Common Bond, an excellent new wave band that had released one album (*Heaven Is Calling* in 1985) on Broken

Steve Hindalong, though best-known as the lyricist and drummer for The Choir, has become a well-respected producer and session percussionist.

Records and then one (*Anger into Passion* in 1986) on Frontline Records. Tamarak was a reggae-inflected pop group featuring Rob Watson and John Mehler. The Lifters were founded by Chris Brigandi, Brian Rey, and Kass Roll (who'd all been part of The Lifesavors' road crew) and released two fun rockabilly records in the Stray Cats tradition. In the mid-1980s, half the band split off and formed Wild Blue Yonder with the vocal talents of young prodigy Crystal Lewis leading the way. Although Wild Blue Yonder released only one album, Lewis would evolve into one of the most successful female vocalists in Christian music in the 1990s.

The MRC functioned for just a few years, and by the mid-1980s Calvary Chapel moved on to other things and even shut down the promising A&S Records. Calvary had jump-started the rock side of Christian music in the early 1980s, just as it had in the early 1970s. But there was much more than just the Calvary-related bands happening in the 1980s.

One of the most exciting and influential musical explosions came out of Sacramento in the early 1980s. Warehouse Christian Ministries (WCM), a nondenominational church under the auspices of Calvary Chapel in Costa Mesa, launched a production company called Sangre Productions in the late 1970s, which evolved into a label called Exit Records by 1982. Some of the artists affiliated with Exit would radically change the face of Christian rock.

WCM really goes back to the 1960s. Louis Neely, a young pastor and world-traveling evangelist, felt called to reach the hippies, who seemed to be so desperate for answers. He didn't have to look far since a growing group of them had begun meeting weekly at his house for Bible study with his wife, Mary, when Louis was traveling. He envisioned purchasing an old warehouse and setting it up as an alternative outreach center. It wasn't going to be a church; instead, it would be a place that all the local churches in his denomination could use for musical outreach and other functions.

The other churches in Sacramento weren't as keyed into the vision as the Neelys were, though. Louis was told to give up his vision or risk losing his ordination. He went ahead with his plans to purchase the building and was dismissed by his denomination.

At about the same time, Mary saw the famous *Life* story of the Jesus Movement and Calvary Chapel. She got a group together and headed to Costa Mesa to meet Chuck Smith (head pastor of Calvary Chapel), who met with her and said that he also believed this was a move of God. He offered to go to Sacramento to dedicate WCM. He also reinstated Louis's ordination. WCM officially opened its doors on April 28, 1974.

WCM used music in the way that Calvary Chapel had. Concerts on Saturday nights were followed by Bible studies. Then, as the Calvary bands began to tour, they came through and played at the warehouse.

Although the first time that Neely held a Sunday service he was the only one in attendance, WCM took off quickly. Unchurched kids flocked there in droves.

The Neelys had a particularly progressive approach to using music as outreach. One of their first major projects was a radio show called *Rock and Religion*. That show evolved into a much slicker show called *Rock Scope*, which at its peak was broadcast on more than 200 radio stations. *Rock Scope* consistently tackled controversial music and media from a perspective of faith without being preachy. The church built a recording studio shortly thereafter for Sangre Productions, with Mary at the helm.

Her background in the music business (producing the radio shows), combined with her specific ministry experience, led her to a much wider vision of what Christians could and should be doing with music. She believed that Christian artists should be engaging the popular culture instead of just singing for each other in churches. This belief would eventually lead WCM to start an in-house record label called Exit Records. The concept of a church running a record company wasn't new, for Calvary had done it with Maranatha!, but a church launching an alternative label with intentions of reaching beyond the Christian scene was a first.

The band that played the Saturday-night concerts was called the Scratch Band (so named because it always had a thrown-together feel). The band got quite good from all the playing, and eventually the members ended up in various serious groups.

Steve Griffith had been an engineer, producer, and full-time professional musician since the mid-1970s. His partner, Jim Abegg (Jimmy A), had played in the early Exit band Thomas Goodlenas and Panacea, an excellent but obscure jazz-pop band. Abegg and Griffith hooked up in 1982, and Vector was formed. Griffith had been influenced by the progressive strains of Yes, Emerson, Lake, and Palmer, and Jethro Tull. Abegg, a Midwestern native, had been more into the classic guitar rock of Hendrix and the newly emerging guitar technique of bands such as U2 and Roxy Music. Griffith's clear tenor voice, excellent songwriting, and stylistically savvy ear mixed well with Abegg's innovative guitar style, Charlie Peacock's textured keyboard sound, and former Temptations and Romeo Void drummer Aaron Smith's drum skills. Vector quickly became one of the early breakout hits on the new Exit label. The band's first album, *Mannequin Virtue*, was a very Police–U2–Fixx-influenced effort, with excellent production and solid songs. Christian rock critics were stunned by the professionalism, and Vector landed big time in the industry.

For their follow-up, the band, who'd lost Peacock to his previously established solo career and Smith to The Seventy Sevens, enlisted the production skills of Chuck Wild (Missing Persons). The result was a much more commercial, keyboard-styled pop record called *Please Stand By*. It scored a major Christian radio hit with the love ballad "Can't Help Falling in Love."

The Scratch Band, for the most part, turned into The Seventy Sevens around 1982. With Jan Eric Volz on bass, Mark Tootle on keys, and Mark Proctor on drums, The Seventy Sevens blended everything from new wave to Zeppelin to The Crampz to U2 into a musical spasm that worked on every level. Mike Roe's performances, which included flailing his skinny body around the stage like Iggy Pop or screaming into the microphone as if he was engaged in some kind of primal therapy, were the stuff of legend. The band was tight, and The Seventy Sevens quickly earned respect as one of the most skilled bands ever to play in the Christian market.

But as catchy as their 1983 debut *Ping Pong over the Abyss* was, it was nothing compared with their sophomore effort. With Proctor gone because of family commitments (though he cowrote several of the songs), The Seventy Sevens swiped Aaron Smith from the mostly inactive Vector lineup. Smith had played on "Papa Was a Rolling Stone" by The Temptations and on Romeo Void's "Girl in Trouble." His chops soon became legendary. In 1984, the band unveiled *All Fall Down*, a sophisticated rock treasure. A heightened sense of texture, lyrical vulnerability, and candor permeated the songs. *All Fall Down* remains one of the most important records in the entire genre. Its influence on the next generation of musicians was immense. The Seventy Sevens had become the hottest band in the underground.

To support *All Fall Down* and *Please Stand By*, in 1984 The Seventy Sevens and Vector toured with Resurrection Band while the suits at home argued over whether they should be promoted in the Christian market or in the mainstream market. Exit had signed a deal with A&M Records for secular distribution, but since the bands were never really active in the club circuits A&M lost interest. Both bands appeared at the first Cornerstone Festival, where they instantly earned national followings.

In 1984, Charlie Peacock also released his debut solo record *Lie Down in the Grass*. The versions of the record distributed in the Christian and secular markets varied slightly. One song was different on each, which confused and annoyed some fans since they had to buy two copies to get all 11 songs. But the brilliant musicianship and artistry more than made up for the hassle. Peacock, it could be heard immediately, was a major talent.

Before becoming a Christian, Peacock (whose given name is Charles Ashworth) was a full-time musician playing the club scene around Sacramento and San Francisco. His experience showed. With an ethnic worldbeat inflection and plaintive vocals somewhat reminiscent of Sting, Peacock exuded a sophistication rare in the Christian market.

Another of the early Exit artists was the British poet Steve Scott. He was originally signed to Larry Norman's Solid Rock label in the late 1970s, but the album that he recorded was never released. He joined the WCM crowd about the same time and soon became a full-time staffer. Although he'd appeared on the 1978 Sangre Productions sampler *Come Back Soon*, *Love in the Western World* (1983) was his real debut. On it, he sounded like the true British new waver that he was. With a sound somewhere between The Cure, Roxy Music, and Simple Minds, and lyrics that were excellently written and startlingly poetic, Scott impressed. He even hinted at his poet's soul in the spoken piece "This Sad Music." *Love in the Western World* was an understated and underappreciated masterpiece. Scott remains a walking art seminar. Whether through his music (which sadly he has seemingly abandoned since the 1980s) or his spoken poetry, he is so far out on the cutting edge that he can hardly be seen without binoculars.

Exit's first artists were all resounding hits with the press, rock radio shows, and fans. It seemed that Exit could do no wrong. There were a few more obscure releases, such as *Rock of Offense* by First Strike, a metal band that showed promise but never got a chance to develop it. But by the close of 1984, Exit was known as a creative hive.

When A&M dropped Exit altogether, the label immediately began looking for a new mainstream distributor. Charlie Peacock had been working with Brent Bourgeois and "Bongo" Bob Smith writing songs for Santana and had thus come to the attention of music mogul Bill Graham. Bill Graham Productions ended up signing management deals with several Exit artists and then hired Lou Maglia as a consultant to help handle this situation. Maglia (who'd later found the successful Zoo Entertainment label) took a job with Island Records, where he pitched the Exit bands to his new boss, Chris Blackwell. Blackwell, undaunted by the faith aspect since he was raking in big bucks from U2, signed Exit to his roster of distributed labels. The efforts to launch Exit's bands to the mainstream then began in earnest.

In 1987, both The Seventy Sevens (who'd turned down big-league secular interests to stay connected to the Exit collective) and Charlie Peacock released records — on Island only. The two albums, both self-titled and stunning, were released exclusively in the general market. It was nearly impossible to find them in a Christian store. Both records got great reviews, and both started to sell through the system as Christian fans found their way to secular stores to pick them up. But in 1987 Island had one priority, an Irish band that had released the most important record of the decade. It was the year of *Joshua Tree*, and all else paled in comparison. Exit had also signed Robert Vaughn and his band The Shadows from San Diego. Their debut, *Love and War*, was also an Island-only release. Although it was possibly the label's best shot at mainstream success (it

Mark Harmon founded the Bay area band The Strawmen before joining The Seventy Sevens in the early '90s.

perfectly balanced the new rock sound gaining a foothold with classic rock licks, and Vaughn's raspy vocals provided a more commercially accessible sound than either The Seventy Sevens or Charlie Peacock had), all three records fell through the cracks. Peacock toured as a mainstream act, but The Seventy Sevens didn't. Other than receiving some decent reviews, the albums went nowhere. The wheels started to fall off the Exit vehicle.

In squabbles that have only been hinted at in interviews, Mike Roe and the Neelys began to disagree on strategy, obligations, and even their overall mission. Tootle left The Seventy Sevens, and Roe left WCM. Roe wanted out of the Exit family, but the leadership of the label, also the leadership of the church, thought that he was "not ready" to go. That opinion didn't sit well with Roe or the remaining members of the band, and they decided, essentially, to pack it in. Roe began recording demos and working in private.

A&M had passed on even releasing Steve Scott's second record, *Emotional Tourist*, so his career as an artist was considered over. He traveled the world representing WCM and conducting seminars. The Neelys decided to shut down the label and get out of the music business. Just like that, after releasing three of the best records in either the Christian market or the secular market, Exit was over.

Charlie Peacock began recording independently as well. In 1990, the Cornerstone Festival set up an Exit reunion night with Vector (a gig that spurred the band back into action), Peacock, and The Seventy Sevens.

The show lasted almost four hours and included a 20-minute jam on Scott's "Ghost Train." Fans, though excited by a night of jaw-dropping music, were left frustrated that once again the Christian underground had offered up artists as excellent as those of "the world" but that they had been shunned.

The Seventy Sevens would reform and dominate the alternative rock scene in the Christian market in the 1990s. Charlie Peacock, similarly, would parlay his independent career into a successful relationship with Sparrow Records as an artist and producer. Even Vector would return with more music that was almost too good to be profitable. Steve Scott recorded CDs full of spoken poetry set to loops of sound effects that he'd recorded all over the world. He'd also become a regular writer for *True Tunes News* and a frequent speaker at the Cornerstone Festival.

Although independent home recording would soon increase in quality and decrease in cost, in the 1980s musicians depended on record labels to make the music available. There were some new rock-oriented Christian labels as well as the big labels from the 1970s that dabbled in rock and roll.

At one time, the most progressive label among the old guard was Benson Records. It had distributed Pat Boone's Lamb and Lion label, which had released rock projects from DeGarmo and Key and Jerusalem. Benson had also handled distribution for NewPax music, which had signed Daniel Amos for their *Alarma!* and *Doppelgänger* albums. Even earlier it had distributed a small label called Pilgrim America Records, which had signed one surprisingly good band from England called Andy McCarroll and Moral Support.

McCarroll had released two solo albums of acoustic music in England in the 1970s, but no one in the United States heard of him until a quirky red album called *Zionic Bonds* hit stores in 1981. The record was straight new wave/post-punk rock in the British tradition of The Clash. Not only was it loud, but it was also as brash lyrically as it was musically. McCarroll's voice was extremely nasal, and the band was beyond hyperactive, but they did set a new standard for both musical adventurousness and lyrical confrontationalism. Although McCarroll produced the debut album for British rockers Split Level many years later, neither he nor Moral Support ever followed up *Zionic Bonds*.

Benson also distributed a rock label called Heartland Records, which featured the progressive rock of Cincinnati-based Prodigal, which had formed in 1975. Its new wave-based art rock was ahead of its time. Prodigal toured nationally and released three excellent but obscure albums in the early 1980s. The music was intricate and aggressive, and the lyrics were layered and symbolic. Prodigal, like Daniel Amos, was the kind of rock band that Christians could play for their non-Christian friends.

Although the band's lyrics reflected a Christian perspective, they were not too obvious.

Heartland also released one album by a southern rock/boogie band called Vision. Its claim to fame was that its keyboard player was none other than Billy Powell of Lynrd Skynrd. Vision released one respectable record and played at Cornerstone '85, but it didn't last much longer than that.

Benson also distributed Rooftop Records, which brought some of the early Servant albums to a wider audience. Although the band was first on Tunesmith, a division of Praise Industries in Canada, its wider distribution by Benson got it increased attention. Eventually, the band moved to Myrrh for their final two albums.

Refuge Records, which shaped much of the alternative scene in the 1980s, was also distributed by Benson. Refuge was founded by music producer Greg Nelson and former Sparrow employee Jack Hafer. They had run the short-lived Spirit Records, a division of Sparrow that had attempted to launch artists such as Benny Hester into the secular market but had been shelved after one year. With the assistance of Ray Nenow, who'd worked with Pilgrim America and other labels, Refuge was launched in 1980. Its vision was to establish a label for secular artists who'd become Christians and wanted to express their faith. The label was supposed to create excellent albums for these artists and then launch them simultaneously into the mainstream and Christian markets.

The label's first signing was Joe English, who'd made a name for himself in the general market as the drummer for Paul McCartney's Wings. English (ironically, the only American in Wings) had a typical testimony of a life with money, drugs, and women that had unraveled at the seams. His music was basic pop rock not unlike McCartney's, but it was his name and his pedigree that earned him a following in the Christian rock scene. English performed at Cornerstone '84, then released an excellent synthesized pop record for Myrrh in 1985 under the name The English Band. English never did get a decent shot at the general market.

Refuge's second signing was even more auspicious to real rock fans than Joe English. Bonnie O'Farrell had sung with Ike and Tina Turner and blues master Albert King before hooking up with Delaney Bramlett in 1967. The two married and formed the hugely successful and influential Delaney and Bonnie Band. When the band toured as the opening act for Blind Faith, Eric Clapton was so impressed that he joined the band, and Delaney and Bonnie became one of the most respected bands in the business.

Bonnie Bramlett was a serious musician with a great voice and a knack for writing compelling music. She became a Christian in the late 1970s and soon signed with Refuge to record Christian music. Her sole recorded output was 1981's *Step by Step*. Although a solid release, the record failed to connect widely with Christian audiences. Refuge wasn't able to land Bramlett in the general market either. In the late 1980s, she dove into acting under the name Bonnie Sheridan and landed a recurring role on TV's *Roseanne* and a part in the film *The Doors*. She is still an active studio musician.

Refuge's third signing was a Syracuse native who'd joined the enormously successful southern rock band The Outlaws. Rick Cua had actually become a Christian in 1977 before joining the band. To him and others who'd deepened their traditional Catholicism into a more intense Christian experience, their music was their job. When Nenow approached him about a Christian record deal, he signed within hours.

Cua's solo debut, 1982's *Koo-Ah*, was a slick and impressive pop-rock record along the lines of Tom Petty and the Heartbreakers. It was followed by 1983's *No Mystery*, which took Cua in a slightly more edgy direction, drawing some comparisons to Rick Springfield. Cua then moved to Sparrow Records, which released his seminal *You're My Road* as well as his most rocking material on *Wear Your Colors*. He then moved again to Reunion Records for four much more pop-oriented records and then to his own label, UCA, for a compilation and *Times Ten*. Cua then joined a Celtic-influenced pop band from Nashville with some friends and old band members called Ceili's Rain. Cua is currently working behind the scenes as a creative director for EMI Christian Music Publishing.

Refuge moved away from signing only secular acts when it ran out of options. Early signings included The Lifesavors, Daniel Amos, and Daniel Band. But Refuge was just getting started. In the mid-1980s, it expanded its roster exponentially and became the label for rock and alternative projects in Christian music. There isn't space here for a complete rundown of Refuge bands, but following are a few highlights.

Sweden's Edin Adahl crafted edgy keyboard-driven new wave rock. Refuge imported a lot of music from Europe actually, including Semaja, Jan Groth, The Technos, and others. Both Simon Adahl and Bertil Edin released solo projects.

The Chicago-based rock band In-3D turned many heads with their debut *No Glasses Needed*. Their sound was reminiscent of The Police — more so on their debut than on their tragically overlooked follow-up, 1995's *Barrage*. The band played Cornerstone '84 and, after having played for years under the name Timepiece, had developed a tight sound. Guitarist Randy Kerkman, upon the dissolution of In-3D, started Mission of Mercy, an even more alternative band. In 1993, the band changed their name to Yonderboy and released their only nationally available album, *A Mission of Mercy*, on Etcetera Records. The other members of In-3D never reentered the Christian music scene.

Refuge launched a heavy metal label in the mid-1980s called Pure Metal. The label was bankrolled by the great sales of Whitecross and Bride. Unfortunately, it also released some of the worst music ever heard. To get Whitecross and Bride on its roster, Star Song bought Pure Metal in the late 1980s and dropped the rest of the bands.

About the same time as the launch of Pure Metal, REX, a hard rock label, popped up in New York. Although distributed by Refuge at first, its founder, Doug Mann, and Refuge employee Gavin Morkel would later join forces to render REX a fully independent label and distribution company. REX entered the 1990s as a force, signing some of the best heavy metal and industrial bands and a few nonmetal bands such as Sixpence None the Richer, Fleming and John, The Waiting, and The Wayside.

Refuge disappeared after the sale of Pure Metal. Rumors of financial mismanagement and contract breaches abounded, and most of the late-1980s bands signed to Refuge had little good to say about the label.

When Benson dropped Refuge from its roster of distributed labels, it filled the spot with an upstart alternative/rock label from Newport Beach, California. Frontline Records was founded in 1986 by Jimmy Kempner, a former pastor at Calvary Chapel in Costa Mesa who'd taken an advisory position at the Ministry Resource Center, an informal label affiliated with Calvary. Calvary also owned Broken Records and used the MRC as a sort of farm league for it. The best of the MRC bands, such as The Altar Boys and Undercover, were eventually moved to Broken, where they released bigger albums that benefited from Maranatha!'s distribution agreement with Word. Kempner oversaw the label and intended to buy it from the church. However, after getting to know the business, he signed most of the artists to personal service contracts and launched Frontline Records.

The first batch of Frontline releases included the classic album *Gut Level Music* by The Altar Boys and *Kiss of Life* by The Lifesavers. Most of the bands came from the southern California scene, but soon Kempner's reach spread around the world. Frontline quickly filled the shoes that Refuge had left by the door. It released a relentless stream of rock, alternative, and metal albums into the Christian market. Bands such as Bloodgood, Deliverance, Mad at the World, Crumbacher, Carson Cole and RU4, Common Bond, Wild Blue Yonder (a version of the MRC rockabilly band The Lifters), and even Daniel Amos all ended up on Frontline. At the end of the 1980s, Frontline bought Graceland and Intense Records, two Chicago-based labels run by Caesar Kalinowski, and added Sacred Warrior and Vengeance Rising to its metal label and Flock 14 founder Tim McAllister's project World Theater to its new Graceland moniker. Frontline also ended up owning the Alarma Records label that Terry Taylor had started. Eventually, Frontline would use its own name for pop bands such as Crystal Lewis and Jon Gibson (a blue-eyed soul singer) and use Alarma and Graceland for alternative bands such as Jacob's Trouble, Daniel Amos, The Swirling Eddies, and Veil of Ashes. Frontline used Intense Records as its hard rock brand for Deliverance, Tourniquet, Bloodgood, Shout, and Mortification, as well as its industrial act Mortal.

Although Frontline's success was built on Benson's distribution system, by the end of the 1980s Frontline was large enough to launch its own distribution company. Although it would never be competitive with the big three, Word, Sparrow, and Benson, Frontline Music Group was a significant presence in the Christian music field.

Frontline was notorious for exploitative record deals inflicted on the bands that trusted the label. Several artists complained in interviews about what they thought were financial abuses. Frontline successfully batted down the charges for years, but eventually it was dragged under by its own weight. In 1995, Frontline filed for bankruptcy protection. Its assets, including the masters to some of the most important Christian rock records in the business, were purchased by the Killen Music Group (KMG) from Nashville. KMG has rereleased some of the classics as double discs, but many are still unavailable.

Sparrow Records developed its identity on the backs of releases such as Keith Green's *For Him Who Has Ears to Hear* and albums by Barry McGuire, John Michael Talbot, and Second Chapter of Acts. By 1975 standards, Sparrow was contemporary, even progressive; by 1980s standards, however, it was lagging behind. Its biggest sellers were children's records such as *The Music Machine* and *Bullfrogs and Butterflies*, so the next logical step was to head into youth music. And rock was youth music.

Sparrow's first and most aggressive step into rock was the signing of Resurrection Band, the hard-rocking group from Chicago's Jesus People community. The band spent the late 1970s and early 1980s with Light Records, a company significant in earlier years but fading fast in the 1980s. The band shortened their name to Rez, and their first project for Sparrow was the 1983 live album *Bootleg*, recorded over two nights at The Odeum, an arena in the Chicago suburb of Villa Park.

Bootleg introduced Rez fans, some unhappily, to the sounds of keyboards, drum machines, and synthetic vocal effects. The band still had a blues-rock style, but it was very 1980s sounding. After 1985's *Hostage*, the band returned to their analog hard rock roots for the album *Between Heaven and Hell*.

Opening the Rez shows at The Odeum was a new Sparrow signing, Steve Taylor, who had a six-song EP for sale called *I Want to Be a Clone*. Taylor was a Denver preacher's kid who tried the Christian college experience in Los Angeles for one year before returning home to attend the University of Colorado to study music performance. What he didn't possess in musical ability he more than made up for in chutzpah and wit. Feeling a vague calling into something musical, he even spent a week at performance camp with John Davidson. Dejected and confused, he returned home looking for a mission. When a fellow student in his film class used The Clash's "Lost in the Supermarket" as a soundtrack, Taylor snapped to attention. He immediately went out and bought *London Calling*, and at that moment "It all fell into place." He identified with the band's use of satire, snarl, and humor to make serious charges about the world. "All they were missing," he said in the liner notes of his 1994 boxed set *Now the Truth Can Be Told*, "was hope." Taylor had found his mission.

His first song was the sneering "Whatcha Gonna Do When Your Number's Up?" It had the delicacy of an Amtrak train on a bad night. Since his first song lashed out at the unsaved, he aimed his second tune squarely at the church. "I Want to Be a Clone" was a campy, sarcastic poke at the all-too-safe Evangelical Church. His protocol was established: equal-opportunity commentary.

Taylor recorded demos of his first few songs and went to California to seek his fortune. The pop labels that he met with liked the music but were afraid of the lyrics, and most of the gospel labels wouldn't even listen to the songs. One person did, though: Jim Chaffee, who worked for The Continentals, a sort of traveling youth group chorus that harkened back to the earliest days of Christian pop music. Taylor took a job as assistant director of The Continentals, a gig that led him to join the Christian musical comedy troupe Jeremiah People. His stint there resulted in one of his compositions being recorded on an album. It also led to his finally getting a showcase concert at the annual Christian Artists Seminar in Estes Park, Colorado. His time was coming.

Taylor played his two songs with a thrown-together band. Although many of the suits from the gospel music business sat stunned as Taylor skewered their preconceptions of "appropriate" Christian behavior, a handful of carefully chosen plants created pandemonium in the hall. Sparrow president Billy Ray Hearn was there and was so impressed that he waited for Taylor with a recording offer. They struck a deal, and within months the debut six-song EP *I Want to Be a Clone* was unleashed upon a Christian music scene becoming drowsy from breathing its own hot air.

Taylor's debut tour, the Rez tour of 1983 mentioned above, introduced the lanky, quirky, funny, and disconcertingly correct singer to rock fans within the church. Taylor was an instant hit. Sparrow, no doubt proud of its gamble, quickly sent Taylor in to record his first full-length album, *Meltdown*. He expanded his repertoire with songs that recklessly dealt with adultery, abortion, politics, celebrity worship, consumerism, and sin in general. *Meltdown* broke nearly every rule of Christian music and was a huge hit. Taylor followed it with an even bigger hit, 1985's *On the Fritz*.

He was on a tear. He continually advanced, making hamburger of sacred cows and earning the respect of thousands of Christians who never thought they'd like Christian music. Since his style was as firmly tied to his lyrics as it was to his quirky alternative-pop music, it was difficult to describe. He had to be heard to be understood. Considering that most rock fans who heard him loved him, it was likely his lack of exposure to the general market that kept him from being a huge star.

As his fourth album percolated, and early demos indicated a darker tone, it became apparent that church-oriented Sparrow mightn't be the best place for it. In a remarkable example of label and artist working together for the greater good, Sparrow let Taylor negotiate a deal with Myrrh Records for the release of *I Predict 1990*. In what many critics and fans considered Taylor's finest hour as a writer, vocalist, and visionary, *I Predict 1990* finally seemed to push things too far. Not only did it predictably push the buttons of the antirock crowd such as Jimmy Swaggart, but it became controversial among credible sources as well. Some folks mistakenly thought that the album cover promoted spiritism or some kind of occultic symbolism, and others thought that his satirical "I Blew Up the Clinic Real Good" was intended literally. Taylor became frazzled from explanation after explanation and decided to take a break.

But his break was short lived. He soon hooked up with some other Christian artists who'd been branded envelope pushers and shown various doors. Along with guitarist Dave Perkins, his own A&R man Lynn Nichols, drummer Mike Mead, and bassist Wade Janes, Taylor formed Chagall Guevara. The group signed with MCA and recorded a stunning debut CD in 1990. At last the world would hear this treasure, make Taylor famous, and vindicate the tireless support of his underground fans. But Chagall Guevara was just too good to be popular.

The band played to a crowd overwhelmed with appreciation at Cornerstone '91. Shortly thereafter, their album was released to Christian stores via Sparrow. Despite great reviews, fans in high places, and a European tour with Squeeze, Chagall Guevara didn't work out.

Taylor reemerged with another solo album (and a live album) in the 1990s, and then he took an unexpected step. He started his own label, Squint Entertainment, which would finally, almost 20 years after Taylor's first foray into the scene, bring quality Christian music to the masses with a resoundingly successful album by the darlings of the alternative Christian underground, Sixpence None the Richer.

Sparrow released many other rock records in the 1980s. It signed a spitfire singer from New York named Margaret Becker. Her sophomore release, *The Reckoning*, stands as one of the best of the genre. Her amazing

Mike Roe brings a healthy dose of the Blues and old-style rock and roll to The Lost Dogs.

voice and writing ability set her apart, and she became the model female rocker in Christian music. As the years moved on, she evolved more and more into an adult-pop artist.

Sparrow's answer to the slick arena rock of Petra was a band of studio players called Whiteheart. Although the band debuted with Chris Christian's Home Sweet Home label, it wasn't until they hooked up with Sparrow that they really became good. The early version of Whiteheart included Steve Green on vocals and a band that was Bill Gaither's band as well. After a shocking turn of events that saw vocalist Scott Douglas sentenced to 15 years in prison for sex-related crimes, the band splintered again. Eventually, founding members Billy Smiley and Mark Gershmehl kept Whiteheart going, while guitarist Dan Huff went on to form the mainstream rock band Giant.

Whiteheart's charismatic front man Rick Florian became one of Christian rock's first pinup boys. But despite the band's slick presentation and slogany lyrics (or maybe because of them), Whiteheart was second only to Petra in album and ticket sales among the rock bands in the mid-1980s. Their Sparrow debut, *Don't Wait for the Movie*, was a big hit in the Christian subculture, and it spawned many hits and a follow-up album called *Emergency Broadcast* that sounded like it had been recorded at the same time. Fans of progressive music didn't really dig Whiteheart, but kids and youth leaders did. The band helped to define "Christian rock" as a genre and was one of the reasons that so many other artists hated, and still hate, being pigeonholed into that genre.

Most of the mid-1980s lineup of Whiteheart went on to new and better things shortly after *Hotline*. Bassist Tommy Simms joined Bruce Springsteen for several tours. Gordon Kennedy (whose writing skills were hinted at on the Whiteheart ballad "Fly Eagle Fly") ended up writing songs for Eric Clapton and Garth Brooks, among many others. Chris McHugh became one of the most in-demand drummers in Nashville. He was replaced by Adam Again's Johnny Knox (a swap that simply horrified Adam Again fans). Whiteheart changed lineups from album to album throughout the 1990s, becoming even more like Petra. They signed with Curb Records, where they recorded their most aggressive album, *Redemption*, before putting the band on hold. Their creative peak was 1989's *Freedom*.

Sparrow briefly operated a rock sublabel called Kerygma (home for Kerry Livgren's excellent *Art of the State*, *Reconstructions*, and *Prime Mover* records, fellow AD member Michael Gleason's elaborate album, and roots rocker/Bryan Adams–sound-alike Kyle Henderson, formerly of The Producers). Sparrow was the typical Christian label of the 1980s. Signing Steve Taylor was its last risk despite the obvious dividends. Sparrow became a safe place for noncontroversial Christian music. The distribution of Star Song in the late 1980s saw some heavy metal come through the system, but the risk taking was over by the time that the label was purchased by EMI in the 1990s.

Between 1972 and 1980, Petra released four albums and sold an impressive 500,000 albums in total. Selling half a million copies in the 1970s was a big deal, especially for a Christian rock band. By the beginning of the 1980s, then, Petra was an established outfit that had even managed to get some mainstream press coverage.

In 1981, Petra hooked up with Mark Hollingsworth, a young fan of Christian rock, and hired him as their manager. Hollingsworth had worked with some of the earliest Christian bands and in mainstream radio. By hiring a fan with real-world experience to run the office, Petra exploded. *More Power to Ya* and *Not of This World* sold over a million copies each and pulled through several hundred thousand new sales of the older albums. And the band was drawing up to 20,000 fans per night at their arena tours. With state-of-the-art set design, lighting, and sound, and music right in step with the reemergence of the arena rock of bands such as Journey, REO Speedwagon, and Triumph, Petra became Christian rock's first supergroup.

Their formula was to marry easily understood lyrics to classic rock riffs and melodic production. They departed from that form for 1985's synthesizer-driven *Beat the System* and began to decline as a result. Still, Petra on a bad day was 10 times bigger than any other Christian rock band. Eventually, their second vocalist, Greg X. Volz, left the band and was replaced by Head East vocalist John Schlitt, who, along with fresh production by John and Dino Elefante (Kansas), reinvigorated Petra for the late 1980s.

Even fans of progressive rock had something to enjoy in the growing Christian rock scene: Arkangel, from Texas. The band's top-notch musicianship and elaborate graphics impressed many a Yes fan. Front man Kemper Crabb also released a solo album called *The Vigil*, which, despite its obviously traditional arrangements, connected with thousands of fans. His exploration of Celtic and medieval musical and lyrical influences exposed an unmined area of Christian faith. Another rare but important progressive rock album was *Beyond the Crystal Sea* by Jimmy Hotz, the producer of Arkangel's *Warrior* album. A true musician's album, the short-lived gem would become a collector's item selling in some cases for over $200.

Star Song frequently experimented with off-the-page bands. One such group was Quickflight. The Canadian band had released one album, *Breakaway*, on the Canadian Tunesmith label in 1980, and it had been embraced by the underground. But 1983's *Decent Beat* was miles ahead in both writing and production.

By 1982, the band was down to Rick deGroot (lead vocal, keys), Greg Johnson (guitars), and Dale Dirksen (bass, vocals, keys). Feeling called to get into the mainstream, they honed their respective chops by playing in clubs and bars around their base in Kelowna, British Columbia. They recorded the tracks that became *Decent Beat* over the course of a year. Star Song heard the songs and expressed interest in releasing them. A few months later, *Decent Beat* was released to a Christian market not quite ready for modern synthesized rock. The lyrics penned by deGroot and Dirksen were also more figurative and symbolic, similar to those of Daniel Amos and Prodigal. Like Andy McCarroll and Moral Support and so many other regional artists, Quickflight was ahead of the game. The band broke up shortly after the release of *Decent Beat*.

Home Sweet Home was a label that Word distributed for contemporary adult singer and producer Chris Christian. He was bankrollable by Word because he had "discovered" Amy Grant back in 1977. Home Sweet Home began its run in 1981 and became one of the most successful Christian pop labels in the business. Although most of its releases couldn't be considered rock, or even that contemporary, the label did release several records by Dan Peek (formerly of the 1970s superband America) as well as the first few records by Whiteheart and one of Christian rock's most revered writers and singers, Mark Heard. Home Sweet Home sold over a million records before shutting down. Christian made a fortune from Grant's catalog and parlayed that into the successful publishing company Bug and Bear.

To many rock fans, though, Home Sweet Home would only be remembered as the label that screwed Heard. Although the details are sketchy, his considerable creative output of the 1980s was controlled by Chris Christian, (except *Appalachian Melody*, released by Larry Norman's Solid Rock label in 1980) and neither seemed to do anything to help Heard get the recognition that he deserved. Unfair record deals were unfortunately all too common in the early days of Christian music as big business. Most artists didn't even know what publishing rights were and quickly signed them over to people such as Christian. According to close friends of Heard, he never made any money from his Home Sweet Home albums. When he died in 1992, fans clamored for Christian to rerelease his back catalog on CD to benefit his wife and daughter. Other than the compilation *Reflections of a Former Life* in 1993, nothing happened until 1999, when Christian put out some low-rent reissues through an on-line distributor. He moved on to television production and other business ventures in the 1990s.

The manager of Word's Nashville office was Mike Blanton, a shrewd businessman who saw the ins and outs of the business and where the money was going. Along with a local banker named Dan Harrell (Amy Grant's brother-in-law), he formed Blanton and Harrell Management for

Phil Madeira is more active than ever after over twenty-five years in and around the business.

three initial clients: Amy Grant, Michael W. Smith, and Kathy Troccoli. Smith had been a songwriter in Nashville with some success, and Troccoli was a Catholic singer from New York. Unable to find the right record deals for Smith and Troccoli, the two formed Reunion Records and secured distribution with Word. Reunion was an instant success. Smith went on to become one of the best-selling Christian artists of all time, second only to Grant.

Reunion, though frequently involved in attempts to launch its artists into the mainstream, made its fortunes by mining the subculture. In 1986, the label unveiled its first real rock signing, Canada's Elim Hall. The band's debut, *Things Break*, was impressively modern sounding. Although it scored some Christian rock hits, the band wasn't successful enough for Reunion and was dropped after only one album. *Things Break* made a splash, though, and was an important first step toward relevant rock and roll by a major label. Reunion released two albums by fellow Canadians The Awakening in the late 1980s. The band's polished sound was reminiscent of the art rock band Yes, and, though they were dropped by Reunion after their second album, the two main writers formed a new band called One Hundred Days and continued to craft excellent power pop and rock into the 1990s.

Word's sublabel Myrrh was known predominantly for one artist in the 1980s: Amy Grant. She can't be called a rock artist, but her role in Christian music is worth addressing. Her first several albums were pure Christian pop, but beginning with her 1985 album *Unguarded* she began to seek a crossover. Her 1988 album *Lead Me On* (arguably her best) was both lyrically and musically rich. There will be more about Grant in the third wave.

Myrrh took on an adventurous A&R rep in the mid-1980s named Tom Willett, a big thinker and a true fan of great music. He created a fresh side of Myrrh based in California called Myrrh LA. That division made a valiant effort to bring Myrrh up to date with events in the mainstream. One of Willett's brightest signings was LA's The Choir, led by Derri Daughtery and Steve Hindalong. Willett was assisted in modernizing Myrrh by Lynn Nichols and Mark Maxwell, who knew that Christian music was lagging behind secular music. Nichols, Maxwell, and Willett were behind some of Myrrh's brightest moments, including the epic Phil Keaggy album of 1988, *Sunday's Child*.

Keaggy was considered royalty in Christian music and the best guitarist in the world by many fans. He enjoyed a respectable string of Christian radio hits and had a fan base that would buy anything he put out. But Keaggy wandered from label to label trying to find the right fit. During the days of Jesus music, he was with New Song Records, an offshoot of the Love Inn community in New York. He then migrated to Sparrow

Records for a series of excellent albums in the late 1970s and early 1980s. He also did some time with Nissi Records, a label distributed by Sparrow but doomed to failure.

Sunday's Child was his first album for Myrrh. Surrounded by friends who knew that Keaggy was better than his album sales indicated, he dug deep and created an album that ranks as one of the best Christian records of all time. With Nichols producing and a list of contributors that included Randy Stonehill, Russ Taff, Mark Heard, Steve Taylor, Derri Daughtery, Alwyn Wall, Rick Cua, and many others, Keaggy brought the best elements of his 1960s rock and pop influences to the fore. With vintage tube amps buzzing, stacked vocals, and even a retro album cover reminiscent of *Meet the Beatles*, he lived up to the expectations. To support the album, he hit the road with Stonehill (who'd also reinvented his sound with the edgy roots rock of his 1986 album *The Wild Frontier*) and a top-notch band dubbed The Keaggy Stonehill Band, with Mike Mead on drums and Tim Chandler (Daniel Amos, The Choir) on bass. In many fans' minds, the tour stands as one of the best in Christian music history.

In 1986, Tom Willett got Word to agree to become more aggressive. Although some Christian artists were in step with the music of the 1980s, the Christian music industry wasn't able to get them out of the "ghetto." Word had secured a high-profile mainstream distribution deal with A&M that seemed to promise improved exposure for the musicians; however, with the exception of Amy Grant, it didn't. Records by The Choir, Steve Taylor, Mylon LeFevre, and Broken Heart, among others, still got dumped into the "gospel" bins at mainstream stores. Anything with the Word logo on it got put into those bins. The struggle came in trying to get the records out of the gospel bins and onto the regular racks.

Willett couldn't wait for that to come about. His idea was to launch a new label without the stigma of "Christian" attached to it. With A&M handling distribution, the artists could at least count on being heard on mainstream radio. The signings would be cutting-edge artists who, though they were Christians, wouldn't be too obvious about their faith. What? Records was thus designed to promote music about what could be "seen by the Light," as T-Bone Burnett had put it.

One of the first projects came from Mark Heard. Under the pseudonym Ideola, Heard recorded a techno-based record that filtered his characteristically brilliant songwriting through more modern music. He'd languished under a terrible contract with Home Sweet Home (also distributed by Word) and, though a respected artist among the underground, had thought that a reinvention was in order. Ideola's only album was 1987's *Tribal Opera*.

Another What? artist was Dave Perkins, a gravelly voiced rocker from Los Angeles. His amazing debut, *The Innocence*, also released in

1987, was way ahead of the curve for Christian music. Although adored by rock fans, Perkins remained obscure to the rest of the world. He'd take a second crack at stardom by joining with Steve Taylor and Lynn Nichols for their Chagall Guevera project in 1991, and he'd release an interesting industrial rock project under the name Passafist through REX Music in the mid-1990s.

What?'s name was really built on the reputation of two albums that the label released by one of the most impressive artists ever to hit the Christian scene. Steven Krikorian had been recording satirical new wave rock since 1978 under his stage name Tonio K. His debut, *Life in the Foodchain*, was a resounding hit with critics and an instant underground classic on AOR and college radio. He followed it in 1980 with *Amerika*, which failed to make Tonio K. a household name but earned Krikorian a well-deserved reputation as an incredible songwriter who could switch gears from laser-tongued satirist to earnest lover within seconds. In 1982, he released the *La Bomba* EP and then slid into the shadows.

In 1986, Tonio K. reemerged as a Christian with something to say. His first release as a Christian was the deeply sarcastic *Romeo Unchained*, a mellower album for the edgy postpunk rocker. With production by T-Bone Burnett and a supporting cast that included Mark Heard, Tim Chandler, David Miner, Charlie Sexton, and many others, *Romeo Unchained* was simultaneously humorous, ironic, and sincere. "I Handle Snakes" poked at the bizarre snake-handling Pentecostals who took scripture a bit too literally and jabbed at the mainstream church and the Christian music subculture at the same time. "Impressed," an ode to the great romances of pop fiction, drew stark parallels to real love and commitment, which were explored on "You Belong with Me" and "You Will Go Free." *Romeo Unchained* was a critical success and scored a number-one hit with "True Confessions"; however, despite being celebrated by the fringe folks, the record failed to make a dent on the pop side. It managed to sell well in the Christian market despite the controversial lyrics.

Krikorian followed *Romeo Unchained* with the more rootsy *Notes from the Lost Civilization* in 1988. The album was thematically the stage upon which the botched relationships in *Romeo Unchained* had played themselves out. A gritty look at the collapse of truth, love, and spirituality in Western civilization, the album was an immediate critical hit. Many Christians ended up rebuying the album when they found out that the A&M version had the hysterical song "What Women Want" on it (the Word version didn't). With production again by T-Bone Burnett, and a cast of players much richer than the Christian market was used to, *Notes from the Lost Civilization* was expected to finally land Tonio K. in the emerging alternative rock landscape of the late 1980s. Unfortunately, A&M seemed to be uninterested in What? Records or the amazing albums that it released. The experiment failed. Once again Christians had attempted to bring their best efforts to the world at large and were ignored. Tonio K.'s 1989 album, *Ole*, was finished and in the can, featuring contributions by David Hidalgo of Los Lobos, Paul Westerberg of The Replacements, Peter Case, and David Miner. A&M didn't even release the album. It was eventually released in 1997 by Gadfly Records.

Myrrh made a commanding jump into modern music through its work with The Choir, Leslie Phillips, Russ Taff, Randy Stonehill, Steve Taylor, Phil Keaggy, and eventually metal bands Holy Soldier and even One Bad Pig. As the 1980s came to a close, Myrrh was actually a leading force in rock production. But despite its best efforts, it couldn't land anyone but Amy Grant outside the underground.

Myrrh's parent company, Word Music, had the largest and most effective distribution system in the business. Executives at Word noted the excitement generated by The Choir and Phil Keaggy and attempted to expand their involvement in rock production. Seeing Frontline rack up considerable sales was likely also a catalyst. As late as 1986, Word was still getting lapped by Benson with its Frontline deal when it came to rock and roll. Most industry insiders knew that as time moved on rock and alternative music would fuel growth. Not wanting to get left behind, Word found some rock labels to distribute through its system. This active pursuit of real rock labels would eventually usher in the third wave of Christian rock in the 1990s.

One of the more promising of the distributed labels for Word was the resurrected Broken Records, run by Undercover's Ojo Taylor and Adam Again's Gene Eugene. The first round of releases included a live Undercover album, a solo project by Taylor, a Canadian band called Level Heads, a promising alternative band that had been kicking around the independent scene for years called 441, and one of the most loved alternative Christian albums of all time.

Adam Again debuted in 1987 with an independent release (actually on the insignificant Blue Collar Records label with sketchy distribution by Lexicon Distributors). The band really landed when they excited those at Cornerstone '86 with their infectious brand of groove-based, guitar-driven, dance rock. Calling to mind bands such as The Talking Heads and Prince and the Revolution, Adam Again had come out of nowhere to become the buzz band of the year. Their debut, *In a New World of Time*, was promising but suffered from poor production.

Mastermind Gene Eugene fixed that for their sophomore effort, simply called *Ten Songs by Adam Again*. Although still relying on programmed drums, the album flowed with a sense of groove like no record before it. Eugene had fused the funky vibe of Minneapolis or Detroit with the guitar squalor of the LA alternative scene. His socially conscious

Adam Again's Paul Valadez, Johnny Knox, "Riki" Michelle Palmer, Andrew Prickett and Greg Lawless.

lyrics and melancholy voice set the whole thing off. Adam Again owned the underground, and *Ten Songs* was the favorite album of many fans.

Adam Again followed *Ten Songs* with another topper, *Homeboys*. For it, the band added the formidable drum skills of Johnny Knox and left most of the keyboards and synthetic ingredients behind. Eugene's voice and guitar and organ playing melted into a gritty backdrop of aggressive groove rock. Just as the heat became unbearable, the sprightly and sensual vocals of covocalist Riki Michelle would chime in to offset the angst. *Homeboys* was brilliant. Adam Again increased its cult following and drove it into a frenzy with jaw-dropping annual shows at the Cornerstone Festival. They remain one of the most celebrated bands in the annals of Christian rock.

Perhaps inspired by the increasing hipness of the Christian music scene in the late 1980s, or possibly the increasing hipness of his own label, Ojo Taylor reformed Undercover after a three-year hiatus. The other members had formed Boys Club hoping to land a mainstream deal. When Undercover got back together, its sound was heavier, darker, and more in step with the emerging alternative sound in hard rock. Their first Brainstorm Artists International (BAI) release was *Balance of Power*, a visceral work that took the themes of *Branded* to new depths. During the recording of *Balance of Power*, guitarist Gym Nicholson's wife died during routine surgery. The pain and confusion, felt by the whole band, was palpable. Even through songs such as "Eyes of Love," written prior to the tragedy, the emotions flowed.

BAI went on to release many of the formative records of the third wave in the 1990s. The Seventy Sevens, Daniel Amos, The Lost Dogs, and many other important artists would find their way to BAI in the coming years.

The Cornerstone Festival

Few events have contributed as much to the popularity and viability of modern Christian music as a festival in Illinois put on each year by a bunch of hippies called Jesus People USA (JPUSA) The Cornerstone Festival, though nowhere near the largest festival in the world, is certainly the most influential when it comes to the fringe scene.

JPUSA is one of the few remaining Christian communes in the country. With its roots firmly planted in the Jesus Movement, it retains the evangelical zeal and countercultural fervor that it had in 1972. The members' desire to reach the world through art has manifested itself in many ways. There is Resurrection Band, which has been performing and recording hard rock and blues since 1974. There was a comedy troupe called the Holy Ghost Players that recorded one album of sketch comedy (quite good actually) in the 1980s with Refuge Records. There have been numerous other musical outreaches, including The Crossing (Celtic folk), Cauzin Effect (rap), Crashdog (punk), Seeds (folk-pop), Ballydowse (Celtic punk), and The Blamed (hardcore), as well as numerous other small projects throughout the years. The publishing arm, Cornerstone Press Chicago, has released numerous books on cults, serving the poor, musical resources, and discipleship, an exposé of a fraudulent Christian "star" named Mike Warnke, and even a trade comic book and the diary of a Chicago bag lady. The commune has housed thousands of transients over the years and provided millions of meals and countless cots for a safe night's sleep for battered women. It has also published *Cornerstone Magazine*, the most consistently challenging Christian magazine available. It was officially that magazine that "sponsored" a festival in 1984 called Cornerstone '84.

Resurrection Band had played many outdoor festivals in the 1970s since they were a major part of the Jesus music system. Festivals in Dallas, Indiana, New York, Ohio, and California had drawn thousands to rural areas with poor facilities. A single-day rock festival in Illinois called Illinois Jam drew people from across the Midwest to see Servant, Barnabas, and many other hard-rocking bands. As contemporary Christian music became more mainstream, many of the fringe festivals began to fade away or evolve into predominantly contemporary adult affairs. Members of Resurrection Band grew frustrated with the increasingly slick and commercial festivals that had more and more rules, less and less good music, and much slighter impacts on audiences. They began discussing the idea of a JPUSA-sponsored festival that would be like the Jesus jams of the early 1970s and even rougher.

Henry Huang had been part of the splinter group that had left the JPUSA commune in Milwaukee to go to Europe. It was there that Huang had managed a touring drama/musical production that had traveled across Europe for several years. He was also part of the team that started the Greenbelt Music and Arts Festival in England (which is still going and is the most progressive Christian arts festival in Europe). By the late 1970s, Huang had returned to Chicago, and in 1983 he was picked to coordinate the Cornerstone Music Festival. It was held at the Lake County Fairgrounds just outside Waukegan, Illinois (between Chicago and Milwaukee). About 4,000 people showed up for the three-day event. Some had anticipated it for months, others just popped in out of curiosity. Either way, Cornerstone '84 was as major as it gets.

It seemed that every good established Christian rock band in the world was there. It wasn't just a collection of the bands big enough to tour. The festival flew out numerous bands from California, including

The Altar Boys, Undercover, and The Seventy Sevens. It also had some big names. Kerry Livgren was booked for his debut concert with his new band AD. For some reason, though, the festival wasn't allowed to advertise that he would be there. Organizers made a big deal about a mainstream band making their Christian music debut and left people guessing. Some thought that it was Donna Summer, others The Call, and others U2 or The Alarm. When it turned out to be the former chief songwriter and guitarist for rock legend Kansas, the crowd churned with anticipation. Also on stage that night was former Paul McCartney and Wings drummer Joe English with his band. But the band that opened main stage may have caused the biggest stir. The Seventy Sevens were still largely unheard of outside northern California. But front man Mike Roe's bizarre stage antics and incredible playing made sure that wasn't the case for long. Christian rock took major steps toward viability during Cornerstone '84, steps that would continue every summer after that.

The early festivals were big money losers, and as such they were pure labors of love. All of the work income at JPUSA went into a common purse, and other JPUSA businesses subsidized the festival for years. The first seven festivals were held at the Lake County Fairgrounds, but just as the festival started to break even the need arose to find a new home. A large farm outside Bushnell, Illinois, was purchased by the community in 1990, and by 1991 the Cornerstone Festival had moved four hours southwest into cattle and corn country. By the mid-1990s, attendance was up to 25,000, and the festival drew people from every state in the union as well as several foreign countries.

Cornerstone represents a lot more than just concerts. It is truly a cultural experience. From children making art projects in the Art Rageous tent to tattooed skaters on the half-pipe, from songwriters singing in coffeehouse tents to hardcore punk bands moshing and stage diving, all extremes are represented. The main stage, at least half a mile from the rest of the festival in a natural basin, draws from 10,000 to 15,000 people per night, and another 15,000 or so wander among the various impromptu stages, food vendors, and campsites. Hundreds of hours of seminars are offered for those who can handle them. Glenn Kaiser's Music, Musicians, and Ministry seminar has, since 1984, provided biblical advice and teaching on operating a successful musical outreach with artistic and spiritual integrity. Other seminars on cults, dating, philosophy, youth ministry, and even science fiction are provided for the betterment of the crowd. Over 200 bands have played in just one year, often five or six simultaneously on various stages. It's pure overload, and for fans of the fringe it's pure bliss. An enormous tent houses an exhibition hall that becomes a sort of bazaar where everything from T-shirts and CDs to percussion instruments and wild clothing are hawked to the max. Ostrich burgers and Thai iced tea are sold in the food area, and volleyball, basketball, and soccer are played wherever there is room. It is a full-tilt party that rivals Woodstock.

Of course, Cornerstone's biggest impact on the music industry has been its willingness to embrace the best artists, even if they aren't the biggest or the easiest to work with. Several bands got their national debuts at the festival. In the early days, getting booked was nearly enough to guarantee a national following. As the festival spread out over more days and threw up more stages, the roster grew to the point that just getting in the door is no longer a guarantee of widespread exposure. Bands playing the minor stages spread flyers and mingle with fans to drum up good crowds for their sets. And, despite the saturation, there are still bands "discovered" each year by clandestine representatives of the labels. Many bands, in fact some of the most influential in the whole scene, play few live shows other than Cornerstone. Adam Again's Gene Eugene once quipped that no one outside that farm had heard of his band but that there they were stars. True, Adam Again never really mounted a national tour and may never have secured a national following had it not wowed an afternoon crowd during Cornerstone '86. But for all the bands that have gotten their jump-start in Waukegan or Bushnell, there are now scores more that thought the magic would work for them but just got lost in the din.

The New Artist Showcase has become one of the hotspots for up-and-coming talent. Begun in the mid-1980s as a competition stage, the event evolved into a featured slot for many artists. Each year, hundreds of bands enter their demos for a chance to play at the showcase. Only about a dozen are picked. Some go on to sign with national labels (Over the Rhine, John Austin, Deitiphobia, The Wayside, Strongarm, This Train, Sarah Masen, POD, and more), and others remain firmly ensconced in their garages. But for many fans and industry types, the showcase is a priority.

Another of the minor stages that has received a lot of attention is called the Impromptu Stage. It began in 1989 when two bands that didn't make the New Band Stage brought their own PA systems and asked if they could set them up in front of a pig barn. Huang agreed, and Vague and Mission of Mercy played on a hot afternoon in front of a large hog sign. Another band asked if they could use the gear the following day. They did, and as a result of their show The Throes got signed. From that point on, a thrown-together stage has been part of the festival landscape. Although the stage may be filled by hacks a plenty, moments of genius have been heard there.

Pressured to provide more slots for label bands, the festival instituted a label showcase as well. For many labels, getting their bands to Cornerstone is a core part of their marketing strategy. Thus, they pay for a spot in the afternoon. And each year there are far more demands from labels than there are spots to play. Even though more bands are booked

Daniel Amos at Cornerstone Festival 2000.

each year, the cry seems to get louder. There are so many bands out there and only four days in which to fit them.

Besides its radical influence on the still stoic Christian music business of the 1980s (seeing major-label salespeople trying to fit into the freak fest was a treat indeed), the Cornerstone Festival represents something much deeper. By keeping things loose, booking every kind of music from gothic grindcore to Peruvian folk, and embracing the progressive edge of culture, the festival has drawn both believers and skeptics. Not all in the crowd are buttoned-up churchgoers, and wafting pot smoke isn't uncommon. Instead of rejecting that element, the Jesus People have embraced it. There are even bands that, though they swear off the Christian music industry and refuse to play "Christian" gigs, look forward to Cornerstone. It is completely nonpolitical, unattached to Nashville labels, and utterly cool. Everyone feels comfortable at Cornerstone. To many, it is their one annual plug in to Christian music. To the bands, the fans, and even the staff, Cornerstone is a four-day example of what they wish the church would be like all year.

In 2000, Cornerstone put on its 17th festival, and it was more energized than ever. Rez drummer John Herrin took over the helm since Huang felt that he needed a change of scenery. Anyone doubting the cultural importance of Christian music should attend Cornerstone, the best example of Christians embracing music to spread the word. Cornerstone remains the focal point of the contemporary Christian music scene, and it will for years to come.

Heavenly Metal

If you ask people on the street if they've heard of Christian rock, Stryper is the band they most often mention. Maybe that's because Stryper was one of the most successful and outrageous (connected?) Christian bands of all time. Although they were signed to the secular metal label Enigma (Ratt), they were obviously Christians. They even placed a scriptural reference under their logo (Isaiah 53:5, which explained the band's name). And, as if that wasn't enough, they actually threw Bibles at fans at their shows.

Stryper formed in 1984 under the name Roxx Regime. Although the lads came from Christian homes, they weren't living Christian lives at the time. However, between the time that they signed their record deal with Enigma and the time that they turned in their album, they'd become full-blown Christians and had changed the lyrics to all their songs. They didn't mention anything to the label, and their A&R rep found out about their conversion only by reading about it in a magazine. Since the band was selling well, he didn't care.

And they did sell well. Their first full-length album, 1985's *Soldiers Under Command*, sold over half a million copies. *To Hell with the Devil* repeated that success in 1986 and added "Grammy nominated" to the band's résumé. *In God We Trust* came close to selling a million copies. The band ruled MTV, on which videos for "Always There for You," "Honestly," and "Reach Out" were more common than Clearasil ads. Stryper nailed the pop metal craze of the 1980s and was as big or bigger than bands such as Def Leppard and Whitesnake. Of course, not everyone was thrilled about these spandex-clad, long-haired, makeup-wearing, girlish guys singing loud music and throwing Bibles around.

Although brothers Michael (vocals) and Robert (drums) Sweet were believers, they didn't even consider looking at a gospel label for their music. Along with their bassist Tim Gaines and their guitarist Oz Fox, they wanted to proclaim the gospel through glam metal without apology. That they did.

Yellow and Black Attack was a huge success by Enigma standards. The Christian market got a hold of it even though it hadn't been distributed to it. Some Christians thought that the effeminate makeup and hair, the chains, and the yellow-and-black spandex were just too much. Although Stryper had some of the tightest playing, sharpest vocals, and best production, not to mention lyrics that were more obviously Christian than those of most bands on Christian labels, they became a constant source of controversy, many on both sides of the faith fence having a hard time believing that the Christian part wasn't just a gimmick. And, to make matters worse, the band always toured with secular bands, never Christian bands, such as the notoriously debauched Armored Saint, White Lion, and Poison.

Stryper's fourth album, *In God We Trust*, was by far its biggest. The RIAA never certified it platinum (one million copies sold), but many thought that sales reached that mark if the Christian market was taken into account. After the tour for that album, the band seemed to succumb to all the years of backbiting and pressure from both the Christian community and the rest of the world. They'd allowed their albums to be distributed to Christian bookstores by Benson Records, which had only increased the rumors and the controversy.

Their fifth album, *Breaking the Law*, showed the band sans the righteous bumble-bee outfits and sporting rough beards instead of makeup. They toned down the Christian content too, opting for angrier songs about how they'd been misunderstood and persecuted. Although the record shipped "gold" (500,000 copies sold immediately upon release), progress halted there. Having outgrown the spandex and the gimmicks, the band attempted to leave them behind (as did the rest of the hair bands) and focus on being a good band. It didn't take. A club tour followed, and then the band called it quits.

After the band split up, the members stayed active in music. Front man Michael Sweet recorded a pair of solo albums for Benson. Oz Fox got into producing (he introduced an LA band named Guardian through Enigma) and played on other albums. Robert Sweet and Tim Gaines backed up a Christian metal band featuring guitar hero Rex Carrol called King James. Currently, Gaines and Fox are working on a new project called SinDizzy, and Michael is planning to release a third solo album. In the spring of 2000, the first Stryper Expo was held, reuniting the band and some of their most die-hard fans. Although the band made it clear that they were not getting back together, ecstatic fans don't accept that. Someday, they believe, the yellow and black will be back!

It's easy to forget, amid the embarrassing memories of metal in the 1980s, that Stryper really had some chops. Although the media may just have been fascinated by the conflicting images of Jesus and glam metal, the millions who bought the albums appreciated that, beneath the tights and the huge hair, the band wrote great pop songs and performed them with confidence and style. They certainly put Christian rock on the map, though many of the more sophisticated artists didn't appreciate being lumped in with a girlie pop metal troupe that threw Bibles into the crowd (an image that they were trying to shake). Three tribute albums have been recorded thus far, and more will appear. Stryper's impact has reverberated throughout the years.

The roots of Christian metal (alternatively called white metal or heavenly metal) go back as far as the LA-based Agape in the early 1970s.

The genealogy goes something like this: Agape, Resurrection Band, Jerusalem, Barnabas, Daniel Band, and then, by the 1980s, a whole batch of Christian metal bands.

Barnabas, originally from California but calling Iowa and Illinois home for a time, was a difficult band to peg. Their first two albums, *Hear the Light* and *Find Your Heart a Home* (recently rereleased as a double CD), featured hard rock, hard blues, and even metal, with powerhouse female lead vocals courtesy of Nancy Jo Mann. She was obviously influenced by Wendy Kaiser (Resurrection Band) and Janis Joplin. Barnabas's first albums were rough, to be sure, but the craving for speaker-trashing hard rock was so great that the band toured the country and developed a considerable following. After migrating to the Light label in the mid-1980s, the band released their high-point album, *Approaching Light Speed*, a futuristic, full-metal, science-fiction record with good production and great album art. They followed it with the sketchy *Little Foxes* and then disappeared into oblivion. Barnabas was more of a metal band than Resurrection Band, which had been more of a hard rock affair. Barnabas fills the gap between Resurrection Band and Jerusalem and Daniel Band, the next band to carry the metal torch.

Daniel Band combined basic power-pop hooks with the obligatory crunch tone and guitar solos. The first two records are really more hard rock than heavy metal. But by the time of 1984's *Run from the Darkness*, the band was slinging licks with the best of them.

Daniel Band was one of the early Refuge Records signings (their debut was on the Lamb and Lion label). Although they hailed from Canada, the band toured the United States extensively, including several jaunts with Larry Norman and Jerusalem. Their following grew exponentially after they performed at several of the earliest Cornerstone Festivals. As the hard rock of the early 1980s morphed into the metal of the mid- to late 1980s, Daniel Band kept pace. Beginning with *Run from the Darkness*, which introduced the "No 666" logo to the lapels and leather jackets of the faithful, and continuing through *Rise Up* and *Running Out of Time*, Daniel Band rode the metal train to the end of the line. Front man Tony Rossi started a solo band and would release one album as TRB (Tony Rossi Band) in the 1990s with REX Records.

Bride, originally known as Matrix (which released several independent projects under that name in the early 1980s), began what is still an active metal ministry on the Refuge label with a debut called *Show No Mercy*. Everything about the band was dark, from the album cover to the vocals (and to some extent the production). Bride married the classic hard rock of Led Zeppelin to the metal of early Whitesnake and came up with a unique sound. Front man Dale Thompson's voice, with its dramatic flair and borderline out-of-control vibrato, was an acquired taste. Several years later, a new metal band from Los Angeles called Guns N' Roses would popularize the vocal style that Thompson had been using for years.

Bride was also famous for its controversial concerts. Never short on attitude and never afraid to lay it on the line, Thompson was always talking about issues such as alcohol and smoking alongside the basic gospel message. As the years rolled on, the band gained considerable maturity in both style and substance. Their sound became a more refined classic rock vibe, even delving into modern rock and alternative styles on their album *The Jesus Experience*. As the century turned, Bride was second only to Resurrection Band in years running.

Messiah Prophet Band was a shape-shifting heavy metal ministry that debuted with a memorable album called *Rock the Flock* on the obscure Morada label. The band also toured extensively, eventually signing with Refuge for their seminal *Master of the Metal* album. Messiah Prophet Band definitely qualified as heavy metal. From painfully loud concerts to spandex clothes to lyrics, they were as over the top as Twisted Sister or Ratt.

But even heavier was Saint, the heaviest on the scene. Their first album, *Warriors of the Son*, featured a front-cover shot of the band, fists clenched, scowls etched on their faces, and clad from head to foot in studded and spiked leather. Looking the part was only half of it. The music was frighteningly heavy, with low and foreboding vocals and walls of nasty guitar crunch. The band ended up on Refuge and released two more albums of equally heavy music and shocking graphics.

Jerusalem wasn't the only Swedish gospel rock outfit in the 1980s. Leviticus churned out some of the heaviest music this side of Iron Maiden. Their English wasn't great, but Refuge unleashed them on the United States anyway. The first albums were almost as heavy as those of Saint, but by the late 1980s the music had become much more accessible and melodic. In 1988, Leviticus actually toured as Larry Norman's backing band (which Daniel Band and Jerusalem had done previously) and released their most commercial effort ever in *Setting Fire to the Earth*.

Philadelphia was another heavy metal group of the early sort. Their albums *Tell the Truth* and *Search and Destroy* similarly embraced heavy metal. *Search and Destroy*'s album packaging included skulls and other graphically "heavy" imagery. Although the band, along with Messiah Prophet Band and Saint, managed to get booked at the Cornerstone Festival, they were a bit too heavy for prime-time. In the late 1990s, *Tell the Truth* was rereleased as a limited-edition collector's item, showing that, even though the band hadn't held together, their music did have an impact.

Progressive metal, as perfected by the multimillion-selling Canadian band Rush, was an important subgenre within the metal universe. A

Chicago three-piece band by the name of Trytan answered with their own screaming guitars, intricate arrangements, and impossibly high vocals. Although they released only two albums (both for REX Records), their impact was significant. Their debut album was rereleased in 1999 on a limited basis. Currently, front man Larry Dean is the head pastor of a church in Joliet, Illinois, called Heart Maneuvers Christian Fellowship. Trytan drummer Scottie Blackman also serves on the leadership team of that church. Dean has been working on original worship music for several years.

Another Chicago-based metal band to make a mighty noise in the 1980s was Whitecross. The band featured the guitar brilliance of Rex Carroll, a shredder who'd begun to earn a name for himself with a secular metal group called Braveheart. His speed and dexterity as a guitarist definitely made Whitecross an early hit. Also signed to Refuge (actually, most of the Refuge metal bands were on the label's Pure Metal imprint), Whitecross got its major launch at the Cornerstone Festival and quickly became one of the top-selling metal bands in the history of Christian rock. With the band's success came a flood of label-promoted copycats, none of which could match Whitecross.

When metal faded in the early 1990s, Carroll left the band to pursue a solo career. At first, he put together another arena rock band called King James (the rhythm section for Stryper played on the album). He then released one album on Star Song (which by then had bought the old Pure Metal catalog) that explored his blues-rock roots. Scott Wenzel, the band's lead singer, also recorded a solo album and kept Whitecross going, though in a more alternative vein more befitting the 1990s.

A hastily assembled punk-metal band from Austin, Texas, on their way to play the Cornerstone Festival in Gurnee, Illinois, stopped in St. Louis for some pizza. Not knowing any better, the band chose the safely homogeneous Pizza Hut instead of a better local joint. The local classic rock station, called K-She 93, was running a promotion through the chain, offering glasses with the station's logo emblazoned on them. The logo was a pig, in a leather jacket, with a rock and roll sneer. One band member looked at the glass and said, "Man, that's one bad pig." The band took the name on the spot. The following year, they showed up to play the festival with an independently produced vinyl EP called *A Christian Banned*.

One Bad Pig was an interesting phenomenon in the history of Christian hard rock. Their first major concert was at Cornerstone, and it led to a recording deal with, you guessed it, Pure Metal/Refuge. Their show blew the house down. Without their lead singer, Kosher, the band took the stage and began making noise. Down the center aisle proceeded Kosher, holding a guitar above his head as if leading it to a sacrifice.

When he got to the stage, the guitar burst into flames, having been rigged with flash pots. Kosher proceeded to thrash the guitar until it was a pile of wood and metal. The band then tore into a new song called, appropriately, "Smash the Guitar." The crowd, for the most part, ate it up.

One Bad Pig, later known by fans simply as The Pig, was an interesting paradox. Although certainly not the first punk or metal band, they used the rebellious nature of punk rock and the flamboyant excess of heavy metal to make a point. In the hands of any other punk band, songs such as "Smash the Guitar" would have been taken as a simple urge for violence. But The Pig imbued it with a spiritual meaning that fans got. The guitar symbolized their dreams, their egos, the rock and roll lifestyle — really anything that was an idol to them. Offering it to God and then destroying it was a simple metaphor for getting rid of any distractions from their primary objective: to bring God to the screaming masses. The visceral atmosphere of that night would be replicated countless times by The Pig on tour, and "Smash the Guitar" became the title song of their first widely distributed album and one of their fans' favorites.

As the years ticked on, One Bad Pig moved from Pure Metal to Myrrh, home of Amy Grant. They released a live album called *Blow the House Down* and a studio album called *I Scream Sunday*, which featured a cover of Johnny Cash's "The Man in Black." One Bad Pig's lasting contribution to Christian rock may be that, even though their concerts were wildly humorous and raucous, their presentation of the gospel was always their priority. Kosher went on to become an ordained pastor after the band dissolved, and guitarist Paul Q-pek began a promising solo career as a pop singer in the vein of Peter Gabriel.

In 1986, the first true metal band emerged from Frontline Records out of Orange County, California. The band, named after its bass player, Michael Bloodgood, presented stinging heavy metal with an operatic and dramatic flair. Their Darrell Mansfield-produced debut was impressive enough to send them to the head of the 1980s metal class, but it was their second album, *Detonation*, that made everyone take notice.

Front man Les Carlson had been in several off-Broadway plays and had developed a unique raspy voice and a boisterously dramatic stage presence. The band's guitarist, David Zaffiro, was surprisingly adept at both copping metal clichés and imbuing his playing with a sense of menace and desperation that gave the band a deadly one-two punch. First the music, led by Zaffiro's deft touch with a guitar, grabbed your ears; then Carlson's voice and lyrics grabbed your mind.

The live shows eclipsed even the considerably appealing albums. Carlson performed like a true stage actor, often taking on different roles and even changing costumes between songs. He climbed speaker towers to kneel and pray on top of them. He dressed as Pilate, the governor who sentenced Jesus to die, in the song "Crucify." And on less weighty songs he scampered around the stage like a cross between David Lee Roth and an Olympic gymnast.

Bloodgood's appeal spread well beyond the United States. The band's last album was a double live record that had actually been recorded in Europe. When metal cooled, Bloodgood did too. The only member who stayed active in Christian music was Zaffiro, who released two solo instrumental albums and got heavily into producing other bands and writing with others. Bloodgood's mark is well remembered, though their music is hard to find. They were a definite bright spot in the Christian metal landscape.

Originally signed to Enigma Records and produced by Oz Fox of Stryper, Guardian was a glam metal band from Los Angeles that turned many heads. Their original look included what seemed to be specially designed BMX bike outfits turned alien getups. Eventually, they left the Power Ranger motif behind and moved toward the safer spandex and long hair. The band's original vocalist, and their deal with Enigma, left after the first album tanked. Fortunately, the band was hard to dissuade.

Recruiting the young Jamie Rowe from a fair Midwest metal band called Tempest, the band refined their sound and signed with Packaderm Records, a rock label distributed by Word and owned by John and Dino Elefante (the former a previous vocalist for Kansas). Their sound was a much-needed addition to the Christian scene. Rowe's raspy but melodic voice was classic metal and 1980s rock to a T. The band pumped out

U2's mocked the artifice of mainstream music
with their massive Popmart tour.

commercial hard rock à la Skid Row, Guns N' Roses, and Bon Jovi and sold many albums. Guardian would tour more than almost any band in Christian metal, developing one of the slickest and tightest stage shows in the business.

In the 1990s, Guardian did their best to stretch the definition of commercial hard rock by recording an acoustic album and then a fully alternative one. Although their sales began to slip, as had those of every metal band by then, they crafted some of their best songs on those last few genre-stretching albums. Bassist and band manager David Bach became an A&R man, and guitarist Tony Palacios (arguably one of the best shredders) recorded an instrumental solo album after spending some time as Michael W. Smith's lead guitarist.

Another spandex-clad hair band from Los Angeles was the promising Star Song act Barren Cross. Their first album was one of the earliest glam metal records to be widely distributed in the Christian market. The band's debut, *Rock for the King*, featured a front-cover photo of the band wearing light-blue-and-white spandex and makeup, and their image was surprisingly similar to that of Stryper. The music was similar, too, but Barren Cross's metal was more heavy and less pop. The band would end up on Enigma (Stryper's label) for their sophomore effort, with the same reverse-marketed distribution into the Christian industry via Benson. The wide availability and big-budget sound set the band apart from the growing din of Christian metal bands. They enjoyed decent sales and a devoted following throughout their tenure with Enigma, which ended after their third studio album. A live album and a 1990s "comeback" effort assured the world that the band was still alive, but the 1990s were hard on metal bands.

If Stryper was slick, Ken Tamplin's Shout was well-greased Teflon. With a major league voice and considerable guitar skills, Tamplin became an instant hit among Christian metal fans. He was the epitome of 1980s arena rock, except that the band never filled arenas. It certainly wasn't for lack of trying, though. Constant touring and recording kept the band on the top-10 list of the faithful, but any crossover success was limited to Japan.

After a few Shout albums, Tamplin began to go solo, and his songwriting skills came to the fore. Musically, he moved away from metal and toward pop. The move gave him a steady and lucrative career as a music writer for television and film, and his music has been used in television shows such as *Dawson's Creek* and *Party of Five*.

House of Lords was a critically acclaimed, if not commercially triumphant, artsy metal band in the late 1980s. Their prodigious guitarist, Lanny Cordola, left the band to pursue a solo career, which led to a deal with Frontline Records in the Christian market, in which he released several instrumental rock, jazz, and vocal records, eventually developing the band Magdalen with his friend Ken Tamplin.

The debut of Magdalen was the culmination of the talents of Tamplin and Cordola, at that time the darling duo of Christian pop metal. The promotion of the band's debut, *Big Bang*, mentioned 96 tracks of recording, countless hours in the studio, and epic production. Nonetheless, *Big Bang* was a big bust. Record numbers of CDs and cassettes were shipped to Christian retailers in anticipation of the biggest album since *To Hell with the Devil*. Unfortunately, the winds of change were blowing, and the alternative explosion landed like a concussion grenade on Frontline's hopes for *Big Bang*.

Returns on the album were devastating. Tamplin left Magdalen shortly thereafter, embracing his pop roots and perfecting his craft, while Cordola, the progressive of the group, labored on, redefining Magdalen as a modern rock affair to some success. He became involved in a lot of session and production work and remains a vital behind-the-scenes man. He also released several obscure but impressive jazz and blues records through Frontline.

In 1989, years after pop metal peaked, Myrrh signed and released a debut by an LA-based band called Holy Soldier. With a sound straight out of the MTV playbook, Holy Soldier was right in step with the metal scene. The debut was well received and included several Christian radio hits. The second album, though, was the band's defining moment. *Last Train* featured a more organic, stripped-down style and a convincing cover version of "Gimme Shelter" by The Rolling Stones. Vocalist Steve Patrick was in top form, and the album featured more Christian radio hits and a successful tour. Following that effort, the band changed lead singers, adopted a new, more "alternative" sound, and moved to Forefront Records. More musical and lyrical developments followed, but in the end the band was unable to survive the 1990s. In 1999, the band's much-sought-after debut was rereleased to great success.

Doug Pinnick, Ty Tabor, and Jerry Gaskill met and formed a band while attending college in Springfield, Missouri, in the early 1980s. That band, Sneak Preview, would record one impressive independent album and play countless club gigs as a cover band. In 1988, their debut release as King's X came out on the Megaforce label (a division of Atlantic). *Out of the Silent Planet* was an instant hit with critics, other bands, and the Christian hard rock underground.

Based in Houston at the time, the band, though signed with a secular label and touring with bands such as AC/DC, was comprised of believers. The lyrics were well-crafted allusions to the writings of C.S. Lewis, the ministry of Dr. Martin Luther King Jr., and various Christian themes. The music was a thick blend of Hendrix-like guitars, gospel vocals, imaginative arrangements, and killer groove. There had never been a band like King's X. Although the multiracial aspect of the band caught some media attention (bassist and lead vocalist Doug Pinnick is black), it was the overall impact of the music that blew listeners away. Pinnick's vocals rode atop Tabor's innovative walls of guitar, and his bass parts locked in with Gaskill's drumming with urgency and drive. Add lyrics with an intensity all their own and you have an amazing package.

King's X was the first openly Christian band to make an impact in the secular hard rock world without marketing faith as a gimmick. Although Stryper had been a good pop-metal band, it was known as a Jesus band. King's X turned heads with their music, and, by the time anyone figured out that they were Christians, they couldn't deny the power of the music. Their videos received extensive play on MTV, they toured arenas and clubs, and their singles got played on hard rock radio stations around the world. King's X was simply one of the most exciting things to happen to the metal scene in years. As the luster of the hair bands faded, King's X was there to remind fans that there could still be heart in hard rock.

The band nonetheless had many connections with the Christian music industry. They signed a deal with Star Song Records, and one of their songs was picked up by Morgan Cryar as the title track for his 1986 *Pray in the USA* album. The band backed him up in the studio and opened for Petra on a national tour. Before that, Pinnick had played in one of the incarnations of Servant and contributed songs to their albums.

The influence of King's X spread to another Texas-based hard rock outfit called The Awful Truth. The band's single release found favor with critics and some King's X fans but never caught on nationally. They soon split up. Some of the members went on to form Atomic Opera, a small but compelling hard rock band. Others began a band called Galactic Cowboys, which has released several excellent albums on various labels and toured with King's X.

A small Chicago-based label introduced some important music into the Christian scene in the late 1980s. The label used the name Intense Records for its metal side and Graceland for its alternative side. Intense debuted with two important metal releases in 1987. The first was from the Chicago-based band Sacred Warrior.

Sacred Warrior had been a secular metal band in the Chicago club scene for years under the name Nomad. All members of the band became Christians at roughly the same time and eventually shut Nomad down. They soon began playing again, with a new Christian message behind their music. Their finely honed chops set them apart as one of the premier heavy bands of the day. Lead singer Ray Parra's almost operatic voice combined with intricate arrangements and a sort of gothic darkness to create a sound reminiscent of one of the band's biggest influences, Queensryche. The debut album, *Rebellion*, was an instant hit among metal fans.

Sacred Warrior would continue well into the 1990s, refining their complex sound and winning new fans as most metal bands were fading. They had an especially devoted following in Germany (as did many metal bands) and did not stop rocking until 1996. Although Sacred Warrior closed up shop, the members have continued to experiment with new sounds and plan a release sometime in the new century.

The next major release for Intense was the death metal of Vengeance. Their debut, *Human Sacrifice*, was the most brutally heavy record to come out in the Christian market up to that point. After the initial release, they discovered that a secular metal band was already using the name, so they changed their name to Vengeance Rising. *Human Sacrifice* featured a close-up simulation of one of Christ's hands nailed to the cross, complete with blood and everything. The band used the violent nature of thrash metal to convey the intensity of Christ's crucifixion. Front man Roger Martinez was an evangelistic fire bomb, instantly relating to his audience as he spoke in the same slang and dialect as his fans.

After the debut releases of Sacred Warrior and Vengeance, Intense and its sister label Graceland were sold to Frontline Records. Both bands released several albums through the new Frontline-Intense company. Vengeance Rising released their follow-up album, *Once Dead*, and then, following a string of financial problems and disputes with the label, the band, with the exception of Martinez, decided to call it quits. Instead of dissolving the group, Martinez took over ownership of the band and ran it himself for several years, releasing albums that were nowhere near as good as the first two. The other members formed a new group called Die Happy (inspired by a JPUSA T-shirt design) and signed with Intense. That band released two albums of classic 1970s-style metal in the vein of Black Sabbath, Deep Purple, or Rainbow.

After running the band into further debt and hitting a sort of personal wall, Martinez was dropped from Intense. In what remains as the most disturbing fall from grace in the annals of the Christian metal scene, Martinez went on a tear, trying to implicate the label or his former bandmates for the problems faced by Vengeance Rising. He eventually renounced his faith and continued with the band in the occultic death metal scene.

The story of Martinez and Vengeance Rising reverberated throughout the industry. Martinez had been a pastor in the Sanctuary Church and one of the most zealous ministers in the medium. Fortunately, the Christian metal scene had years of positive results and strong leaders, and

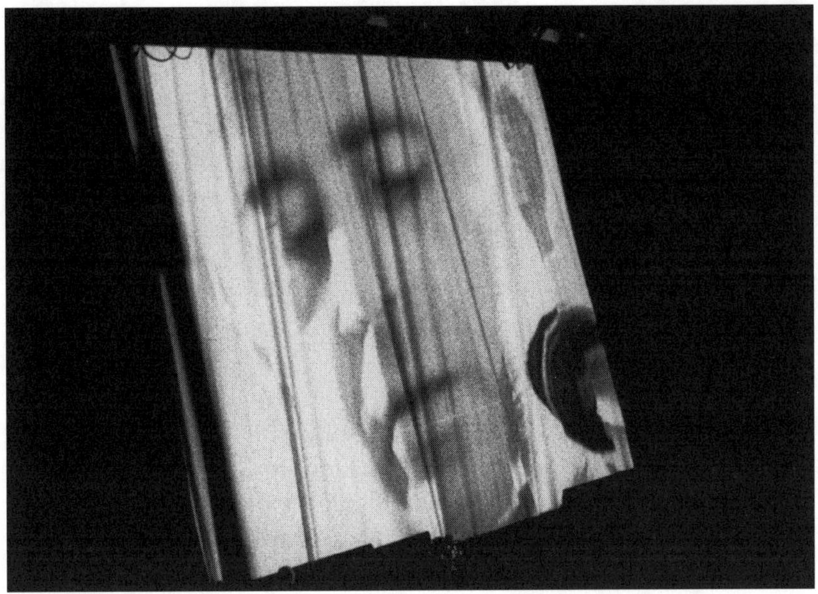

Gene "Eugene" Andrusco was honored with a special video tribute at the Adam Again concert at Cornerstone 2000.

his departure, though sad, didn't set back the spread of hard-music ministry on a wide scale.

One of the heaviest bands ever to hit the Christian scene is Australia's Mortification. The thrash/death metal band, led by guitarist/vocalist Steve Rowe, originally debuted in the mid-1980s with a less than brilliant album under the name Light Force on Pure Metal/Refuge. Light Force became Mortification, and Rowe suddenly had one of the most credible Christian death metal bands in the world on his hands. Every release on Frontline/Intense, beginning with their self-titled debut, was a blatantly evangelistic work of shredding death metal. Their second album, *Scrolls of the Megilloth*, got some marketing in the secular industry, where fans of bands such as Deicide ate it up.

Rowe faced a battle with cancer in the late 1990s but never let it get him down. He has launched his own label and is currently still regaling the world with Mortification music and records by other Christian death metal bands from around the world.

Another thrash band from Los Angeles picked up by Frontline/Intense was a group called Deliverance. They debuted on a hugely successful and influential compilation called *California Metal* on the short-lived Regency label. Deliverance found instant favor with Vengeance Rising fans and expanded on it. Their music combined what had become by then a relatively staid formula for thrash metal with more experimental alternative tones. One of their albums was produced by Daniel Amos's Terry Taylor, who gave it a sonic depth missing in most thrash albums. Deliverance continued well into the 1990s, finally calling it quits with their final release, *River Disturbance*, in 1996.

One of the most durable and influential metal bands has been Ted Kirkpatrick's Tourniquet. The band, which derived most of its album titles and lyrical themes from a medical dictionary, created music that was intricate, aggressive, and progressive. Where most metal was satisfied to be heavy with the music, Kirkpatrick imbued his band with controversial lyrics and a vocabulary that gave brain cramps to many a teenager.

The band's debut, *Stop the Bleeding*, was released to critical acclaim and strong sales in 1989. It was followed by albums such as *Psycho Surgery* and *Pathogenic Ocular Dissonance*, and the binding on Ted's father's medical dictionary wore thin. Although Tourniquet liked to use scientific terms as analogies for the basic problems of humanity, occasionally Kirkpatrick tackled more basic issues such as animal cruelty and politics.

As the major labels finally caught up with the alternative revolution, Tourniquet was one of the few bands (along with Bride) that rose to the challenge and survived. 1996's *Crawl to China* showed that the band could adapt without sacrificing what made them unique. After that one slight departure from form, and an excellent acoustic trip down memory lane, the band returned to its vocabulary-rich form with the 2000 release of *A Microscopic View of a Telescopic Realm*.

Along with these bands, literally hundreds of others added their efforts to the heavenly metal scene. Many released one or two albums and then either evolved or disappeared. Many of the albums were flat-out awful, and some of the bands weren't really Christian but nonetheless found their way to Christian labels, and others just couldn't survive Curt Cobain's revolution. Christian metal fan Doug Van Pelt kept fuel on the fire with his magazine *Heaven's Metal* (which became HM magazine in the late 1990s). HM remains the pivotal voice of the Christian hard music underground. For over 20 years, Christians have been crafting heavy metal of every flavor. The intensity and confrontational nature of the music are perfectly suited to the message of the gospel.

Getting the Word Out

A number of Christian rock radio shows emerged in the 1980s. Although mostly in smaller towns and as special one- or two-hour programs in the middle of the night, Christian rock was being broadcast. There were even charts for rock songs by the mid-1980s, but since there were so few rock radio stations a highly charting single didn't necessarily translate into great sales.

In the absence of solid radio, and since MTV wasn't interested in Christian music, the only way for new bands to be promoted nationally was either to tour or to receive coverage in magazines.

John Styll's CCM magazine flourished in the 1980s. Broadening the magazine beyond music and changing the name to *Contemporary Christian Magazine* lasted for a while, but eventually the name went back to *Contemporary Christian Music* or CCM. Although his mandate was to cover all Christian music, from the contemporary adult of Dallas Holm, to the gospel pop of The Imperials, to the rock of Daniel Amos, Styll consistently managed to cover the progressive fringe with authority. As rock slid into mainstream music, CCM leaned more and more toward the mainstream. However, by keeping an eye on the rock side, and consistently publishing thought-provoking editorials by John Fischer, the magazine has always retained its usefulness.

A batch of underground magazines reminiscent of the 1960s "rags" began to circulate across the country. The *Activist* from Ohio covered punk music, ran cartoons, and questioned the viability of major-label music. In Orlando, Dan Kennedy published the *Cutting Edge*, a newsletter that featured reviews of cassette-only demos as well as label releases. *Notebored Magazine* eventually came along with a more slick product but a cool perspective nonetheless. Also launched was an excellent resource from the Pacific Northwest called the *Alternative Christian Music Journal*. Others followed and flourished into the 1990s until they were replaced by web sites that accomplished the same things.

A Christian rock fan in Chicago by the name of Paul Emery started promoting Christian rock concerts in 1980. His company was called Harvest Productions, and he began by putting together a one-day "festival" of bands such as Servant, Rez Band, and Barnabas. Emery brought bands such as Daniel Amos, Phil Keaggy, DeGarmo and Key, and scores of others to Chicago.

When 103.9 FM adopted a Christian format in 1983, WCRM became a major partner for Emery. He hosted a Saturday-night radio show called the *Harvest Rock Show* that played music by all the bands that he was going to bring to Chicago. It was the first time that bands such as Jerusalem, Larry Norman, Daniel Band, or Rez Band were played on the air in the city. Harvest Productions grew quickly and became the largest Christian-concert production company in the Midwest.

In 1986, Emery enlisted the help of writer Brian Quincy Newcomb to start a magazine dedicated to the emerging rock scene. Originally distributed in Chicago at Harvest Productions concerts, the *Harvest Rock Syndicate* eventually made its way around the world, reaching over 10,000 people with reviews of records, in-depth interviews, and news about the rock underground in the Christian music business. Newcomb also regularly looked beyond Christian labels and established Christian bands to find nuggets of truth in secular pop culture. Often mainstream bands with Christian members or lyrical overtones would be explored alongside albums by Petra and Rez Band. This approach positioned Christian rock in relation to secular rock. For instance, compared to Steve Green, Whiteheart sounded very intense, edgy, and raw. But what did they sound like next to Bon Jovi, Guns N' Roses, or Huey Lewis and the News? By placing Christian music in the larger secular context, Newcomb and the other writers gradually matured the tastes and critical abilities of their readers. And many artists were inspired to work harder knowing that their music would get honestly critiqued.

Shortening its name to the *Syndicate* and changing ownership, the magazine lost much of its impact in the 1990s. Eventually, it was shut down, and Harvest Productions was sold to an out-of-town concert promoter who focused on arena concerts. WCRM changed formats, and the days of the *Harvest Rock Show* in Chicago came to an end.

A Zondervan-family bookstore in Carol Stream, Illinois, became known for its progressive music department. The manager, music fan Russ Schwartz, hired a music buyer who could really help to create a department that would reach people. The man for the job turned out to be Mike Delaney, who'd eventually become known as one of the foremost collectors and dealers of hard-to-find Christian music in the world. Delaney networked with other progressive music fans and got albums into the store from California, Europe, and nearly everywhere else. Not only did he stock every rock and alternative release from Word, Sparrow, Benson, Lexicon, and the catch-all Spring-Arbor distribution system, but he also carried releases from Kosher Records and Imports of California, Embryo Arts of Belgium, and MRC albums from California that hadn't made it into a major distribution system. Delaney's department became part of the underground distribution network. Other stores may have tried similar approaches, but certainly none was as thorough.

Eventually, Schwartz left the store to become a sales rep for Word, and Delaney left to move to Michigan. He launched a company called RadRockers Emporium (The Itinerant Iconoclast), which he used to set up massive booths at Cornerstone Festivals to sell hard-to-find music. RadRockers evolved into a successful dealer of collector's items.

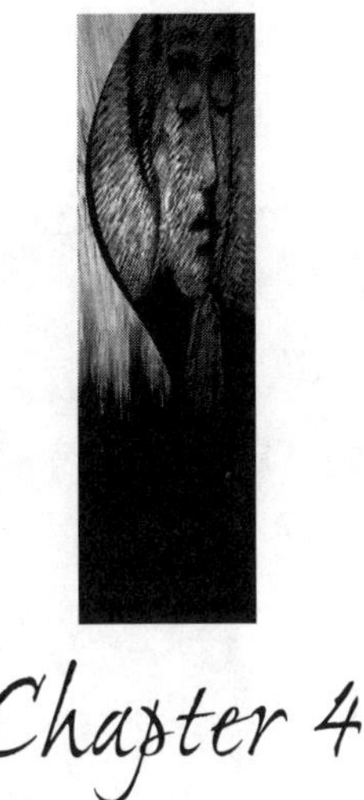

Chapter 4

The Third Wave (1990–99)

If the 1980s marked the adolescence of Christian rock, the 1990s marked its young adulthood. In the latter decade, MTV and cable TV in general brought an explosion of revenue potential. Then along came the Internet. By 1996, almost every band, label, retailer, radio station, and advertiser had a web site. Information and entertainment went supernova. Information flowed like cheap beer at a frat party, and society's appetite for entertainment seemed to be insatiable. Musically, we'd all "been there, done that." Every imaginable musical genre had been explored. The only thing left was shock.

Into a scene dominated by overdone pop divas, bad-boy rappers, and indulgent college rockers strode the perfect antidote, Kurt Cobain and his Seattle band Nirvana. Although the band's music was certainly good, it was the image of the slacker, the disenfranchised, the hopeless case that connected with media-crazed teens like a raw wire in a thunderstorm. Having been overfed by the overly sweet and too fabulous pop scene of the late 1980s, youth were primed for something new.

By the early 1990s, Michael Jackson, dubbed the King of Pop in the 1980s, was little more than a cartoon character to the youth of the cities of America. The African American crowd had moved on to hip-hop,

Michael Pritzl injected intensity and emotion into alternative Christian music with his band The Violet Burning.

gangsta rap, and Boys II Men, and the white kids had left Jackson's camp as soon as the *Thriller* video became boring. When Nirvana bumped Jackson off the top spot on the Billboard Album Charts in 1991, it sent a jolt through the music industry. Highly marketed pop music suddenly became old news. The cutting edge was grunge and later, simply, "alternative." The alternative bands of the early 1990s created a rallying point for youth. Long on image (or the intentional lack thereof) and sometimes short on content, one-hit wonders returned as radio discovered a new vein to mine, full of bands with names such as Bush, Weezer, and Belly. The edgy style of the 1980s as perfected by groups such as U2, The Red Hot Chili Peppers, and The Cure became the pop music of the 1990s.

Hardcore amorality became commodified as a legitimate response to the world's hypocrisy and emptiness. Not only did the music of Nine Inch Nails become mainstream, but its message of hatred, sexual aggression, and nihilism and its vehement anti-Christian stance became just as acceptable. Even rape, murder, and cop killing became fair lyrical game in the marketplace. The fringe had become the mainstream, much to the delight of the marketing and sales people for the various record companies and broadcast outlets. The Western world sailed beyond postmodernity. Moral relativism, the celebration of excess, and hyperconsumerism coalesced, and the big guns of Madison Avenue and Hollywood perfected their co-opting of legitimate social paradigm shifts into marketing coups. Instead of searching for integrity in art, people celebrated emptiness, downplaying anything with meaning or purpose. Any attempt to offer an answer was met with a sneer. No one was to be trusted, and life was to be lived instinctively, with no reference to the past and no concern for the future.

In Hollywood, a new generation of films emerged that, had they been made in the 1970s or 1980s, would have been underground at best. *Natural Born Killers*, for example, ostensibly an attempt to explore the dark underbelly of media saturation of society, instead served as a thrill ride of violence and sex. With its prominent alternative music soundtrack and its mainstream actors, it played like a long MTV video minus any censorship. Americans, especially youth, were being entertained by increasingly intense doses of bloodshed and mayhem. Religious and community leaders snapped out of their 30-year lull and called for tougher standards, rating labels on records, and more restrictions. But this was a battle that they'd already lost.

Traditional interests, especially the church, had abdicated their role in pop culture long before. The music industry that they had created served as insulation between them and the rest of the great unwashed. Even their churches, once the centers of community life, had become fragmented "family centers" where members could gather throughout the week to be surrounded by sound teaching, uplifting music, safe socializing, and family-oriented entertainment. There was little need to worry about the world outside. By 1988, in fact, when Martin Scorcese released his film version of *The Last Temptation of Christ*, the church had become so disconnected from secular society as to be predictable. Instead of having rendered Jesus as accurately as possible in film, they'd allowed the void to be filled by Scorcese and then protested about his treatment of Christ. Their calls for boycotts rang in the air like cap guns at a battle on China Beach.

Tipper Gore and her Parental Music Resource Center (PMRC) convened high-profile hearings on the effects of rock and rap on kids. Calling for record ratings similar to what the MPAA did for movies, the PMRC played right into the hands of a cynical music industry, which knew full well that one of the best ways to shock listeners, and thereby connect with them in some way, was through graphic sexual and violent lyrics and coarse language. Thus, the PMRC stickers affixed to albums by Two Live Crew and just about every gangsta rap album became additional promotion. If the record companies had dared to place stickers on their albums that said "Buy this album — it contains bad words and lewd content," they would have been laughed out of the business. But the PMRC, in effect, allowed them to do just that.

Television was no exception. Always trying to compete with cable channels that had no content boundaries for sex and language, mainstream television pushed its standards lower and lower. Sexual content and nudity became acceptable, and shows such as *NYPD Blue* intentionally pushed the envelope. MTV brought bikini beach parties to the after-school hours. Advertisers often drove the "progress" by making their 30-second spots as sexual and aggressive as possible. In an environment where anything goes, and the only way to register your product (whether it be a band, a pair of jeans, or a can of Coke) is to get a bigger rise out of an audience than competitors are able to, restraint and judgment have no role.

In the music industry, it was no different. The bottom line had always been, and will always be, about money. What had changed, though, was the industry's ability to generate cash from the youth culture. Teens in the 1980s and 1990s had more disposable money than had any generation before them, and it became the goal of the music industry to get as much of that money as possible. The more kids could be wedged away from their parents or any connection to anything bigger than themselves, the easier it would be to get them to throw their cash and attention around like pearls before swine. The influential power of music was well known. Since the 1970s, there had hardly been a television ad without a melodic hook or jingle, and major corporations took advantage of the suggestive power of music by sponsoring concert tours.

Tim Taber and Eric Campuzano of The Prayer Chain.

Meanwhile, the Christian music industry was also growing by leaps and bounds. The bookstore networks had a firm monopoly on distribution, often exerting significant influence on what was released or promoted. Christian radio had become increasingly popular, especially in larger markets such as Chicago and Dallas, and concert tours filled stadiums and churches with Christians. The Christian community had nearly completed its total retreat from mainstream society. It even had its own television networks. Many Christians were able to live in a world within a world, one that would protect them from ever brushing up against non-Christians. And the ghetto was large enough that many people made millions of dollars selling Christian CDs to Christians, Christian books to Christians, and even Christian toys, paintings, videos, and clothes to Christians.

A handful of Christian artists, however, wanted nothing to do with that ghetto. They wanted to be out in the "real world" playing concerts in clubs and bars, selling CDs in mainstream record outlets, and being played on secular radio. Unfortunately, it wasn't that easy. If their faith was detected by the power brokers in the mainstream music business, they were labeled as Christian artists, and their music was placed in the gospel or "Contemporary Christian" bins at music stores. Many radio stations and MTV wouldn't touch them, and if their audiences didn't drink enough beer they found it hard to get booked in mainstream venues. All of this had nothing to do with the music; it was about marketing and cash. This left many artists of faith extremely frustrated. On one side, they were shut out of the Christian scene because they were too controversial or didn't play the game right. On the other, they were ignored as irrelevant. Fans were frustrated too. The small community of alternative Christian artists boasted an incredibly loyal fan base; many fans would drive 10 hours to see The Seventy Sevens perform one show. Even more would buy all their music through mail-order catalogs because local secular and Christian retailers refused to stock anything good. Events such as the Cornerstone Festival became increasingly important to this network of between 10,000 and 50,000 people.

However, when Nirvana and Nine Inch Nails became mainstream, youth pastors across the country simultaneously convulsed. Suddenly, the church's irrelevance was staring them in the face as their own youth became increasingly pierced, tattooed, and successfully wooed by the machinations of the entertainment industry. Youth pastors had long been an important part of the equation in Christian music. Often younger than head pastors, they wanted to be considered hip by their charges. Music was a cheap and easy way to demonstrate their relatability, and it often served as a teaching aid to boot. Youth pastors would take groups of kids to festivals and concerts and would promote Christian music to them. By and large, though, youth pastors wanted music that was easy to justify to the parents and pastors to whom they had to answer. They wanted music with a high ratio of JPM (mentions of Jesus per minute). With the alternative revolution, however, the chasm of relevance between the mainstream Christian rock bands and the secular music that kids heard on MTV turned into the Grand Canyon. Eventually, many of the big names, DC Talk notably, evolved to meet the trends. But there all along, lurking in the shadows, were a bunch of bands stuck between the church and pop culture, just like their predecessors in the Jesus Movement had been.

Distributing Fringe Music

These fringe bands had recordings that needed to be distributed. Word Distribution, having had some earlier success with distributed labels such as Maranatha! and later Brainstorm, rushed into the distributed-label craze. The biggest distributor of Christian music soon started to mine the fringes for sellable albums, and a group of labels known as the Word Associated Labels, or WAL, emerged. They were Brainstorm (which had debuted in the late 1980s as Broken Records), Packaderm (the arena rock label headed by John and Dino Elefante, who brought out most of Guardian's albums as well as the first series of rock praise albums), Wonderland (the Chicago label started by Caesar Kalinowski and Gavin Morkel of REX after they sold Graceland/Intense to Frontline), Glasshouse (a dreamy little label run by The Choir that released the stunning *At the Foot of the Cross* records as well as albums by John Austin and blues man Dan Smith), and Rode Dog (a division of Reunion, which featured The Prayer Chain and The Throes and was run by Dave Palmer). The WAL pushed out between 30 and 50 albums a year between 1990 and 1993.

Jimmy Kempner's Frontline Music Group tried to be a distributor on its own, but after a few years the system fell apart. Its distribution was taken over by a new company called Diamante Music Group, which essentially moved into the Frontline office and took over. When it came to cutting-edge rock music in the 1990s, Diamante was the place. All the smaller alternative labels ended up at Diamante at one time or another.

Founded in New York City in the late 1980s, REX Music was the brainchild of Doug Mann, a music fan and producer. His original stylistic slant was toward heavy metal. The first signing on REX was a Chicago-based Rush sound-alike called Trytan. Next was an astoundingly good (even for people who hated the genre) speed metal/thrash band called Believer. REX also signed a classic metal band called Rage of Angels. With spotty distribution, REX struggled to get on the national map. The quality was there, but the product was just too aggressive to get into some stores

Marc Ludena, Chris Wicklas, Michelle Thompson,
and John Thompson of The Wayside.

without the push of a major label behind it. Mann ended up setting up his own distribution system along with co-owner Gavin Morkel and moving the company to Chicago and then to Nashville. REX eventually found its way to Diamante for distribution.

Although it was still known for the heaviest music out there, such as the death metal of Living Sacrifice, the industrial rock of Passafist, and the industrial noise of Circle of Dust, in the early 1990s REX sought to broaden its appeal. Mann looked for alternative bands that could offset the label's image. One of his first efforts was an acoustic/new folk label called Storyville run by industry veteran David Bunker. Storyville released projects by Pam Mark Hall, Nancy Honeytree, and other folk artists. Mann also sought out a band from Chicago called The Wayside that played rootsy acoustic-based pop and rock. The Wayside's founder (your author) became convinced that he should start his own label, Etcetera Records, which could bring The Wayside and other nonmetal bands to the REX family. About the same time, Mann signed a band from Texas called Sixpence None the Richer and a Nashville alternative band getting rave reviews in the club scene called Fleming and John, but within days he announced that he was leaving to take a position at Forefront. Etcetera released albums by The Wayside, Love Coma (featuring future solo artist Chris Taylor and Sixpence None the Richer's Matt Slocum on guitar), and industry veterans Greg and Rebecca Sparks. REX also signed an indie label from Atlanta that brought pop bands The Waiting and Villanelle (later renamed Smalltown Poets) to the REX system.

In the mid-1990s, REX was convinced to leave the Diamante system and move to Platinum Entertainment, a major general market label that handled distribution for The Beach Boys and various country labels and had recently purchased the old Light Records catalog. The deal looked good on paper, but after REX pulled up stakes and moved to Platinum the system didn't work well. Sales dropped and eventually forced REX to begin bankruptcy proceedings. At the last minute, Platinum stepped in and assumed ownership of REX without taking on the debts that REX had incurred. As a result, many of the bands never got paid, and REX, which had showed so much promise a short time before, was history. The Waiting got signed by Sparrow, and Smalltown Poets signed with Forefront. Fleming and John moved to the mainstream Universal Records label. After vocal protests and basic refusals to work with the new owners of REX, Sixpence None the Richer was sold to Steve Taylor's Squint Records. The Wayside, Greg and Rebecca Sparks, and most of the other artists returned to the indie scene.

The breakout story from Diamante was a start-up label called Tooth and Nail. A young entrepreneur named Brandon Ebel was about to change everything. He'd moved to southern California to find a way into the music business. He landed a job as a phone-sales person at Frontline. He was quickly promoted to radio promotions and then to director of alternative and metal. Frontline was on the way down, and many of the staff were on their way out, so Ebel had room to move up.

In his free time, he went to clubs and churches to check out local bands. The scene had exploded, and there were dozens to pick from every weekend, few of whom had record deals. He had a vision for a label as cool as the up-and-coming secular labels of the day, such as Rough Trade, Wax Trax, and Caroline. Those labels had developed such a strong brand identity that a certain crowd would buy an album just because they liked the label. Ebel secured a small-business loan and in 1993 launched Tooth and Nail with new band Wish for Eden's album *Pet the Fish*.

Tooth and Nail secured distribution through Diamante and in the first year released a hardcore album by Focused, an alternative pop record by Starflyer 59, a retro techno-synth pop album by Joy Electric, an industrial album by Chatterbox, a Seattle grunge record by Sometime Sunday, a punk rock record by MxPx, a hardcore record by The Blamed, and an alternative pop record by Plankeye, among others. The records were all at the progressive fringes of their various genres. The label used "gang ads," as Frontline and others had done, to get the most exposure for each band. Tooth and Nail quickly became known as an edgy, cool new label. Bands flocked to it willing to take smaller offers than labels had been forced to hand out in previous years. By taking advantage of lower recording costs, hype over the alternative music scene, and sheer momentum, Tooth and Nail became the lone success story among the early 1990s label scene.

As Tooth and Nail gained speed, many other labels finally disappeared. Word dumped its distributed-label program and focused on rebuilding Myrrh with California alternative pop band Dakoda Motor Company (featuring Peter King of MTV fame) and eventually Guardian and The Seventy Sevens. Brainstorm managed to stay on track through the mid-1990s and then shut down.

Tooth and Nail began spin-off sublabel Solid State for the heaviest stuff. It would eventually release about 30 albums per year, nearly owning the alternative scene in the Christian market. In 1997, Ebel launched a new label called BEC (the Brandon Ebel Company) and secured Christian and general market distribution with EMI. This was a controversial move to some since Ebel moved some Tooth and Nail bands to the new label. Diamante, which had allowed Tooth and Nail "the run of the place," as one employee put it, was worried about losing its top label. Sure enough, just as Diamante finally started to get the attention of more than just the most devoted retailers, Tooth and Nail left its system. Talk of a lawsuit spread, but eventually Ebel and Diamante president Bill

Conine resolved their dispute through mediation. Tooth and Nail moved to the EMI system, actually setting up its own distribution system (Sonic Fuel) within the EMI superstructure. In 1999, all of Tooth and Nail's roster was moved into the general EMI system.

Tooth and Nail has succeeded on two major fronts. In terms of momentum, it has released hundreds of albums for over 100 bands and has sold millions of copies, mostly 10,000 or so at a time. But it has also had some breakout hits. The ska craze of the 1990s was largely centered on Tooth and Nail, and its band The Supertones led the way. The Supertones have sold hundreds of thousands of albums and had numerous successful tours as headliners. Even bigger was the punk pop of the Washington-based band MxPx. The band was among the first to sign with Tooth and Nail, its members inking the deal before they were even old enough to legally sign the contract. It was MxPx's popularity outside the Christian scene that led A&M to sign a special distribution deal with Tooth and Nail to handle the label in the mainstream. That deal eventually led to A&M buying MxPx's contract from Tooth and Nail.

It hasn't been all hugs and kisses for Tooth and Nail. Ebel caught some flak for going on record saying that Tooth and Nail wasn't a Christian label. His point was that a record label couldn't be a Christian. The bands were Christian, but the label was just a label. In fact, it later turned out that a couple of Tooth and Nail bands didn't consider themselves Christians. Ebel and his label reignited the "Christian band" versus "Christians in a band" debate that had existed for years. Some retailers, publications, and even bands bristled at the label's seeming cockiness as time went on, but most kept their opinions to themselves while they sold records.

Others complained that Tooth and Nail had flooded the market, leaving no room for smaller labels. Retailers complained when the label set up its own mail-order company and retail store in direct competition with them. Many wondered if any thought went into the spiritual content of the music as more and more of it sounded just like secular pop music. As with any success story, there were many who weren't fully enthusiastic about Ebel's dominance over the alternative Christian scene.

Tooth and Nail's impact, for better or worse, has been thorough. As one of the most profitable labels in the Christian music business, and one of the most profitable indie labels in the general market, it continues to dominate. For the second half of the 1990s, Tooth and Nail *was* alternative Christian music, leaving little room for anyone else.

Beginning in the early 1990s, the Christian market began to look like a flea market to major mainstream entertainment companies. Jimmy Bowen, the mogul behind the rise of "new country" music in general and Garth Brooks in particular, saw similar potential in Christian music. His

David Bazan's band Pedro The Lion became an underground favorite in the late '90s.

target became the biggest and most profitable independent Christian label in the business, Sparrow Records. Bowen arranged for EMI Music to buy Sparrow in October 1992. (In the same week, Word was purchased by Thomas Nelson, the largest Bible publisher in the world. Nelson ended up selling Word a few years later to Gaylord Entertainment, the owners of Country Music Television, the Nashville Network, and Opryland.) Since Sparrow had its own distribution company, EMI set it up as EMI Christian Music and then changed the name to Chordant Distribution. Sparrow had handled distribution for Star Song (The Newsboys) and Forefront (DC Talk). EMI ended up buying those companies as well.

Shortly thereafter, the Music Entertainment Group, a massive conglomerate run by Wes Farrell (a mogul whose first conquests were *The Partridge Family* and *The Brady Bunch*) bought Benson Music. BMG bought half of Reunion and Blanton and Harrell Management, and a year later the Zomba Corporation bought Brentwood Music, which had launched a rock label called Essential.

In a few short years, the whole landscape had changed. The distribution of Christian music into secular markets increased, at least for the top five percent of the releases. Basically, Point of Grace and Michael W. Smith were easier to find in Target stores, but, with the exceptions of The Supertones, DC Talk, and a few other bands, the real rockers were not part of the growth.

As the 1990s wound down, the massive breakthrough wasn't materializing for the majors. The titles that did break through were almost all of the rock/modern pop variety, so the major labels began seeking more of it. EMI secured the distribution of Tooth and Nail, giving it a solid position within the rock market. Brentwood/Essential launched but quickly abandoned an alternative label called Sub*Lime. Benson did the same with Tattoo.

Meanwhile, Word, once the leader in general gospel music distribution, and once the leader in rock and alternative distribution, was left behind. Especially when it came to rock, Word had little as the decade wound down. It did have one asset, though, a little start-up run by Steve Taylor called Squint Entertainment.

Basically, in the 1990s, the business side of the Christian music scene was a cacophony of start-ups, shutdowns, changeovers, and bankruptcies. With a few notable exceptions, the entire decade resembled an uncomfortable junior high dance. Throughout the chaos, though, some albums garnered a lot of attention, as did some artists.

Artists Old and New

In 1990, at the Gospel Music Week in Nashville, Michael Knott launched the subversive label Blonde Vinyl Records. He moved his own bands (LSU and The Lifesavers as separate entities) and gathered up a number of young indie bands such as California's Black and White World (featuring lead vocalist Rob Gallas, who'd later join Undercover), Texas industrial pioneers Deitiphobia, Dancehouse Children with its groundbreaking electronica, and the ever-strange Breakfast with Amy. Within the first year of its existence, Blonde Vinyl had released over a dozen of the most adventurous albums that Christian music had ever seen. For an ad to appear in *True Tunes News* at the Cornerstone Festival in 1991, Knott gathered the album covers of most of his label's acts and added the caption "A New Alternative," implying that Christians could now choose a new type of music. It may have been the first time that the word *alternative* was officially used to describe a style of music.

Blonde Vinyl cranked out records for two years until its distributor, Spectra Distribution, filed for bankruptcy, owing Knott a lot of money. Blonde Vinyl was shut down shortly thereafter, but Knott went on. He started up Siren Music and released a few significant records. One was an LSU project called *Cash in Chaos*, and another was the first post-Dancehouse Children album by Ronnie Martin under the name Rainbow Rider. Although the record was panned by some critics, it endured as a classic among fans of the genre.

By 1995, Knott gave up trying to run a label and became busy as an artist. He recorded a new (and incredible) LSU album, *Grace Shaker*, for Frontline, a Lifesavors record called *Huntington Beach*, and an acclaimed solo album, *Rocket and a Bomb* for Brainstorm. He also recorded a solo album for Tooth and Nail called *Strip Cycle*, a solo album called *Fluid* for Frontline, and an LSU album called *Dogfish Jones* for Flying Tart. Between 1994 and 1996, Knott released seven albums, including a live LSU record on Grey Dot Records.

Then he revisited an old agenda. Back in the 1980s, he'd tried to infiltrate the secular scene with a band called Bomb Bay Babies and a solo single. In 1996, his new "secular" band, The Aunt Bettys, comprised of former LSU members, was signed to a major-label deal with Elektra. Their self-titled debut was a shock to Knott's Christian fans, for it definitely pushed the envelope in terms of language and subject. He maintained that the songs, though certainly darker at times, were consistent with his past work and were a conscious effort to connect with a larger rock audience. The Aunt Bettys developed a solid following in the LA club scene and got rave reviews in the local press. Unfortunately, shortly after the release of their debut, the band became the victim of label politics. When it became clear that the new leadership at Elektra (the band had been signed by Seymour Stein, the founder of Sire Records, who'd originally signed Madonna and The Ramones, among others) had no intention of supporting the band, they arranged for their own release from their contract with Elektra. Eventually, The Aunt Bettys hung it up (after releasing a CD of rarities, demos, and outtakes from their Elektra album called *Ford Supersonic* on the indie Marathon label). Knott continued to write and record, including an unreleased project on the life of King David.

As the 1990s came to a close, he was preparing two new ventures. First, he put together a new mainstream band with Dennis Dannell of Social Distortion called The Strung Gurus. The duo wrote and recorded a project and shopped it to several mainstream labels. Just as they were gaining momentum, tragedy struck. Dannell died of a massive brain aneurysm at the age of 38. Although known more as the founder of the seminal punk band Social Distortion, Dannell had become increasingly involved in the alternative Christian scene in Orange County. He'd produced albums by Fanmail, Deluxetone Rockets, Value Pak, and others. His faith, combined with Knott's, could have broken down the division between secular and Christian rock. Second, Knott joined a new band with Eric Campuzano, Wayne Everett, and Andy Pricket, formerly of The Prayer Chain. The new band, called Cush, made its debut at the Cornerstone 2000 Festival.

Although The Violet Burning front man Michael Pritzl had experienced the earliest days of the Orange County Christian alternative scene as a member of a promising band called The Children, it wasn't until he

Michael Knott, who is also an accomplished painter,
has released over twenty albums.

formed The Violet Burning that this explosive figure was unleashed. Pritzl, along with Michael Misiuk (who'd later form several bands, including Acoustic Shack, Autumn Rose, and The Kreepdowns), Lonnie Tubbs, and Kirt Gentry formed this dynamic band in the late 1980s. They convened at Gentry's church to record some demos. The church (the Vineyard) happened to have a label with access to the Christian market. It signed the band and released the demos as their first album, *Chosen*, in 1989. The record, on New Breed Records and distributed by Frontline, was a surprising hit. Bookings at Cornerstone and all over Los Angeles followed. The band members were a bit stunned.

After Misiuk and Gentry left and were replaced by Shawn and Scott Tubbs, the band recorded their follow-up. In the midst of the 1992 explosion of brash grunge bands like Nirvana and Alice in Chains, the band opted for a more textured, smooth, and emotional record, *Strength*. It came together quickly, with most of the songs coming from the pain of several of Pritzl's friends' deaths and a close friend who went through a divorce. In a very Psalm-like fashion, Pritzl's pain was therapeutic to his listeners. *Strength* was a resounding hit in the underground and placed The Violet Burning right up there with The Seventy Sevens, The Choir, and Mike Knott.

Conflicts between the church-owned New Breed and Pritzl led to the band's opting to have the record released through Blue Stone Records, a label out of a church in Denver. Controversy erupted almost immediately as some individuals from one church sent a fax to dozens of others that The Violet Burning were fornicators and drunkards, charges that the band denied, adding that two of the members were virgins and that two were married. Although the details of just what was said have been a source of contention for years, the fax drove a wedge between the band and the Christian community. With emotions raging, Scott and Shawn quit the band, leaving it to Michael and Lonnie.

The two rebuilt the band and continued to play shows, though mostly at bars and clubs. A few demos were recorded and sold at shows, but not until 1996 did The Violet Burning return with a new album. Having been picked up by the secular indie label Domo, Pritzl vented his spleen on that self-titled album. With the camaraderie of former Prayer Chain member Andy Prickett (guitars) and The Choir's Steve Hindalong added to the lineup, The Violet Burning exploded with anger, tears, and the tiniest glimmer of hope. The catharsis was too much for some fans, but most went along for the ride. Domo shot a video for the band that aired on MTV France and in Europe, where the band toured. Unfortunately, as is too often the case, the label couldn't make it work, and the record failed commercially.

The band got out of the deal with Domo, Tubbs finally said goodbye, and Pritzl was left to himself. He'd written a bunch of songs inspired by the time he'd spent in Berlin, and in 1998 he recorded and released *The Violet Burning Demonstrates Plastic and Elastic*, which he believes best captures the purpose and vision of his band. Recorded independently of any label and sold only through the band's web site and a handful of dealers such as True Tunes, the album sold out several times. The band, then consisting of Herb Grimmaud Jr. on bass, Robbie Farr on guitar, and Michael Kalmar on drums, proceeded to play some carefully selected shows. The sound had become reminiscent of Bowie glam, and the band sported heavy makeup, fingernail polish, and feather boas. The Violet Burning, though still coming from a basic position of Christian faith, was pushing the limits further than any other band had before them. Members were seen smoking in album art, and to the Christian market this was troubling. But they'd distanced themselves from the market part of the Christian scene by taking their music directly to the fans. Despite the controversy, the band turned in some of their most passionate live concerts during this phase. They followed *Demonstrates* with the release of *I Am a Stranger in This Place* (a collection of older songs redone in a live setting) and *Prayers of a Satellite Heart*, a worship record, both for the new Sovereign Productions label.

There may not be a better example of a third-wave band than the LA-based alternative rockers The Prayer Chain. In addition to their sound (which evolved from a youthful guitar-hook-dominated anthem format to a dark, brooding, and neopsychedelic swirl by the time of their final album, *Mercury*), they were one of the first successful bands to have grown up listening to Christian bands such as The Violet Burning, The Choir, and The Seventy Sevens. The influence, especially of the first two of those bands, was most apparent on the band's 1992 debut EP or their 1991 indie release *The Neverland Sessions* (recorded at The Choir's Neverland Studio and produced by Steve Hindalong).

1993's *Shawl* boldly proclaimed that "Shine Is Dead," referring to their hit single "Shine," which earned them their record deal and national hype. The band, on a fast track of stylistic growth, seemed to hate anything as soon as it was committed to tape. Regular touring earned them a significant following, and on 1995's *Mercury* they stretched themselves even further creatively. The band broke up after the *Mercury* tour but have done a few reunion shows. Guitarist Andy Prickett, bassist Eric Campuzano, and drummer Wayne Everett have remained active with other bands such as Lassie Foundation, The Violet Burning, and most recently Cush, with Michael Knott.

Charlie Peacock, though he released several excellent records in the

1990s, shifted his influence toward nonmusical work. First he launched a label called Re:Think designed to foster artistic independence and forward thinking in its artists. He then took a long hiatus and wrote an influential book titled *Christian Music at the Crossroads*, targeted at the industry itself. In 1999, he returned to recording with the stellar *Kingdom Come* record. He also continues to produce many artists for Sparrow.

Hailing from Seattle, Poor Old Lu was one of the highpoints of Frontline's existence. Their debut in 1993, *Mindsize*, came when none of the members was even 18 years old. Despite their youth, producer Terry Taylor called them one of the most exciting bands he'd heard in years. The album blew critics and fans away with its fresh alternative sound. Over a mere four years of active recording, the band released five albums. Scott Hunter (vocals), Nick Barber (bass), Jesse Sprinkle (drums), and Aaron Sprinkle (guitar) proved that alternative rock in the 1990s could simultaneously be edgy, imaginative, and musically excellent.

Back in 1990, in the sweltering heat of Athens, Georgia, a musical phenomenon known as Vigilantes of Love arose. Fronted by Bill Mallonee (the only original member), the band debuted with a stripped-down record called *Jugular*. Mallonee was a Christian, and his hard-worn faith was evident in his songwriting. With acoustic guitar, accordion, and reedy vocals, he and the other Vigilantes of Love made their entrance.

Although a bad record deal with an obscure local label made the band's more fleshed-out acoustic rock second album, *Driving the Nails*, hard to find, the band hooked up with Fingerprint Records, an indie label run by Mark Heard and Dan Russell. The first fruit of that relationship was the Mark Heard– and Peter Buck (REM)–produced *Killing Floor* of 1992. Heard and Russell knew better than to launch Mallonee into the Christian market, where his brutal honesty would be squelched. But they also knew that the portion of the Christian underground, the same folks whom Heard was reaching, would love the band. They released *Killing Floor* independently and began shopping for a major-label deal.

Killing Floor combined the energy of post-punk rock like that of Elvis Costello with the southern storytelling drama of Flannery O'Connor or Tom Petty. Reviews were fantastic, and — when the band debuted at the Cornerstone Festival in 1992 to choruses of "Who the heck are the Vigilantes of Love?" — they proceeded to show the skeptics. By the end of their set on the afternoon stage, the verdict was in. There was a new favorite band in town, and they were from the same town that had brought the world REM and The B-52s.

Mallonee built a significant following of Christians by playing Cornerstone every year and granting interviews to Christian publications such as the *Syndicate* and *True Tunes News*. Although he was a believer, he didn't feel like existing exclusively within the confines of the Christian

The Vigilantes of Love refused to limit their faith-infused rock to the Christian underground.

market. And, by the early 1990s, most fans could care less what label a band was on. The existence of the Vigilantes of Love outside the Christian label scene may only have enhanced their appeal among listeners less and less interested in the Christian industry.

Fingerprint got Mallonee signed to Capricorn Records, the mainstream label that handled Sonia Dada, 311, and Rusted Root. The band (always changing personnel) emerged with *Welcome to Struggleville*, their most polished and band-oriented album yet. Produced by Sting producer Jim Scott, the album got the band noticed by *Rolling Stone* and some of the cooler AOR stations, such as WXRT in Chicago. The band toured clubs as a headliner, already able to generate considerable crowds wherever they played. They also toured as the opening band for others, such as The Freddy Jones Band.

The Vigilantes of Love released two more records for Capricorn, *Blister Soul* in 1995 and *Slow Dark Train* in 1997. In between those albums, upstart gospel label Warner Resound released a compilation of the band's most "spiritual" songs to the Christian market. Disputes with Capricorn followed the release of *Slow Dark Train* (the band's most hard-rocking record of all), and the band asked to be released from the contract. Thus, in 1998, they returned (again with significant lineup changes) to the independent scene. At that point, Mallonee even parted with longtime manager Dan Russell. He released a home-grown record called *To the Roof of the Sky*, which mellowed the band considerably and aimed more toward the

Over The Rhine is best characterized by the breathy and vulnerable voice of their front-person Karin Bergquist.

emerging alternative country scene. The album, as with all of Mallonee's, was loved by his fans, and even without a record deal or a manager the band was able to tour constantly.

Things started looking up in 1998 when Pioneer Music Group was launched by some people with experience in both the gospel and the mainstream markets. Pioneer was designed to capitalize on Christian market sales but to focus on landing artists in the mainstream. Run in part by REX veteran Tyler Bacon, Pioneer was the buzz story of 1998. Vigilantes of Love, with a new lineup in place, hit the studio with producer Buddy Miller (Steve Earl, Emmylou Harris, Julie Miller) and recorded their strongest effort yet, a slick but dusty album called *Audible Sigh*. With the added dynamic of Kenny Hutson (the closest that Mallonee came to an equal member) on mandolin, pedal steel guitar, and leads, the band staked a claim deep in alternative country territory, which was exploding in popularity due to bands such as Wilco and The Jayhawks. When some prereleases were sent out to industry people, word came back that finally the Vigilantes of Love were going to hit the big time.

Unfortunately, bad luck struck again. A deep financial recession in Japan forced Pioneer to shut down immediately, mere days before the release of *Audible Sigh*. The band, shocked, to say the least, began to look for alternative deals. Pirated copies of *Audible Sigh* made from the prereleases started to show up on E-Bay, and the momentum that the band had built was threatening to implode. At Cornerstone '99, the band, with the assistance of Etcetera Records and True Tunes, released a limited quantity of CDs to their fans. Two thousand CDs sold out in days, generating more buzz and encouragement for the band.

In the absence of another option, Mallonee licensed *Audible Sigh* to the new True Tunes Records label (an indie label that licensed the name from TrueTunes.com), and in March 2000 a "final" version of *Audible Sigh* was released under the name Bill Mallonee and the Vigilantes of Love. The band ended up signing with the mainstream indie Compass Records for the release of a slightly different version of *Audible Sigh* in the general market.

Formed in Cincinnati in the late 1980s, Over the Rhine developed a significant local following prior to the release of their independent debut, *Til We Have Faces*. Self-described as "post-nuclear, pseudo-alternative, folk-tinged art-pop," Over the Rhine enchanted fans at their debut at Cornerstone '91's New Band Stage.

The band launched what would become one of the most successful independent careers in all of pop music. They sold *Til We Have Faces* and their 1992 follow-up, *Patience*, directly to fans and through a handful of retail outlets. Their sound hung on the breathy vocals of Karin Bergquist, the insanely good guitar playing of Rich Hordinski, and the artsy writing of Linford Detwiler. They quickly rose to the top of the independent scene and then to the mainstream.

Although Over the Rhine received several offers for record deals within the Christian market, they held out. Too many other excellent bands had taken that route only to exist in obscurity, never able to impact culture at large. Their patience was rewarded when in 1993 they signed a deal with IRS Records, one of the hippest alternative labels in the world. IRS rereleased the band's first two records and then a new album, *Eve*, in 1994. The album was darker and more aggressive that the previous work, possibly better suited for the mainstream alternative market. IRS, however, failed to do anything for Over the Rhine that they hadn't done for themselves. Thus, when IRS was sold in 1995, the band secured a release from their contract. They returned to the autonomy of the independent scene.

In 1996, the band released two new recordings. The first, *Good Dog Bad Dog*, is considered by many to be their finest work. The second, *Darkest Night of the Year*, was a hauntingly beautiful Christmas album. The band continued to tour regularly, including several high-profile tours with The Cowboy Junkies. Also in 1996, Detwiler and Bergquist were married. Shortly after, guitarist Rich Hordinski left the band to form his own band, Monk. He was followed by drummer Brian Kelly.

In 1999, Over the Rhine signed a multialbum deal with Virgin/Backporch that offers the band total creative freedom and the ability to rerelease their back catalog. They have added Don Heffington (Lone Justice, Emmylou Harris) on drums and will release a new album in early 2001.

Over the Rhine contributed to the rising hipness of being an indie. Along with Vigilantes of Love, The Violet Burning, The Choir, and many others, they chose to be independent. Their lead would have an enormous impact on the Christian music underground throughout and beyond the 1990s.

There may not have been a more successful or significant songwriter in contemporary Christian music than Rich Mullins. Although he was firmly ensconced in the most mainstream areas of Christian music, he had a decidedly rock and roll heart.

Mullins entered the Christian music scene through a publishing deal with Reunion Records. In 1982, Amy Grant recorded his song "Sing Your Praise to the Lord" on her *Age to Age* album. From that point on, Mullins was "in" whether he liked it or not. He signed his own deal with Reunion as an artist and debuted with a self-titled pop record in 1986. His sophomore effort, *Pictures in the Sky*, yielded some serious Christian radio play, but it was his 1989 release, *Winds of Heaven Stuff of Earth*, that saw him begin to gel as a serious artist. By combining his classical training with decidedly folk performances (and an increasing interest in the musical inflections of his Irish heritage), he created songs that were casual and inspirational at the same time. One of the songs from *Winds of Heaven Stuff of Earth* would go on to become the biggest Christian hit of the past 20 years. "Awesome God" has already been granted modern-hymn status by most members of the Christian community.

Mullins wasn't your average adult contemporary Christian singer, though. Although his songs flourished in the white-bread world of Christian pop, he was a bare-footed, messy-haired, overtanned misfit. He approached the Christian music scene with much graciousness considering how silly he thought it was. Unlike other artists who'd soured on the subculture thoroughly, he always seemed to separate the humans, be they fans or industry folks, from the "machine." As a result, he could stretch the boundaries within which people had put Christian music. He had a more practical impact as well. As he grew as an artist, he deepened the musical arrangement and presentation of his songs and thereby moved Christian pop closer to the aesthetic sensibilities of the mainstream.

In September 1997, Mullins, on his way to a benefit concert in Wichita, Kansas, was killed in a car accident on a rural Illinois highway. He'd just finished production on a solo album for one of his musical compatriots, Mitch McVicker, and had written the songs for his upcoming album, his most ambitious project to date. He'd decided to call it the *Jesus Record*, and on it he explored the personality, ministry, and characteristics of Jesus from a real-life perspective. He'd told friends and members of his Ragamuffin Band (Rick Elias, Mark Robertson, Jimmy A., and Aaron Smith) that it was the album he'd been put on Earth to make. Just hours before getting into his truck to drive to Wichita, he'd bought a cheap boom box and recorded his song ideas for his new label, Myrrh.

The Ragamuffin Band decided to record the album as a tribute to Mullins and to Jesus. In 1998, they released the *Jesus Record*, with special guests such as Amy Grant, Ashley Cleveland, and others singing the songs. They also cleaned up the cassette demo as much as possible and inserted a separate CD of Mullin's final recording in the package. The record was a resounding success. The following year, Mullins posthumously won the prestigious Artist of the Year Dove Award. It was his first. The Ragamuffins continue on as a band, and each member has continued a solo career.

All of the Ragamuffins were active musicians before hooking up with Mullins. Drummer Aaron Smith was part of the seminal Sacramento band The Seventy Sevens. Jimmy Abegg (also temporarily based in Sacramento) played with Vector and Charlie Peacock. Bassist Mark Robertson played with The Altar Boys, The Stand, The Allies, Under Midnight (under the name dB Allen), and his own rock-a-billy power pop band This Train. But musical director, guitarist, and vocalist Rick Elias had been searching for his niche for years when Mullins recruited him.

Elias emerged in 1990 as a roots rocker on the Frontline label out of California. With his wife, Linda, and his band, The Confessions, Elias released an album that caught the industry off guard. Although Frontline didn't really have the muscle to launch Elias into the mainstream Christian music scene, his Springsteen-meets-Mellancamp sound wowed the rock underground. Elias followed that album with 1991's *Ten Stories*, another critical success that Frontline made sure few people heard. To support *Ten Stories*, Elias toured with Margaret Becker, but his music and vivid songwriting were a bit too much for the sleepy Christian pop scene of the early 1990s.

Elias stayed involved by producing albums for bands such as The Wayside, Split Level, Tuesday's Child, Randy Stonehill, and many others. He was recruited to join the Ragamuffin Band, really the first time that most fans of Christian music got to hear his amazingly expressive voice and unique guitar skills. Another break came in 1996 when Elias was hired as a producer, guitarist, and songwriter for the Tom Hanks film *That Thing You Do*. Elias wrote or cowrote five of the soundtrack's songs and played most of the guitar parts. He even made a brief cameo appearance as a member of the bandstand in the background during the film. His talents had finally been recognized.

The Christian scene soon began to catch up to Elias. In 1998, he released a collection of demos and home recordings in England and then in the United States called *Blink*. The album yielded a modest radio hit, but Elias was too busy working with the Ragamuffins to worry about *Blink*. He continues to be one of the most in-demand producers and recently launched his own studio in Nashville. In 1999, he produced Chris Taylor's breakthrough album *Chris Taylor's Worthless Pursuit of Things on the Earth* along with Mark Robertson.

In 1991, four of the most important artists in the annals of Christian music came together. Inspired by The Traveling Wilburys, a "supergroup" comprised of Roy Orbison, Bob Dylan, Tom Petty, Jeff Linn, and George Harrison, the Christian group called themselves The Lost Dogs and was comprised of Daniel Amos's Terry Scott Taylor, The Seventy Sevens's Michael Roe, The Choir's Derri Daughtery, and Adam Again's Gene Eugene. Their union resulted in far more than a novelty record.

The Lost Dogs embraced all the musical elements of Americana, from bluegrass country to Delta blues. Each member had various strengths. Taylor had a well-documented background in country music and Beatlesque pop. Roe had let his love for the blues show more than once during his work with The Seventy Sevens. Daughtery had been a fan of country and folk ballads. Eugene was the one who surprised some people. In Adam Again, he'd always played basic R&B-inflected alternative rock. In The Lost Dogs, his voice took on an emotional depth that was tangible.

Each artist brought some songs he'd written or some traditional songs he wanted to cover. They got together in a studio, set up their gear, and recorded. The results were stunning. Their first project, 1992's *Scenic Routes*, caught the industry off guard. The single "Breathe Deep" climbed all the way to the top of the Christian Hit Radio charts. *Scenic Routes*, with its decidedly untrendy country-folk-blues sound, ended up selling more units than each artist's previous records combined.

The Lost Dogs toured, including a rousing performance at Cornerstone '92. Although they maintained their primary bands, a bond formed between the four that was obvious. Each had spent at least a decade (Eugene maybe just under that) out in the trenches creating music that was artistically important and personally satisfying but not always commercially successful. Daughtery and The Choir were probably the best-selling band represented, but not by much.

Also in 1992, The Seventy Sevens released their most controversial album to date. Although the band submitted it with the title "Pray Naked" (about leaving baggage at the door when going to God), Word changed the title to *Seventy Sevens*, obviously not realizing that the band had released a self-titled record five years earlier. *True Tunes News* and other magazines covered the album under its intended name, and the censorship that was supposed to avoid controversy backfired. But the real story was the album itself. Although Roe had recorded some solo songs under the name Seven and Seven Is, and Brainstorm had released the off-years collection *Sticks and Stones*, this was the first all-new Seventy Sevens record since the 1987 Island release. The sound was much more hard rock, showing influences as diverse as Edgar Winter and Led Zeppelin.

In 1992, Adam Again released *Dig*, the band's most intensely personal and musically aggressive record yet. The following year saw the release of a second Lost Dogs album, the more planned-out but just as engaging *Little Red Riding Hood*. The single "Pray Where You Are" was a huge Christian radio hit. The Lost Dogs were no fluke. *Little Red Riding Hood* built on the musical themes, concepts, and humor of the debut. And, while it sold very well, The Choir released the independent *Kissers and Killers*, and Daniel Amos released one of their most astonishing records to that point, a sweeping pop road trip called *Motorcycle*.

1995 was a busy year for the four artists. Adam Again released their troublingly beautiful *Perfecta*, The Seventy Sevens released *Tom Tom Blues*, and Daniel Amos released *Songs from the Heart*. The Choir had released *Speckled Bird* in 1994 and was working on their forthcoming 1996 release *Free Flying Soul*. Yet the four somehow found time to gather again in 1996 and record *The Green Room Serenade*. It took more steps toward rock but managed to retain the trademark sound of The Lost Dogs.

The group got together in 1999 and recorded their debut for BEC

Terry Taylor with The Lost Dogs at Cornerstone 2000.

Recordings, a much more polished album called *Gift Horse*. With most of the songs written by Taylor, the album had a more cohesive sound. The first single, "Diamonds to Coal," charted on Christian rock radio. The extra muscle of the BEC label, combined with the slicker songs and the increasing interest in Americana music in the general market, all pointed toward good things for The Lost Dogs in the new millennium.

Tragedy struck fans of Christian music on March 19, 2000. Gene "Eugene" Andrusco passed away in his sleep from a massive aneurism and heart failure. The outpouring of grief from many parts of the world was astounding. Eugene had not only impacted fans with his music in Adam Again and The Lost Dogs but also produced countless albums at his Green Room studio in Huntington Beach, California. In fact, his studio (also his home) had been ground zero for the alternative Christian music scene in California. Andrusco had recorded over 60 albums for Tooth and Nail alone. Most importantly, he was a friend to many artists and fans. His loss has been among the most significant in the Christian music community.

Cornerstone 2000 commemorated the millennium by bringing back some of the most important bands from years past, some of which had broken up long before. The Lost Dogs, Daniel Amos, The Seventy Sevens, The Choir, and Adam Again were all booked to play. The directors decided to have the rest of Adam Again play and to have various friends of Andrusco sing in his place as a tribute. Mike Knott, Mike Roe, Derri Daughtery, and others participated.

Although Resurrection Band never officially quit, throughout the 1990s front man Glenn Kaiser spent a lot of time exploring various roots of the rock experience and the Christian experience. He released two acoustic blues albums, an electric blues record, an R&B album, a singer-songwriter acoustic record, two worship albums, a three-piece rock ensemble record, and several Rez projects. His impact goes far beyond his music. One of the head pastors at the Jesus People USA community, he has also functioned as an unofficial pastor for Christian rock over the years. In many ways, he has acted as the musical and spiritual conscience of Christian rock.

Mark Heard has been another great influence. He's been quietly subverting the status quo in Christian music since the beginning. Heard has never accepted that Christian music should be safe, sanitized, and limited to Sunday mornings and Wednesday nights.

Beginning in 1990, Heard released one album a year on his own Fingerprint label. The three albums would become a sort of trilogy. The series began with *Dry Bones Dance*, a basic acoustic return to form for the singer-songwriter. Heard had been doing acoustic before acoustic was cool, and on *Dry Bones Dance* he reminded all that a powerful song doesn't need a lot of noise to drive it home. As the "alternative" revolution took off, Heard came up with an alternative all his own, good music. *Second Hand* (1991) put more of a band sound back in, taking the music closer to the mainstream. *Satellite Sky* (1992) was off the page. Although still focused on acoustic instruments, many of the songs centered on a 1939 National Steel mandolin. Whether run acoustically or through an overdriven amp, the mandolin added an edge to *Satellite Sky* that created a natural crescendo for the trilogy. The album closed with one of the most hopeful and poignant songs that Heard had ever written, "Treasure of the Broken Land."

After performing a rare late-night concert at Cornerstone '92, Heard suffered a mild heart attack. He finished the show and then was taken to a hospital from which he was air-lifted to a bigger hospital in Springfield, Illinois. He was released a few days later but suffered a massive heart attack across the street from the hospital in a hotel room. He lingered in a coma for a month and then finally passed away on August 16. His death stunned the Christian music underground and caused some introspection among mainstream industry folks as they realized that they'd taken a treasure for granted.

Heard's songs had the ability to be painfully honest, awkwardly vulnerable, and deeply inspiring at the same time. Heard has been cited as a favorite songwriter of heavyweights such as Bruce Cockburn, Michael Been (The Call), Larry Norman, Bill Mallonee, and Steve Taylor. Two tribute discs were released after his death: the single disc *Strong Hand of Love* and a double-disc set called *Orphans of God*. Many of Heard's best songs were compiled on an album called *High Noon*. His early albums have been cheaply rereleased by Home Sweet Home in what many fans consider to be one last insult. A collection called *Reflections of a Former Life* compiled some of his 1980s material. The new wave album that Heard did under the name Ideola is among the most precious collector's items in all of Christian music.

The 1990s were dominated by new faces, young bands, and the frenzied pursuit of the "next big thing." But amid the cacophony, Randy Stonehill, one of Christian music's greatest treasures, was still working away. In 1991, he hooked up with Terry Taylor, who'd produced his album *Between the Glory and the Flame* 10 years earlier. The two created *Wonderama*, the most sweeping and beautiful of Stonehill's records. With a sound somewhere between *Pet Sounds* by The Beach Boys and *Abbey Road* by The Beatles, the album brought Stonehill into the 1990s. *Wonderama* was astounding, yet it failed to connect on a widespread basis.

In 1994, Stonehill launched his own label in partnership with his booking agency. The label was called Street Level Records, and its distribution went through the doomed REX system. Also signed to Street Level was the inimitable Julie Miller (also a refugee from Myrrh). The two released beautiful records and did a tour together, but when REX collapsed the label also folded. Miller made her way to the mainstream Hightone Records label, and Stonehill was on his own.

Then, in 1998, Stonehill landed at Brentwood, the home of Jars of Clay, and released the Rick Elias-produced *Thirst*. It was, once again, an amazing album. Stonehill's recorded output in the 1990s was flawless, yet his audience dwindled back down to the die-hard fans. Stonehill is currently working on a children's project with Terry Taylor.

Stonehill is one of the few artists from the first generation of Jesus music who is as vital and artistically important now as he was back then. His songwriting has never faltered, and he is widely revered as Christian rock's wacky Uncle Rand. But beneath the humor and wild stage antics beats the heart of a great songwriter. In retrospect, his name seems to have been prophetic, for Stonehill has been a touchstone for Christian music that avoids commercial pitfalls and snares. In Old Testament times, the Hebrews would set up a pile of stones as a memorial whenever God had delivered them from their enemies or provided for them miraculously. The stone hills were monuments to the faithfulness of their God. As of 1998's *Thirst*, Stonehill has released 19 albums and is still going strong.

Hand in hand with Stonehill's return to his roots was that of guitar hero Phil Keaggy, who began the decade with 1990's *Find Me in These Fields*. Being the master that he is, Keaggy's 1991 acoustic instrumental album *Beyond Nature* was no surprise. But to folks who thought that he'd emptied his bag of tricks in 1988 with *Sunday's Child*, 1994's *Crimson and Blue* was a wake-up call.

There were extended jams on the album, but there was also incredible songwriting and killer production. The general market version, simply called *Blue*, featured a cover of Badfinger's "Baby Blue," and both the Christian market and the general market versions featured his cover of Van Morrison's "When Will I Ever Learn." *Crimson and Blue* thrilled Keaggy fans, and, if there had been doubts about the viability of Keaggy in the 1990s, they were obliterated in 1994.

With vital new music in the 1990s from Daniel Amos, Randy Stonehill, Phil Keaggy, and Glenn Kaiser, who'd all been involved with Christian rock from the beginning, fans finally had a sense of history or heritage. They would have preferred that their heroes' music was respected by the world at large, but records such as *Thirst* and *Crimson and Blue* assured them that their years of support hadn't been for naught.

Artists Breaking Through

One of the main distinctions about the third wave of Christian rock is that more rock bands sold over 200,000 units in the 1990s than adult contemporary bands did. Several factors coalesced to bring rock to the fore in the 1990s, but perhaps the most important were retail and radio.

The last bastions of resistance to the extremes of the emerging alternative scene were retail and radio. They often flexed their muscles. If an album package was deemed controversial, it was returned. Major chains such as Family Bookstores could affect a label's very policies simply by deciding not to carry certain records. Christian radio clung desperately to its "only game in town" status and often refused to play new music unless other stations around the country were already playing it. Yet, despite the objections, Refuge, Frontline, REX, and eventually Tooth and Nail managed to get their "extreme" music (as Diamante calls it) into the stores and onto radio shows.

A perfect example of the changing frames of reference was DC Talk. When they debuted in 1988, they were a bright-eyed, fresh-faced, church-ready pop band. Sure they rapped a little, but their music had all the bite of an Annette Funicello movie. It was safe, blatantly Christian, and quite awful. In 1988, that's exactly what the industry ordered. However, as the band grew, so did their music. Although their second album, *Nu Thang*, was still terrible by any mainstream standards, it added a slight edge to the band's sound. But 1992's *Free at Last* was a different story. With a more authoritative voice and a radical improvement in songwriting, DC Talk became a legitimate pop band. The album sold incredibly well (way past gold), and DC Talk became the new darlings of the Christian music industry.

U2's Bono on the Popmart tour.

Now, despite the improvements in songwriting, production, and overall savvy, to call *Free at Last* a rock record is a stretch. By and large, DC Talk had created something beyond classification. To a kid immersed in secular music, they still would have been considered a cheesy pop band, but compared with the other Christian releases the album was revolutionary.

Unlike many Christian bands that reflexively reduced the faith content of their songs whenever they attempted to reach beyond the subculture, DC Talk, perhaps instinctively, did the opposite. Knowing that their 1995 release would have the full muscle of Virgin Records behind its mainstream distribution, and aware of the breakthroughs of gangsta rap acts such as Snoop Doggy Dog and Public Enemy, and the alternative-cum-mainstream coup pulled off by Nirvana, Soundgarden, and Metallica, the members of DC Talk were ready to step into the spotlight. Industry insiders predicted a slick pop record with little to no spiritual content — just the kind of album that Virgin was great at peddling. When the working title leaked out, the buzz started.

While fellow Christian artists were diluting their spiritual content so as not to offend mainstream ears, DC Talk decided to call the album *Jesus Freak*. Its title cut was a brazen statement of faith:

> What will people think
> When they hear that I'm a Jesus freak
> What will people do when they find that it's true
> I don't really care if they label me a Jesus freak
> There ain't no disguising the truth

If these guys had plans to infiltrate mainstream pop music, they certainly weren't doing so by stealth. Other songs were just as "bold" (as Christians like to call it when someone states his or her faith plainly): "So Help Me God," "Like It Love It Need It," and Charlie Peacock's "In the Light." The boys were creating music as celebratory and emboldening as Kurt Cobain's philosophy was pointless.

Musically, the band embraced their pop roots as filtered through an alternative lens. "Jesus Freak" sounded a lot like a certain Nirvana song in the chorus, but beyond that the album stretched in many directions. From the arena rock of "Like It Love It Need It" to the R&B reflections in "Just between You and Me" and "What Have We Become" to the pure pop of "In the Light," *Jesus Freak* was an amazingly diverse yet cohesive work.

Established fans loved the new sound, as did a respectable number of mainstream kids. *Jesus Freak* sold well over a million copies. The Christian music industry was smitten with the album as well. "Jesus Freak" won the Dove Award for Song of the Year. Not "Rock Song of the Year," mind you, just plain "Song of the Year," the award usually given to the most "moving" tune on Christian radio. That moment caught many people off guard. When the band members went up to the stage to collect the award, the crowd (almost all industry people gathered for the annual gospel music week) went nuts. Artists such as Steven Curtis Chapman and Michael W. Smith seemed to be the most excited. Suddenly, it seemed as though the Christian industry was finally opening the doors to rock artists. Sure, it wasn't Michael Knott or Daniel Amos, but this was big news. In one deliberate move, DC Talk had brought the industry, kicking and screaming as some of its reps may have been, into, well, into the 1970s.

Meanwhile, the band took a break before commencing to record their next album. In the time off, Toby McKeehan launched his own label, Gotee Records. (Gotee would end up one of the leading labels in the industry, releasing major records by singer-songwriter Jennifer Knapp and alternative pop worship by Sonic Flood, among other successes.) Michael Tait got into producing and writing and even launched a funky hard rock band called Curious George. Tait earned major chutzpah points for taking his new band straight to Cornerstone to test it on one of the toughest, most musically sophisticated audiences in the world. Although DC Talk had become a "joke" among the cooler-than-thou alternative set, Tait slammed the crowd with funk-based hard rock that rivaled anything released by Lenny Kravitz or King's X. Kevin Smith (who changed his name to Kevin Max at some point in the interim) released *At the Foot of Heaven*, an impressive book of poetry accompanied by original paintings by Jimmy A. and recorded one song, "Lonely Moon," for the Mark Heard tribute *Strong Hand of Love*.

In 1998, the band released their long-awaited follow-up. *Supernatural* exceeded all expectations. It is an epic pop album, on par in terms of writing and production with classics such as ELO and Queen. Wisely steering away from the easy trappings of the deflated alternative scene, the band crafted a lush, sweeping album full of clever, inspiring, and sometimes humorous songs. Although the album has yet to be certified platinum (it's currently sitting at about 750,000 copies sold), it has solidified DC Talk as a band that Christian rock and pop bands will be compared to for decades. In 1999, after their wildly successful *Supernatural* tour, the band announced that they were taking a break to pursue individual interests.

DC Talk, by taking risks and bothering to grow as artists, has pushed the whole industry forward. With DC Talk considered to be right in the middle of the mainstream, some ska and punk bands such as The Supertones and MxPx have exploded past the 250,000 sales mark.

A small Christian college in southern Illinois called Greenville College began offering a major in contemporary Christian music in the early 1990s. Some joked that it would be a good major for future youth pastors

Daniel Amos's Ed McTaggart.

but that it would never help any band or solo artist to make it in the actual business. They'd soon be eating their words.

In 1993, four students at Greenville started writing songs together and doing shows. Actually, all of the students in the program wrote songs and performed together. Most would work with one group and then move along to another. Songwriting and demo recording were homework. But that year a group formed around their love of a particular style of alternative music. Citing acoustic groups such as Toad the Wet Sprocket as influences, and then developing a friendship that kept them at it, Dan Haseltine, Charlie Lowell, Matt Bronleewe, and Steve Mason wrote and recorded a techno song called "Fade to Grey." Although it was for a class project, the four decided to write more together. Following Christmas break, they began writing in earnest, both to increase their repertoire for live shows and to satisfy writing requirements. Lowell, looking for a name for the band, remembered a verse in the Bible (2 Corinthians 4.7) in which the Apostle Paul talks about the mystery of God pouring his blessings into fragile and flawed human hearts: "But we have this treasure in jars of clay, to show that this all-surpassing power is from God and not from us."

The band became known as Jars of Clay in January 1994. In the coming months, they wrote more songs together, including "Love Song for a Savior." On a whim, Lowell submitted a tape to a contest publicized in CCM magazine. The competition was for independent bands to play during the Gospel Music Week in front of various record labels. The band members were surprised when, out of all the submissions, they were chosen to be among the 10 bands to perform at GMA (Gospel Music Association) '94. The band won the competition. They returned home to Greenville to find that Christian labels had been calling the pay phone in their dorm looking for them. Their popularity on campus exploded. Within a month, they manufactured 1,000 copies of a CD demo called *Frail.* The thousand sold out immediately, and the band ran another 500 copies. (These early CDs have reportedly sold for more than $500 among collectors.) Upon completion of the school year, the band, minus Bronleewe, who was about to get married, moved to Nashville to seek a record deal.

They convinced Lowell's high school friend Matt Odmark to move to Nashville and replace Bronleewe. The band entertained offers from several labels, working at various jobs to pay the rent on the two-room apartment that they shared. Eventually, they chose to sign with the new Essential Records label, citing its affiliation with Silvertone in the general market, the significant financial backing of Brentwood Music, and a general sense of family at the small label. The man who pursued and signed them was Essential's director, Robert Beeson. (Just a few years before, Beeson had been the front man for a California alternative pop band called Uthanda.) Beeson got the band into the studio to begin their debut album. An office intern got a copy of the *Frail* CD into the hands of her uncle, the imaginative guitar master and producer Adrian Belew (Talking Heads, Nine Inch Nails, Frank Zappa, David Bowie, and member of King Crimson), who liked what he heard and agreed to produce a couple of the songs. Belew handled "Flood" and "Liquid," while the band produced the rest of their self-titled debut themselves. Having Belew's name on the CD would come in very handy down the road.

The album was released in 1995. Tight vocal harmonies and shimmering acoustic instrumentation blended with percussion loops and keyboard patches, earning the band a significant buzz within the industry. Christian radio stations loved the first single, "Flood," and sent it to the top position almost immediately. The band toured with PFR and Brent Bourgeois for the better part of 1995 and 1996, and things started to take off. "Flood" developed a life of its own at secular radio. Silvertone, Essential's mainstream counterpart, jumped on it and got it to the top position on several radio charts. The album climbed into the Billboard Hot 100 and didn't drop out of the Top 200 for the entire year of 1996. The song was tearing up the charts and became the most successful Christian "crossover" single ever. The band began headlining club dates, wanting to take their music to the mainstream crowds as well as to the Christian crowds. They had bands such as Matchbox 20 and Duncan Sheik opening for them (as well as Christian groups such as Sixpence

None the Richer and Sarah Masen). Jars of Clay entered 1997 as one of the hottest bands in the world. The album *Jars of Clay* was certified gold in 1996 and soon went platinum and then eventually double platinum.

The band followed their amazing debut with their Grammy Award-winning 1997 album *Much Afraid*. The title was a literal description of how the band approached the dreaded sophomore effort. The album, though not generating the mainstream radio buzz that the first album had, did reach the platinum level. The band dominated Christian radio and contributed songs to several major motion pictures, including *Liar Liar*, *Long Kiss Goodnight*, *Hard Rain*, and *Prince of Egypt*. Some secular stations played songs from *Much Afraid*, but the buzz was mainly in the Christian market.

The band released *What if I Left the Zoo?* — by far their best record to date — in late 1999. The album asks, in unclouded terms, what would happen if we left our "comfort zones" and got out into the world. The band members should know the answer. With production by Dennis Herring (Counting Crows, Innocence Mission, Cracker, Bruce Hornsby, Concrete Blonde, The Temptations), the band achieved their most cohesive and mature-sounding album to date. At the turn of the century, Jars of Clay stands as one of the most promising bands in the pop scene and is among the best within the Christian scene.

In 1992, two friends from an Episcopal church in New Braunfels, Texas, got together and recorded a demo tape. One, Matt Slocum, was a proficient cellist and guitarist and had written some impressive songs. The other, Leigh Bingham, was a 16 year old who grew up listening to Patsy Cline, loved singing, but hadn't really considered it as a career. After hearing Bingham sing at church, Slocum asked for her help on his demo. Little did either know that they'd become one of the most successful bands in the history of faith-informed music.

Slocum dubbed the duo Sixpence None the Richer, after a story from a C.S. Lewis book called *Mere Christianity*. In the story, a boy asks his father for a sixpence so that he can buy his father a gift. The father gladly gives his son the coin, though he knows that he is buying his own gift. It is therefore not the gift that is of value to the father but the heart of his child. Slocum saw a parallel: music, like art in general, is a gift from God that Slocum could give back. It isn't something for which humans deserve credit.

The first demo tape circulated among some in the industry and was sold in the underground by True Tunes. A friend of the band gave a copy to David Bunker at REX Records. Bunker heard a great deal of potential in the rough demo and proceeded to sign the band to the label. Their first three projects would be released through REX, with significant distribution only in the Christian market.

In 1993, the band released their debut, *The Fatherless and the Widow*, to mild critical acclaim. They were still a very young band, longer in writing and playing talent than they were in stage presence or experience. But their fresh sound (a blend of alternative sensibilities with sensitive and vulnerable vocals) earned them a niche in the burgeoning alternative Christian music scene. The band performed a Steve Taylor song ("Bouquet") for a tribute record (*I Predict a Clone*) and at a special showcase concert in Nashville with Taylor, The Wayside, and Circle of Dust. As the band played, Taylor watched from the wings, excited by the music but surprised by the static stage presence of Bingham, who seemed to be terrified of the crowd. The connection with Taylor through the album and the concert would prove valuable down the road.

The band had picked up drummer Dale Baker and later bassist J.J. Placensio and honed their stage presence with incessant touring. In 1994, their second effort, *This Beautiful Mess*, was released to overwhelming praise from critics, fans, and even the industry. The album won the GMA's Dove Award for Best Alternative Album in 1995. *This Beautiful Mess* featured more aggressive music, including a greater rock edge from Slocum's guitar, the additional vocal interplay of rhythm guitarist Tess Wiley, and the live drumming of Baker. The album was miles ahead of *The Fatherless and the Widow*, and the demand for concerts from churches and coffeehouses allowed the band to go full time, which in turn allowed them to improve even more. By 1996, Sixpence None the Richer was the premier band in alternative Christian music. Their concerts got tighter, and their songs got stronger.

The band's label, REX, was going through various financial struggles as the band rose. Many thought that with more effort from REX Sixpence None the Richer could have broken into the mainstream. Alas, the label floundered and in 1996 officially filed for bankruptcy. The band released an EP called *Tickets to a Prayer Wheel*, which featured new songs, cover tunes, and remixes and bought them some time for their follow-up. In a move that is still being argued in the courts, REX's distributor, Platinum Entertainment, assumed ownership of all of REX's assets, including Sixpence None the Richer's contract and masters. Suddenly, the band went from having a strained relationship with its label to a flat-out impasse. They would not record for Platinum or Light, and they found an ally in Steve Taylor.

Taylor had become one of the most respected individuals in the Christian music industry. As an artist and producer, he'd set the standards for integrity, vision, and relevance. Few knew at the time that his greatest contribution lay just ahead. Taylor took up the band's cause and went so far as to meet with the label to help the band get out of their deal. Although that meeting was unfruitful, Taylor would eventually prevail.

Platinum continued to run REX, though completely apart from all of the label's founding staff. The members of Sixpence None the Richer, discouraged by events beyond their control, continued to tour. In private, they began writing and even recording what would eventually become their next album. The songs reflected the despair of their situation.

Meanwhile, Taylor founded a label of his own with the help of Word Records. Squint, named after his own album of 1992, was to be a new breed of Christian label, one that would find the best bands and endeavor to launch them far beyond the Christian subculture. Sixpence None the Richer was his template and his immediate goal. Finally, with the financial assistance of Word and the willingness of the band to break up rather than record for Platinum, the deal was made. The band was sold to Squint, though Platinum retained the rights to their back catalog. Almost immediately, the band released their secretly recorded self-titled masterpiece. With Taylor handling production, the band had blossomed into one of the most important voices in the 30 years of Christian rock.

While the band toiled on, their personal lives went through massive changes. First they decided to relocate to Nashville from Texas since it was far more central to their tours. Then Leigh courted and married Mark Nash of the band PFR in 1996. Slocum and Baker also found love in the midst of the pain. However, Wiley, who'd become an increasingly significant part of the band's sound and stage presence, departed in 1996. Placensio, though he played all the bass parts and helped to arrange parts of the self-titled album, couldn't endure the strain of the label struggle. He departed amicably in 1997 and spent some time in the alternative pop band Plumb, another female-fronted Christian band taking full advantage of the absence of Sixpence None the Richer. His tenure with Plumb was short, and in 1998 he and his wife, Tonia, returned to Texas, where he became the pastor of arts at a church in Austin. Placensio and Wiley have both begun solo projects and promise to return to the musical arena soon. Placensio was replaced by Justin Cary, and Wiley's spot was eventually filled by Sean Kelly.

On *Sixpence None the Richer*, Slocum went through the complete range of human emotions. The blissful side of love was playfully celebrated in "Kiss Me," while the more sober side was explored on "Love." But the overall tone of the album was dark since the legal and business struggles preoccupied Slocum. The album was embraced by fans, critics, radio, retail, and even concert promoters. Although its tone was darker than the Christian establishment usually preferred, all could relate to the struggle, and the redemptive content was overwhelming. Not only had Slocum risen to the upper ranks of songwriters, but he'd also completely come out of his artistic shell. With full orchestration and hints at various Americana sounds, *Sixpence None the Richer* was a powerful artistic state-

Matt Slocum left Love Coma to start Sixpence None The Richer, which broke out with their huge 1999 hit "Kiss Me."

ment. *True Tunes News* called it the best album of 1997, as did several other publications.

Part of Squint's vision was to launch Sixpence None the Richer into the general market on their own terms. Thus, as the record was distributed to Christian stores, a single, "Love," was released to college radio to modest success. The real break came over a year after the album's release. Through previous relationships, the label's LA partner found some interest in using the album's lightest tune, "Kiss Me," in a movie. Before it appeared in the fairly awful *She's All That*, a teen romantic comedy, it was placed in the television shows *Dawson's Creek* and *Party of Five*. "Kiss Me" was released as a single and distributed by Columbia in lieu of a full soundtrack to *She's All That*. It would go on to sell over 200,000 copies and would pull the album sales well beyond the two-million mark. It also led to appearances on *Late Night with David Letterman*, *The Tonight Show*, *Live! With Regis & Kathy Lee*, *Later*, *The Martin Short Show*, *The Rosie O'Donnell Show*, and many more. An early video for the song, set in Paris and shot in black and white, was added to the rotation at VH1. The network became a major marketing vehicle for the band and Miramax Films as "Kiss Me" became one of the most played videos of the year. A second video was shot and included footage from and appearances by the principle actors in the movie. A third version would also appear later, featuring footage from *Dawson's Creek*. Nash became a regular on various VH1 shows, and other Sixpence None the Richer songs would land in even more movies, including their cover of Abba's "Dancing Queen" in the Nixon comedy *Dick*.

The members of Sixpence None the Richer have handled the articulation of their faith masterfully. Never the first to bring it up, but never shying away from the fact that they are believers, they've walked the line carefully. They've severed ties with most Christian concert promoters, but they also appeared at the 2000 Dove Awards performing a new song from their upcoming album and graciously accepting the award for Group of the Year. They won't do a headlining tour of Christian venues, opting instead to tour as an opening act for various mainstream artists, but they'll still play a few select Christian festivals. During Gospel Music Week 2000, they graced the cover of *CCM* magazine alongside their producer, mentor, and career savior, Steve Taylor. Their last two Christian market singles have been specially recorded songs from the *Streams* and *Roaring Lambs* albums (both focusing on specific spiritual themes). They are certainly not turning their backs on the Christian market altogether, but they are not embracing it fully either. They have found themselves in a rare position that warrants efforts in both the Christian and the general markets. Sixpence None the Richer's career closely follows the chronological and social dynamics of the third wave of Christian rock. More than any other band, they also mark the end of that wave and the beginning of the fourth. Can openly Christian artists have careers in mainstream pop music?

As the decade wound down, one more band had a few surprises for the industry. Payable on Death (POD) exploded out of the San Diego "southtown" scene. In 1993, the band launched their own indie label, Rescue Records, and released their debut, *Snuff the Punk*. The band premiered their particular blend of hip-hop and hardcore at the Cornerstone Festival. The buzz was huge. POD instantly became one of the hottest bands in the underground. But even before playing Cornerstone, the band shook the San Diego scene big time. Their second show was opening for Green Day, and within a year they had played with Cypress Hill, HR, Mighty Mighty Bosstones, and The Vandals. The word was out in both the Christian and the secular rock undergrounds that POD was the bomb.

The members of POD are Christians, though they avoid the tag "Christian band." Instead, front man Sonny prefers to say that they are just Christians in a band. Whatever the description, the explosion of POD has many people excited.

The band released another studio album, *Brown*, and then a live album before hooking up with Tooth and Nail to release an EP early in 1999. But later that year, when their new label, Atlantic, released *The Fundamental Elements of Southtown*, POD really took off. They were all over MTV, on the road with Korn, and covered in every major hard music magazine in the country. Sure, fans eventually knew that they were Christians, but their album and live shows were so devastatingly good that few were going to hold that against them. The album has been certified gold, and most fans think that there's much more to come. The band was given a coveted mainstage spot on the Ozzfest 2000 tour and at Cornerstone 2000, and its singles are climbing the rock charts. With exuberant coverage in *Rolling Stone*, *Billboard*, and a host of hard rock magazines, POD may be the biggest hard rock band of 2000, unless Creed beats them.

Artists of Faith

As both fans and artists became increasingly dissatisfied with the "Christian music" tag in the 1990s, two distinct phenomena occurred. First, a flood of Christian bands emerged but wanted to avoid being tagged "Christian," knowing that the label would limit their ability to make a mark in the pop field. Although they'd take the sales generated by the Christian market, and they'd give their teeth to get a gig at Cornerstone, they simply didn't want that label attached to their music. Second, a number of new artists who signed to general market labels believed in Christ

Adam Clayton of U2.

and reflected their beliefs in their music but simply refused to call themselves or their bands Christians.

Ed Roland had been putting bands together and taking them apart for 12 years before he finally got the right combination. In 1994, after giving up on finding a record deal for his band Collective Soul, he dissolved the band, holed up in a studio in his hometown of Stockbridge, Georgia, and recorded demos that he hoped would land him a songwriting deal. The recording was typical: drum machines, minor overdubs, and an intentional diversity of styles to show potential publishers his songwriting range. To get a response to his project, he sent a CD, under the false name Brothers and Brides, to the local college station at Georgia State University. One of the songs was called "Shine," which Roland had originally written in 1987. It was a hit at the station and led Roland to pull a slightly different version of the band back together for some shows.

Independently pressed copies of the demo, called *Hints, Allegations, and Things Left Unsaid*, were promoted at concerts and local record shops. Then in late 1993 a mainstream commercial rock station in Orlando played "Shine." It became a hit there and began to take off around the country. With an indie song hitting the charts, the industry took notice. Labels began scouting the band, and in February 1994 Roland signed with Atlantic, the same label that had turned him down twice before. To capitalize on the success of "Shine," Atlantic released the demo as an album. Roland was horrified that his first national release would be such a roughshod collection of low-budget demos, but his years of working for a break had taught him that, to an industry that raised attention deficit disorder to an art form, the band that hesitates is lost. "Shine" flew up the charts as soon as the Atlantic version made its way across the country. The tune combined a simple rock guitar lick, a quirky vocal hook, and an anthemic chorus in a way that connected with listeners immediately.

The inspirational lyrics were reminiscent of early U2 and The Alarm, and people immediately began asking if they were a Christian band. Roland quickly said no. Yet the lyrics often referred to God, the Lord, heaven, and the kind of love that's much bigger than human affection. In fact, the Christian content was higher on that album than on many releases in the Christian market that year.

Christian rock fans who picked up on the Collective Soul phenomenon noticed one other interesting fact. Roland, in both voice and musical style, sounded surprisingly similar to Terry Taylor and Daniel Amos. A few DA fans even theorized that Taylor had pulled another Swirling Eddies move and had totally reinvented Daniel Amos into a hit secular band. That wasn't the case, of course, but the theory was intriguing while it lasted.

Early on, *True Tunes News* sought an interview with Roland to discuss the band, its musical influences, and the faith element. An employee of Real to Reel studio, where the band had recorded the debut album and Roland had been employed, told *True Tunes News* that the band members were Christians, that they'd all grown up in the same church youth group and cub scouts troupe run out of Roland's father's church (his father was a strict Baptist preacher), and that they were very familiar with Christian alternative music, including Daniel Amos, but that they didn't want to be typecast as a "Christian" band. The interview never materialized, and over time Roland would increase his efforts to keep his band from getting pegged as a Christian band. The strategy was wise. Before any flak for Christian content could hit the band, "Shine" had become the top rock song of 1994, had been certified gold as a single, and had launched Collective Soul as one of the biggest rock bands in the world.

The newly formed version of Collective Soul was comprised of Roland (vocals, guitars), his brother Dean Roland (guitars), Ross Childress (lead guitars), Will Turpin (bass), and Shane Evans (drums). They opened a whirlwind tour with Aerosmith, then a headlining spot at Woodstock '94, and then numerous television appearances on *The Tonight Show* with Jay Leno, *Late Night with David Letterman*, and *Late Night* with Conan O'Brien. The debut record went on to sell over three million copies, and the follow-up, the first real Collective Soul album, sold two million copies and scored three chart-topping hits at AOR radio and adult alternative radio. That self-titled album featured massive hooks, indelible choruses, and walls of old-fashioned guitar bliss. While techno, rave, rap, and hardcore bands were taking over pop radio, *Collective Soul* injected a healthy dose of old-fashioned rock and roll into modern music. Although Roland had tempered some of the spiritual content, the album contained enough Christian content to get the band distributed into the Christian bookstore scene via the fence-hopping Warner Resound label. Resound reps told Christian retailers that the band wouldn't accept the label "Christian" since they feared that it would end their ability to make music for the rest of the world but that the band had confirmed to the label that they were believers and that the stores could sell their music. To many Christian fans, that was the end of the debate. Roland obviously knew enough about Christian music to stay mainstream. It was all part of his grand design.

Legal disputes with the band's manager led to a lawsuit in 1996. The band set up shop in a rural shack and recorded their most personal and introspective work yet. The resulting album was called *Disciplined Breakdown*. The difficult times faced by the band resulted in Roland's most compelling, emotional, and faith-stirring songs to date. Themes of determination, forgiveness, and belief permeated the album. It went on to sell over half a million copies.

1999 saw the release of the band's fourth album, *Dosage*, again with inspirational yet vague lyrics. More radio success and more headlining tours followed. Collective Soul albums are no longer sold in Christian retail outlets since Resound closed up shop, but the band still counts many Christians among its fans. The group's hopefulness has helped to create an atmosphere in pop music much more conducive to positive lyrics.

One of the most surprising stories of the 1990s was that Alice Cooper, perfector of shock rock, master of mock macabre, and prime target of antirock preachers since 1971, became a Christian. Although the stories first started circulating about 1992, when Cooper released his 1994 album *The Last Temptation*, the jig was up. He avoided any public statements at the time, but his lyrics were loud and clear. *The Last Temptation* was a gospel record if ever there was one.

Alice Cooper was born Vincent Furnier in 1948. When he was 13, his family moved to Phoenix, where his father, Ether Moroni Furnier, became a missionary to the Apache Indians. A couple of months after settling in Phoenix, the young Furnier became violently ill. By the time he got to the hospital, he had peritonitis throughout his abdomen. His appendix had ruptured a week before, and his entire digestive system was literally rotting away. The doctors closed him up, inserted a draining tube, and told his parents that he would die. Refusing to accept that God would move them across the country to be missionaries and then let their son die, they called for friends and family around the country to pray. Miraculously, he pulled through. Even before becoming a recommitted

Bruce Spencer played with Charlie Peacock and Vector before setting in with The Seventy Sevens.

Christian, Cooper credited his healing to Jesus. In his biography, *Me, Alice*, he explained, "It was a miracle that I pulled through — thanks to Jesus, and the church and the faith of everyone around me. Years later, whenever my father would tell this story to people, they'd laugh. 'Why would the Lord save the life of Alice Cooper?'"

Vincent grew up in the church but had a fascination with horror movies and music. As a teenager, he formed a blues-rock band called The Earwigs, which later changed its name to The Spiders and then to Alice Cooper. The band moved to Los Angeles, got a record deal, and released their first album, *Love It to Death*, in 1971.

At first, Alice Cooper was the name of the band only. Furnier legally changed his name to Alice Cooper, however, and, when the original lineup of his band broke up, he continued as a solo artist under the name. Although public relations efforts played up the demonic aspects of the band by saying that the name came from a dead witch that the band believed possessed them, Cooper always made it clear that the grotesque stage shows and lyrics were nothing more than simple entertainment. He'd admit years later, though, that he was a raging alcoholic driven by sex, fame, and money, but he was no Satanist. Cooper maintained a close relationship with his parents all the while.

Although the details of Cooper's coming to faith are sketchy, it was somehow through the ministry of R.C. Sproul that Cooper and his wife became Christians. He reportedly attends a small Baptist church in Phoenix and has been personally discipled (trained in the faith) by Sproul and other believers. He and his wife teach Sunday school, and he has become friends with other believing musicians such as Amy Grant and Glenn Campbell.

Again, though, the most convincing exploration of Cooper's faith is his astounding album of 1994. Through the use of his tried-and-true dramatic flair, and with the visual aid of a three-volume set of comic books (assisted by Sandman creator Neil Gaiman) in lieu of music videos, Cooper traced the story of one young man's (his own?) moment of truth. Not only was the album stunning lyrically in its obvious promotion of goodness and even Christ over selfishness and evil, but it was also the best music that Cooper had released since the 1970s. In 1997, Cooper did admit that he was a Christian, but he downplayed his conversion as far as the music was concerned. His label was reportedly unthrilled with the news, as were some of his fans, but when he took the Alice Cooper Carnival on the road in 1997 and 1998 and included classics such as "School's Out" and "Eighteen" in his set the controversy calmed. Cooper had wisely decided to let his music do the talking.

In 2000, Cooper posted a new song called "Brutal Planet" at www.alicecoopershow.com for free download. With a sound completely in step with the postalternative sound of the day, and lyrics that trace societal ills from the Holocaust to modern crimes and violence back to the Garden of Eden and the lies of "the snake," it continues to spread the "good news" through what Cooper knows best.

While Nirvana and Pearl Jam were making Seattle into a pop music capital in the early 1990s, a band gathered with a radically different sound than most of the slouch rock emanating from the rain factory. They were called Sunny Day Real Estate, and they defied categorization. The original trio included guitarist Dan Hoerner, bassist Nate Mendel, and drummer William Goldsmith, but they were enhanced by the unique vocals of Jeremy Enigk.

The band commenced to trade in the type of antics that earn a band loads of indie credibility and permanent marginalization in the marketplace. They refused to do interviews or even to have their picture taken. They defied anyone who dared to use words to describe their music, and they wouldn't tour. Although they released one critically acclaimed album on the always hip Sub Pop label called *Diary* in 1994, rough roads were ahead.

In 1995, in the middle of recording their second album, *LP2* ("the pink album"), Enigk went through a radical spiritual revolution and became a born-again Christian. Although he rejoined the band long enough to finish the album, upon its release the band split up. *LP2*, while not perfect, showed that Sunny Day Real Estate could have been the next big thing. Mendel and Goldsmith joined Dave Grohl's Foo Fighters and rode that train to the top of the rock charts. Enigk lent his voice to projects by Poor Old Lu and recorded an amazing solo album, *The Return of the Frog Queen*, for Sub Pop. Again defying categorization, the album featured Enigk with acoustic guitar and orchestra. In a scene in which inaccessibly adventurous artistic gestures render rockers heroes to a postmodern audience, Enigk was a king. He leveraged his credibility to get fellow believer Damien Jurado a deal with Sub Pop.

In 1998, sans Mendel, the band reunited with the release of *How It Feels to Be Something On*, and then they released a live album in 1999. With Enigk still the only believer in the band, there is some tension, but both fans and band members think that it adds to the group's appeal. Enigk's vocal yet sensitive articulation of his faith has certainly gone a long way toward creating some openness to faith issues within the cynical underground and indie rock scene.

Other Christians would also successfully engage that culture. Examples include the bizarre Danielson Famile, which took its quirky pop all the way to feature spreads in *Spin* and packed out clubs in New York, and Pedro the Lion, a band fronted by David Bazan that started at Tooth and Nail but ended up releasing many records for various mainstream indie labels. In fact, the indie rock scene may be among the most hospitable to faith-informed music because of the contributions of Enigk, Jurado, and Bazan.

Formed in Tallahassee, Florida, in 1995, the rock band Creed took the industry by surprise. In less than four years, they sold over eight million records without any significant coverage by MTV or the music press. And Creed deals with issues of faith more blatantly than do most Christian bands. For the record, they do not consider themselves a Christian band.

Creed was formed by vocalist Scott Stapp and his high school friend Mark Tremonti (guitars). The two recruited bass player Brian Marshall and drummer Scott Phillips, and Creed was born. The band recorded their debut album, *My Own Prison*, independently on a budget of $6,000. Originally released on their own Blue Collar Records label (no connection to the Blue Collar Records out of California in the mid-1980s) and then released through Wind-Up Entertainment, *My Own Prison* sold four million albums on the strength of word of mouth, strong live performances, and four number-one rock radio singles, a first for a debut band.

Stylistically, the band has been called postgrunge, which seems to mean that they incorporate huge guitar sounds and devastating hooks (à la Soundgarden) with lower-register and intensely emotional vocals (à la Pearl Jam). Yet Creed's sound is far more accessible than most of the

The Prayer Chain has reunited several times since their break-up in the late '90s.

Seattle grunge scene ever was. Interestingly, when Pearl Jam, Chris Cornell, and other grunge classics were struggling to reemerge, Creed quietly became the biggest rock band of the late 1990s.

Although dismissed as a fluke by critics who'd ignored the band's bare-bones debut, the fluke struck again with 1999's *Human Clay*, a hard rock spectacle of mammoth proportions. It debuted at the top position on Billboard's Hot Albums chart and lingered there for months, selling over four million units. The industry is finally starting to accept that Creed is a phenomenon, which fans have known all along.

Creed's lyrics focus on giving life meaning and finding forgiveness, peace, and ultimate truth. Frequently using biblical imagery, Creed developed a reputation as a Christian band early on. Although Stapp acknowledged that he is a Christian in an interview with Youngleader.org, he doesn't consider Creed a Christian band, and he doesn't speak for the others about their faith. Yet fans often still debate whether Creed is or isn't a Christian band.

Stapp was raised in a strict Pentecostal home where all rock, even Christian rock, was considered off-limits. His parents confiscated any rock music that he secretly brought into the house, and he wasn't allowed to go to dances or on dates. At 17, he left home and began searching for his own way. Although he has certainly abandoned the strict faith of his parents, he can't get far from the basics. In an interview in *Spin* magazine in

July 2000, the band made it clear that all members are believers but that they don't ever want to be considered a Christian band, for they want to create music for everyone.

Where *My Own Prison* left off, *Human Clay* picks up. Lyrically, the debut album dealt with coming to grips with personal responsibility instead of blaming others for one's woes. On *Human Clay*, the lyrics center on how personal choices affect not only the individual but also those around him or her. The album's first single (an immediate hit), "Higher," sounds like a song about heaven (though Stapp later explained that it was about "lucid dreaming"), and "Faceless Man" is clearly about the search for God. Basically, all of Creed's lyrics deal with the search for truth and peace. The Christian message is presented whether the band wants to label it that or not.

Mainstream Artists

Another characteristic of the third wave was the increased number of Christian rock bands that became big business strictly within the Christian underground. With LSU and Scattered Few serving to define the edges, some mainstream rock and pop bands that may have been too edgy for the more conservative aspects of Christian culture flourished.

One such band was The Newsboys, formed in Australia in the mid-1980s. Refuge Records, in one of its last moves, signed the band and re-

Bill Mallonee of The Vigilantes of Love.

leased their debut, *Read All about It*, in 1988. The record presented a raw alternative pop band in the making. With stage energy that outpaced musicianship, The Newsboys at least made an impression.

In 1990, the band migrated (with some of the heavy metal bands from Refuge) to Star Song. Their 1990 album *Hell Is for Wimps* and their 1991 outing *Boyz Will Be Boyz* were simply awful collections of bumper sticker lyrics set to shallow, hyperactive pop tunes. But the band persisted, touring constantly, and their determination paid off.

By 1992, executives at Star Song figured out that something needed to be done with the boys. The label recruited Steve Taylor to produce a new record for The Newsboys, and he did much more than that. His sophistication and credibility were somehow passed on to the group. When *Not Ashamed* emerged in 1992, people wondered what kind of Svengali this Taylor really was. He wrote or cowrote most of the lyrics on the album, adding his deft touch with a rhyme. He encouraged the band to dive into their honest musical influences instead of trying to rehash what they thought people wanted to hear. Although their enthusiastic Jesus-focused style wasn't sacrificed, *Not Ashamed* showed the boys to be a viable Christian pop band for the 1990s.

Taylor continued to work his magic, maturing the band in the process. He produced their following two albums, 1994's *Going Public* and 1996's *Take Me to Your Leader*. By the time that Taylor was done with them, The Newsboys had evolved into a polished pop band at the top of the Christian heap. Their tours were regularly among the highest drawing in the business, and their albums sold exceptionally well. *Take Me to Your Leader* was the first Newsboys record to reach the general market via EMI Christian Music's relationship with Virgin, but nothing really came of it there.

In 1998, founding front man John James left the band to head back to Australia. Drummer (and unofficial band leader) Peter Furler came out from behind the drums for that year's *Step Up to the Microphone*, and it turned out that he was a better front man than James had been. The group's sound became smoother, and in 1999 *Love Liberty Disco* completed the transformation.

The Newsboys have never been very cutting edge musically, but at least now they are exceptionally good at what they do. They are a pop band, and within the Christian music scene they are one of the best.

Audio Adrenaline was formed in 1992 by Kentucky Christian College students Mark Stuart, Bob Herdman, Barry Blair, Will McGiniss, and Brian Hayes. They recorded an indie project that received airplay on a college station and was heard by Forefront Records president Dan Brock. The band moved to Nashville and signed with DC Talk's label . . . any Christian rock band's dream.

The members of Audio Adrenaline are typical third wavers. They grew up hearing Christian rock by the likes of Petra and DeGarmo and Key (and cooler music by The Seventy Sevens and LSU). Attending a Christian college brought them together, and cheap recording facilities got them a record deal.

Although it would take a while for the band to grow into their own sound, their 1992 debut was produced by industry veteran Steve Griffith (Vector) and thus had a sound that masked the group's inexperience. In 1992, Forefront was new as well. In many ways, Audio Adrenaline and Forefront figured things out together. For their 1993 release, *Don't Sensor Me*, the band had the benefit of a new A&R rep, Doug Mann, who'd launched REX Records and had considerable experience in alternative music. Mann's savvy, Griffith's production skills, and the band's continuing growth led to a much better release. The industry began to take notice. Just as the alternative movement was taking off, Forefront was grooming Audio Adrenaline to fit the bill.

By 1996, the band had their act down to a science. *Bloom* was not only their best effort but also by far their most successful (it eventually went gold). Audio Adrenaline was now in the big leagues of Christian rock. The band got better and better. 1997's *Some Kind of Zombie* and 1999's self-produced *Underdog* continued the success.

In 2000, the band launched their own label called Flicker Records, whose goal is to find bands that "let their light shine." Although Audio Adrenaline may not have had much of a mainstream market influence, it has had a profound and positive influence within the Christian music scene.

Similarly influential has been Third Day. Largely on the strength of moving live shows, it built a massive following as an independent band in Atlanta. Third Day signed with the indie label Gray Dot in 1995 and released their self-titled debut. Due to tremendous radio support, the band became bigger than the tiny Gray Dot could handle. They moved to Reunion Records, where their debut was rereleased with new packaging. Within months, the band was headlining shows around the country. Their sound falls somewhere between the classic southern rock of The Allman Brothers or The Black Crowes and the more modern alternative rock of The Dave Matthews Band or Hootie and the Blowfish.

Their 1996 effort, *Conspiracy #5*, saw them edging toward a sound that was a little more alternative and noisy than what came naturally to them. It was far from a failure, though. It won critics over and stretched their audience at the same time. The band continued to tour and win new fans, including some from colleges who heard their music on mainstream college radio.

In 1999, Third Day released the album that many regard as among the best Christian rock records of the 1990s. Called *Time*, it was recorded

Kevin Heuer played drums for My Friend Stephanie before joining The Vigilantes of Love in 1998.

mostly live in-the-round at the legendary Southern Tracks (Black Crowes, Lynrd Skynrd) studio in Atlanta. Producer Jim Dineen (Camper Van Beethoven, The Outfield) made sure that the instruments all sounded warm. By far the band's best work, *Time* scored several number-one hits. In June 2000, the band released *Offerings*, a worship album.

Although underrepresented, women have made significant contributions to the Christian rock scene. One is a rootsy folk rocker from Manhattan, Kansas, named Jennifer Knapp. She released an independent cassette in 1994 that was sold at her concerts and through True Tunes and a few other sources. She sold over 2,000 copies and then released an independent CD called *Wishing Well* in 1996. Eventually, she was signed to Toby McKeehan's (DC Talk) Gotee label, where her major-label debut, *Kansas*, was released in 1998. Before the decade was over, Knapp generated several number-one radio hits, toured with major names such as Jars of Clay and The Newsboys, and won the Dove Award for Best New Artist. In 1999, she was invited by Sarah McLaughlin to join the Lilith Fair tour.

In 2000, Knapp continued her steady rise with the release of *Lay It Down*, a more gritty and vibrant release. It immediately flew up the sales and radio charts.

Of course, the reigning queen of Christian music in the 1990s was still Amy Grant. Although she never really embraced rock and roll as her style, her impact on Christian music was enormous. 1991's *Heart in Motion* featured the hits "That's What Love Is For" and "Every Heartbeat," but it is probably most remembered for its ubiquitous single and video "Baby Baby." The record was a smash hit, selling millions of copies and etching Grant's name on the big lists along with those of Madonna and Whitney Houston.

Grant returned in 1994 with the nice but not particularly gospel *House of Love*. Gone was the youthful verve of *Heart in Motion*. *House of Love* was adult contemporary music with only the slightest lyrical hints that Grant was anything other than a pop singer. Critics renewed complaints from the mid-1980s about her selling out for success. She insisted that she was just doing what came naturally to her.

1997's *Behind the Eyes* was a stark contrast to any of Grant's 1990s releases. Harkening back to the plaintive and introspective tone of *Lead Me On*, Grant explored some darker alleys of the soul. It was her best material in a decade. But when word got out that she and her husband of 15 years, Gary Chapman, were separating, and then divorcing, and that she was marrying country star Vince Gill (who'd just left his wife), fans were left reeling. Suddenly, songs that had been taken one way sounded totally different. In many ways, *Behind the Eyes* sounds like a good-bye album — at least to Grant's Christian fans.

Grant brought Christian music to the big time and vice versa. Her tours were spectacles on par with any other major act. She was just as beautiful as any other pop singer. Finally, there was an artist that Christian music fans and their secular counterparts could relate to. Her success was also one of the forces behind the major-label buying craze of Christian companies in the 1990s. Warner Brothers, EMI, Sony, and Zamba all bought into the business due partly to Grant's breakthrough in 1991–92.

Christian Rappers

Considering rap music's close connection to gospel music, it makes sense that Christian rap is popular. However, even though some of the best-selling artists have been rappers, the genre has been even more marginalized than rock and alternative music. Yet gospel rap has been a powerful force in many lives.

The earliest example of Christian rap is probably Pete McSweet's 12-inch single "Adam and Eve, the Gospel Beat" from 1982. The disc was released on Lection Records and distributed by Polygram. The single was fairly good, with a lyric that went on and on. It was a sort of introduction to gospel rap, which in some circles was a tougher sell than Christian rock. McSweet never really made much of an impact nationally, but many of the early rappers knew him. His single was reissued in 1989. Another early example was the rap of Steven Wiley. His music was well received at youth conventions and other live settings, and many of the kids bought his tapes. But his success hinged on the fact that he was a great speaker without any competition at the time. Michael Peace was another early rapper. His *RRRock It Right* CD of 1986 came out on Reunion Records, therefore getting a distribution push that Wiley hadn't gotten to that point. Peace released six more albums between 1988 and 1996.

PID (Preachers in Disguise) was the first real ghetto-sounding rap band. Their 1988 debut came out on Graceland Records before it moved over to Frontline. The band stayed with Frontline for many years. A humorous shot at rap came from the Star Song act The Rap Sures, which, considering that it was a joke, created some interesting work. Although the identities of the members were kept secret, no one has ever seen the members of The Swirling Eddies and The Rap Sures in the same place at the same time. . . . D-Boy came along in 1989 with a fresh Latin-inflected hip-hop style. D-Boy (Danny Rodriguez) was shot and killed before his second album was even released. He was 22 years old.

A wave of increasingly credible rap music started coming out of Los Angeles in 1989. Largely because of Gene Eugene at Brainstorm, groups such as SFC (Soldiers for Christ), Freedom of Soul, JC and the Boys, and Dynamic Twins added serious street credibility to gospel rap. Grits came out on Gotee Records, as did the powerhouse *Knowdaverb* record in 1999. SFC's Chris Cooper became a sort of A&R man for the rap scene, producing albums and finding new talent all the time. He released a new SFC album on Tooth and Nail in 1999.

When alternative music became more intense and extreme in the early 1990s, so did rap music. With gang violence at an all-time high, people looked to music to reach the young people. The Gospel Gangsters rose to the challenge in 1994 with the shockingly good *Gang Affiliated* CD. The band threw down an album full of legitimate gangster rap. Their breakthrough ushered in a bunch of gangster rap, hard hip-hop, and eventually even rapcore releases.

At about the same time, a young rapper named Knolly "Rubadub" Williams launched an all-rap label called Grapetree Records and the first gospel-rap magazine, *Heaven's Hip Hop*. Knolly's combination of business acumen and love for the genre led Grapetree to become the world's leading Christian rap label. Grapetree radically expanded the amount of hardcore rap, hip-hop, urban, and even Latin rap available.

Mainstream secular rap occasionally inspired Christian rap as well. Although Hammer's blatantly Christian lyrics were hard to respect alongside his standard sleazy raps, in the late 1990s Hammer recommitted himself to his faith and principles. He independently released *Family Affair*, a fully Christian record.

Arrested Development was one of the biggest success stories of

1992. Its eclectic blend of funk, pop, hip-hop, and R&B connected with white and black audiences, and the single "Tennessee" spent many weeks in the top 10. The album *Three Years Five Months and Two Days in the Life Of . . .* went on to sell four million copies. Behind the music and the lyrics was Todd "Speech" Thomas, a believer and political activist from Milwaukee. Speech framed the spirituality in vague terms, but his Christian influence could clearly be heard. After some major lineup changes, the band released a follow-up album that, though successful by rap standards, saw Arrested Development slipping. Speech then released an excellent solo album that further explored his faith. He also produced another Christian-based rap band called Gumbo.

Christians also had much to celebrate in 1999 as one of the top albums of the year, *The Miseducation of Lauren Hill*, brought a Christian perspective to the mainstream urban music scene in a huge way. Hill owned the 1999 Grammies, and her album was considered the best of the year by numerous critics and magazines.

Christian rap, hip-hop, and urban music continue to expand. They have frequently cross-pollinated with rock and alternative music, as in the case of bands such as POD, PAX 217, and Native Son and the Foundation.

Dancing Christians

Despite the biblical account of King David dancing so wildly before the Lord that his clothes fell off, many evangelicals still fear dancing as if it were a direct portal to hell. In the 1970s, when Noel Paul Stookey of Peter, Paul, and Mary fame prepared to release his debut Christian album, the photo that he submitted for the album cover was rejected by the label. It was a picture of Stookey dancing with his wife at a restaurant. In the background was an open bottle of Perrier water. The label knew that retailers and church folks would wonder if the Perrier was in fact alcoholic and would balk at a picture of a husband dancing with his wife. Stookey was understandably baffled.

By the late 1980s, though, what had begun as techno/synth pop developed into full-fledged dance music. No, not everyone was happy with that. Some youth pastors would gladly take their kids to a death metal or hardcore punk concert but not to a Christian rave or dance night.

One of Frontline's earliest signings was a keyboard-driven group that, though they sounded like they were from England, hailed from southern California. Mad at the World released their self-titled debut in 1987. It was a fully digital experience à la Pet Shop Boys or Depeche Mode. There had been nothing like it in the Christian market, and rock fans ate it up. The band's second effort, *Flowers in the Rain*, tempered the keys with a smattering of guitar, creating a sound not unlike that of The Smiths. The band went on to release five additional albums, ranging in style from hooky pop to gnarly rock and 1960s pop. Despite their ensuing identity crises in the 1990s, those first two albums were crucial ingredients in the burgeoning dance-electronica scene.

An independent band called Painted Orange released a pair of popular underground tapes in the late 1980s and then signed with Star Song for one national release in 1991. A young musician going by the name of Barry Blaze started a band called Code of Ethics around 1990 and released a promising indie tape called *Out of Egypt*. Code of Ethics was signed by REX and then Forefront and Word, releasing eight albums over eight years.

Also in the late 1980s, a Wheaton College student named Ian Eskelin entered the scene. He saw some action as a DJ and dance music artist on the East Coast before going to Wheaton. He stopped in at the True Tunes store in 1989 and heard what was being done in the name of dance music. Inspired, he recorded and released an independent tape under the band name Brand New Language that True Tunes sold. Eskelin eventually hooked up with Chicago-based Wonderland Records and recorded a solo album (also under the band name Brand New Language) as well as one of the first rave records in the Christian market under the name Zero. Eskelin also joined Code of Ethics for a brief time and recorded a second solo album, called *Supersonic Dream Day*, before forming the power-pop band All Star United.

At the same time, a young man was recording techno demos in his bedroom and sending them to True Tunes for reviews. His name was Joey Belville, and the "band" name that he used was Adagio. Finally, in 1991, he made a tape that was professionally reproduced, and True Tunes sold it for him. In time, he'd change his "band" name to The Echoing Green and would release seven excellent albums of what he called "aggressive smile pop." The Echoing Green enjoyed one of the most devoted underground followings in all of Christian music.

Also at about this time, two brothers began recording demos in their home. Ronnie and Jason Martin, both of whom had grown up as huge fans of Daniel Amos, 441, and other early Orange County bands, recorded under the name Dancehouse Children. They signed with Blonde Vinyl Records and released their first album, *Songs and Stories* (a.k.a. *Love Children*), in 1991 and *Jesus* in 1992. Although the records were low budget in terms of production, they established a devoted underground following strong enough for the two albums to be rereleased 10 years later.

In 1993, Jason left to start a guitar-based band, and Ronnie continued under the name Rainbow Rider and released *Beautiful Dazzling Music #1* on Knott's Siren label. Although the record got panned by some critics (mostly for its liner notes), history was on the side of the band, for the record became an underground classic of the genre. Rainbow Rider set the stage for Ronnie to create a new all-synth pop band called Joy Electric that was one of the first signings by Tooth and Nail. Joy Electric recorded eight projects between 1994 and 1999, at which point Ronnie launched his own label, Plastiq Music. Jason started the critically acclaimed and popular Starflyer 59 band and signed with Tooth and Nail in 1994. Described as "shoegazer" or "dream pop," Starflyer 59 crafted neopsychedelic drones with shimmering instrumentation and mostly melancholy lyrics. The band would release nine projects plus a boxed set between 1994 and 2000, all on Tooth and Nail.

The other major development in dance music was when Scott Blackwell, a producer and DJ who'd been a fixture in the New York club scene, became a Christian and got involved in the underground in California. At first, he focused on releasing his own albums of house music for a new division of Frontline called Myx Records. Eventually, he became more of a producer and A&R man discovering various techno, rave, and house bands such as The Raving Loonatics and launching them into the Christian market. Blackwell later launched his own label, N-Soul Records, which focused on dance music. His Nitro Praise series (last count, it was up to Nitro Praise Eight) was a huge success. Blackwell sold that label and in 2000 relaunched Myx as his own project.

By the end of the 1990s, dance music was, for the most part, treated like any other kind of music. It could certainly be abused, but it was also a valid forum for worship and entertainment. Various strains, such as trip-hop, ambient, jungle, and acid house, evolved from what was basically called dance music in the 1980s.

The Industrial Revolution

The cold, synthetic aggression of the industrial sound (early on simply called industrial noise, when the music lacked even rudimentary song structure in lieu of howling and screeching chaos) made a surprisingly fertile field for the development of a Christian variant. Although the invention of industrial music is most often credited to the German band Kraftwerk, Christian bands popped up early on.

The most enigmatic was a band from the Pacific Northwest called Blackhouse. It was comprised of two pseudonymously named artists, Ivo Cutler and Sterling Cross. All of the band's albums were released by Ladd Frith, an independent label from the West Coast. Although the band found a small but loyal following in the Christian underground, most of its notoriety came from the secular industrial scene. The albums *Five*

After debuting as a part of techno-pop band Dancehouse Children, Jason Martin formed Starflyer 59.

Minutes after I Die and *Hope like a Candle* were released in the early 1980s and were followed up by the classic *Holy War* LP. The band kept recording, in the 1990s even evolving toward the more commercial style of bands such as Nine Inch Nails. The true identities of Cutler and Cross were never revealed, and the band refused to grant interviews, so not much is known about the members' backgrounds. But Blackhouse certainly opened the door for several other industrial bands.

An underground scene developed around a few key "zines" in the 1980s, including *Cutting Edge* from Florida. Through the zines, garage bands could distribute their cassette demos via direct mail to a few hundred die-hard fans around the world. Although the production was often awful, and the packaging crude, the earliest strains of punk, noise rock, and industrial found a small but devoted audience. One such band, Gadget, released a few tapes of experimental industrial noise distributed primarily by a couple of progressive mail-order outfits, including a new Chicago-based indie shop called True Tunes.

The first Christian industrial act to be signed to a label and distributed to Christian stores was the Austin-based Deitiphobia. The band was comprised of two friends, Wally Shaw, a mere teenager, and Brent Stackhouse, who'd graduated from Wheaton College. The band originally went by the name Donderfleigen, and their national premiere was on the Cornerstone Festival's New Artist Stage in 1991 (alongside Over the Rhine, John Austin, The Wayside, and others). Their song "Attack the City Walls" was featured on a cassette sampler given away at the festival that contained songs by various Myrrh artists, such as One Bad Pig and Holy Soldier, and each of the indie bands that had been selected to play the stage that year. Word spread about Donderfleigen, and the band found itself with an offer to record for the upstart Blonde Vinyl Records.

The band changed its name to Deitiphobia and released an indie demo called *Digital Priests* and then its Blonde Vinyl debut, *Fear of God*. To fans of industrial music, Deitiphobia was the equivalent of a full solar eclipse. The music was raw and low budget, but it ushered in a wave of spin-offs, sound-alikes, and a new awareness of the genre, just as Nine Inch Nails and Ministry were beginning to grip the national scene. In what was a rarity for the Christian scene, Deitiphobia wasn't several years behind the times. The band was featured in the second issue of *True Tunes News* in 1991. That feature, combined with the deal with Blonde Vinyl, got Deitiphobia on the national scene for good.

Fear of God was followed by a rerelease of *Digital Priests: The Remixes*. Stackhouse's wife, Heather, released a female industrial project called *Wigtop*, and other groups, such as Global Wave System, followed in the slipstream. After two records, Stackhouse quit, and Shaw continued on. When Blonde Vinyl shut down, Deitiphobia moved to Myx Records, a division of Frontline, and released the more commercial but still very industrial *Clean*.

Eventually, Shaw hit the pause button on Deitiphobia and moved into more techno-rock-electronica music with his new "band" Massivivid, with his wife, Sheri. Massivivid's one record, *Brightblur*, won a Dove Award for Alternative Album in 1998, illustrating the irrelevance of the awards since the album still failed to sell well enough for the band to record again. The Shaws continue to explore various postindustrial sounds and have recently rekindled the Deitiphobia flames with a new record for N-Soul Records.

The other main voice in the Christian industrial scene came from one Jyro Zhan and his partner, Jerome. The two formed Mortal, which shocked the scene with its amazing debut, *Lusis*. Mortal's music was aggressive and intense but included catchy hooks and thoughtful lyrics. The debut was followed by the even more impressive *Fathom*, the guitar-based *Wake*, and a live EP, all for Frontline/Intense. Jyro and Jerome experimented with electronica/rave as Jyradelix and then moved to Five Minute Walk to release *Pura*, their finale as Mortal.

Growing tired of the constrictions of the industrial scene, they evolved into a more modern pop-electronic band, changed their name to Fold Zandura, and released an indie album as well as two label releases, including *Ultraforever* for BEC. In 1999, they returned to the indie scene

Common Children released two amazing albums on Tattoo Records before disbanding — they reunited in 2000.

and released another EP. Gyro and Jerome remain firmly planted at the progressive edge of electronic Christian music.

Also making quite a noise was New York's Circle of Dust, featuring producer-musician Scott Albert. Circle of Dust recorded for REX Records, and their debut ranks among the true highpoints of the genre. As with most of the REX bands, Circle of Dust's relationship with the label was strained. Releases were few and far between, culminating in the 1998 release *Disengage*. Albert, changing his name to Clay Scott, formed the performance art band/magic act Angel Dust and kissed the Christian scene good-bye.

Two bands associated with Albert and Circle of Dust were Argyle Park (also on REX) and Tooth and Nail's Klank. Both bands remain active and continue to tweak the industrial formulas to keep their music fresh and challenging.

Chatterbox released one album for Tooth and Nail, as did Technocracy on REX. Word, through its distribution deal with Wonderland Records out of Chicago, released two impressive discs by Under Midnight, a conceptual band comprised of producers Mark Robertson and Caesar Kalinowski.

Christian retailers often shied away from the industrial acts since the music and packaging scared them. Even the heaviest rock shows couldn't play a lot of the music. The bands, for the most part, longed for acceptance beyond the Christian scene but found that elusive.

The dance side of industrial evolved into rave music, which attracted a few artists and fans. Eventually, the industrial bands evolved into either rave/electronica bands or hardcore/thrash bands. Time had run out on the industrial scene overall, but many fans recognized that the Christian scene had produced some impressive efforts. By the end of the 1990s, the industrial scene, by then closely linked to the goth scene, returned to the underground, but this time with the advantage of high-quality, low-cost recording and the ultimate underground networking tool, the Internet. New indie labels such as Flaming Fish and Blacklight are carrying the music forward in greater quality and quantity than ever before.

Gothic Christians

Anyone who thinks that gothic art doesn't go well with Christianity must not be very familiar with that art. There's hardly an art form more in touch with Christianity than gothic art. Even the gargoyles, vampires, and cemeteries often associated with gothicism are directly tied to various Christian images of the day. And Christianity is based on the premise that humanity is basically sinful because of free will and the cunning of Satan. At its core is the murder of an innocent man. Even its primary symbol, the cross, represents death.

As far as music is concerned, "gothic" usually refers to minor keys, droning melodies, and macabre lyrics. The earliest Christian music to fit that description (with the exception of some of Larry Norman's early work) is the obscure Mike Knott album recorded with his band Idle Lovell in 1983. Full of drama and drone, *Surge et Illuminare* was a six-song independent vinyl release. Idle Lovell performed in various clubs around the LA area after Knott left The Lifesavors and before he restarted the band on his own. Many unrecorded Idle Lovell tunes ended up on future LSU albums, such as *Shaded Pain* (a goth masterpiece) and *Wakin' Up the Dead*.

Another early goth masterpiece is Undercover's 1986 release *Branded*. Full of pain and self-loathing, *Branded* maintained one of the most scriptural perspectives on the human condition of early alternative Christian music.

One of Idle Lovell's biggest fans was Knott's friend and sometime manager/mentor, Brian Heally. He'd been fluttering around the embryonic Orange County scene since the beginning, helping bands to get shows, promoting them, buying them food, and so forth. The perennial enabler, Heally called in a few favors in 1989 and had members of Undercover back him up for his debut, *Prints of Darkness*, under the band name Dead Artists Syndrome. Heally's somber baritone, combined with songs about stalking, lost love, blindness, and isolation, made for the feel-bad hit of the summer of 1989. Heally premiered his project at the Cornerstone Festival that summer and was instantly crowned the father of goth, though few fans really knew what that meant.

Heally followed the album with two more Dead Artists Syndrome projects, 1992's *Devils Angels Saints* and 1995's *Happy Hour*. Both records featured members of The Choir and The Seventy Sevens as his band. Heally remains in the shadows of Christian music, waiting for his moment.

Also congealing in the darkness of the late 1980s was an LA club band called Saviour Machine. Although the lead singer was a Christian, his interests leaned toward the dramatic. With a clean-shaven head covered in white makeup, the deepest and clearest baritone this side of better opera singers, and a flair for the dramatic reminiscent of Alice Cooper without the humor, Eric Clayton and his band scared the hell out of more than a few people. As the band grew, their "epic metal" sound deepened, as did their lyrics. As of 1998, Clayton began a trilogy of albums based in painstaking detail on the Book of Revelation (talk about goth!). With the oversight of Pastor Dave Hart (a "goth pastor" from San Diego), Saviour Machine has accomplished amazing levels of performance artistry. Concerts are likely to involve fire, blood, gold, chains, skulls, and other icons. Anyone who thinks that Christian music is a bunch of fluff should see this incredible band in action.

Clayton started his own label, and as a result a host of other under-

Jacob Bradley of The Vigilantes of Love.

ground gospel-goth projects have come to light. The Wedding Party released a haunting album called *Anthems* before breaking up in 2000. Eva O., formerly of the secular Christian Death goth band, became a Christian and released the disturbing *Damnation — Ride the Madness* album, deemed too intense for Christian bookstores by the label's distributor.

Also in 2000, a compilation of dark wave, gothic, and ambient industrial artists was released called *We the Living Volume 3*. Other underground labels, such as Blacklight, Velvet Empire, and Flaming Fish, have released compilations and albums dedicated to Christian goth and dark music.

Back to the Roots

The mainstreaming of alternative music had one other interesting effect in the 1990s. Roots rock made a huge comeback in both the general and the Christian markets. The buzzword in the secular scene became "Americana." Described by some as country music for people who don't like country music, the Americana scene featured some encouraging releases for Christians.

Buddy Miller, a believer who'd been playing guitar and producing records in the Christian market steadily for years (though usually for fringe labels), signed with Hightone Records, as did his wife, Julie Miller. Buddy's records were some of the twangiest, old-style country ever released. Although most of the songs were about relationships, a few songs pointed to a bigger picture. Julie's albums were even more gospel oriented. Buddy became the main guitarist for Emmylou Harris's band and Steve Earl's band. The two performed at Cornerstone '99 amid all the hard rock and alternative music and received an incredible response.

Close friends of the Millers, Victoria Williams and Mark Olson, started an indie band to run parallel to Victoria's solo career. That band was called The Original Harmony Ridge Creekdippers. It released three full-length albums independently.

Even mainstream bands such as The Jayhawks, Gillian Welch, Wilco, and Uncle Tupelo reflected extensively spiritual tones on their records. The Americana scene was remarkably willing to tolerate Christian content as long as it wasn't too preachy. This tolerance was encouraging to bands and solo artists such as Fred Haring and The Wayside.

Another type of roots rock is rockabilly. This Train (featuring Mark Robertson of The Ragamuffin Band) crafted several records of humorous rockabilly music.

The Lost Dogs, however, probably remain the major Christian example of roots music. Their albums are still in demand.

The Ska Revival

It seemed like every third band between 1995 and 1999 was a ska band. Although not the first to capture the attention of the nation, The Israelites, a traditional ska band, was the first to get into the game back in 1989. With a following in both the Christian and the secular scenes, The Israelites flourished in the mid-1990s as an alternative to the more modern-sounding strains of ska coming from the rest of the scene. The band released two studio albums, *Washaway* (1995) and *Montego Bay* (1998).

However, The Supertones were the first of the ska bands to capture a national crowd. After forming in 1992, the band hounded Tooth and Nail president Brandon Ebel into signing them. Hopefully, he's thanked them for their persistence, for the band has sold hundreds of thousands of albums, making them one of the top bands in the business. They've also managed to break out of the Christian box somewhat. Between 1996 and 1999, the band released four albums.

The Insyderz play a brand of ska called "ska-core," which combines the basic ska feel with hardcore rock. The band is famous for intense live shows, which often include familiar worship songs in the band's unique style. They got their big break when, after being rejected for a spot at Cornerstone '96, they brought their gear and set up at a campsite. A label cat heard them jamming and invited them to play at his label's tent. Gene Eugene heard them there, loved them, and signed them to Brainstorm. Within the next year, they were sold to Gumshoe Records and released their debut, *Motor City Ska*. They were an instant hit and followed the album with one more regular album and two collections of ska worship tunes, including a version of Rich Mullins's "Awesome God."

Five Iron Frenzy took the madness to a whole new level. Their "third-wave" ska is infused with punk, pop, and camp. Their shows are usually dangerous but always fun. They have toured the country countless times and even joined the mainstream Ska against Racism tour. Between 1997 and 2000, they released four albums and destroyed several innocent tour vans.

Other ska and ska-related bands come and go all the time. Most of the smaller labels put out various ska samplers of dubious quality to try to cash in on the craze. Despite oversaturation and sometimes overplaying, the stuff just won't go away.

The Independent Revolution

The cost of making music plummeted in the 1990s and gave artists greater freedom and power since they were no longer as dependent on

Erik Brandt of Urban Hillbilly Quartet.

record labels for their livelihood. Meanwhile, technological advances ensured higher-quality independent records.

Bands such as Over the Rhine, Vigilantes of Love, and John Austin were among the first to record big-league-quality albums on their own. Bands struggling to make a living on a label were the next in line. The Seventy Sevens released three independent projects in the late 1990s. As early as 1992, The Choir released their album *Kissers and Killers* independently. They also released a new album in the summer of 2000 that wasn't financed by a label.

A folky acoustic band from Texas called Caedmon's Call made news in the Christian industry by selling over 40,000 units of their two indie titles. Finally, in 1997, they signed a major deal with Warner Brothers. When it became known that Warner was exiting the Christian market, Caedmon's Call got out of the deal and signed with Essential Records, where they used their indie-label experience to launch a new label. They also started a wholesale distributor for indie bands called Grassroots.

With stories such as Collective Soul's indie demo selling two million units floating around, it seemed that every band had a record in the 1990s. Although it became harder for consumers to tell the good from the bad, zines such as *Awakening Records*, *True Tunes News*, and *Phantom Tollbooth* helped people to hear through the din. By 1998, the indie scene was many fans' music of choice.

Alternative Worship Music

Similar to the radical modernization of worship music in the 1960s during the Jesus Movement, a movement that seems to have started in the early 1990s has led to numerous examples of alternative (rock, acoustic, ethnic) worship music.

In 1992, Steve Hindalong and Derri Daughtery (The Choir) produced an interesting album called *At the Foot of the Cross*. It was a collaboration with various other "alternative" and not so "alternative" artists. Basically, they composed original songs around the text of traditional liturgical (in their case, Anglican) services set to music that was delicate, somber, and reverential but rhythmic in a Paul Simon kind of way. The album was a huge hit among fans of alternative music and led to a second volume. The *At the Foot of the Cross* CDs brought forth songs such as "Beautiful Scandalous Night," which have been added to church services as modern hymns.

In 1993, Glenn Kaiser of Resurrection Band compiled various worship songs he'd written over the years for the Jesus People USA community. The songs were recorded in a mostly acoustic style and then released as the *All My Days* album. Kaiser repeated the process for a follow-up called

Throw Down Your Crowns. Also coming from the Jesus People community was an excellent album by the in-house acoustic band Seeds.

Charlie Peacock brought two of the earliest major-label alternative worship projects to the scene. Under the title *Coram Deo*, Peacock pulled together two albums of excellent worship music with his characteristic flair and professionalism.

The Insyderz included various worship songs in their ska-core concerts from the beginning. They recorded some for Squint Entertainment and called the album *Skalleluia*. They followed it with another collection of ska worship called *Skalleluia 2*.

In 1996, a British band called Delirious formed as the house worship band for a monthly service at Arun Community Church of Littlehampton. The band recorded some projects so that audience members could have the music personally. They began performing at other events as well and developed a growing following. Somehow one of the worship tunes, a song called "Deeper," cracked the BBC Top 20, a shocking accomplishment for a religious group. The band quickly signed with EMI, which imported their music to America via the Sparrow imprint. Delirious brought their worship music, slick British pop, to America in force. Suddenly, their songs were sung in youth groups from coast to coast. Most of the worship labels rushed to release more of this style of music.

In 1998, a Nashville group called Sonic Flood took the music a step further. Their debut on Gotee Records was a runaway hit. Meanwhile, back in Europe, a group took the "alternative" part to heart and created some truly alternative worship environments, including a labyrinth. Techno and rave worship music was recorded as an accompaniment. The Nitro Praise series took contemporary worship songs and dressed them up as dance pop songs to great success throughout the 1990s.

Several various-artists compilations came out in the 1990s and centered on worship themes. The *Exodus* album on Michael W. Smith's Rocketown label featured rocking worship tunes by Third Day and Sixpence None the Richer, among others. Word released a similar project, bent more toward adult alternative tones, called *Streams*, and it featured songs with Jon Anderson of the legendary progressive rock band Yes.

In 2000, Rhythmhouse Records released a compelling world-music worship album that featured music from the United States and Europe. The album, *Tongues of Fire*, included music from a particularly modern church in Seattle called Mars Hill Church. That church had recorded one of the best alternative worship albums of all in 1998. Simply titled *Mars Hill Worship*, the CD became an underground hit. It featured rhythmic alternative songs, techno songs, and acoustic songs. (For more up-to-date information on the modern worship scene, visit the Raised by Wolves web site.)

Getting the Word Out

The whole machinery for disseminating information about new bands changed radically in the 1990s. New publications, new festivals, and new technologies combined to spread the word faster and farther than ever before.

Inspired by the rising national significance of the Cornerstone Festival, several smaller regional festivals popped up around the country, and several old-school festivals set up alternative stages in an attempt to reach kids. In Pennsylvania, Creation Festival (the largest Christian festival in the country) spun off a small alternative fest called Purple Door. In Atlanta, the staff of Gray Dot and the local *Visions of Gray* magazine launched the Inner Seeds festival. Inner Seeds ran for a few crucial years, providing some of the few southeastern performances of bands such as The Violet Burning and Adam Again. In the Columbia River gorge, a fest was launched by Mikee Bridges of the band Sometime Sunday. It was called the Tom Fest, and by the end of the 1990s it had spread to Los Angeles and beyond. Tooth and Nail even set up its own festivals. Just like compilation CDs, fests with multiple bands drew big crowds and were an effective way to get new bands some needed exposure.

By 1993, *True Tunes News* had become the widest circulated of all the rock-oriented magazines in the Christian music scene. With a peak mailing list of 50,000 worldwide (in 24 countries), it became the lead dog when it came to the fringe.

The *Syndicate* kept going into the 1990s, but the magazine was sold to new owners, who let it flounder. Newcomb stepped down as editor and was replaced by Chris Well, an experienced writer who'd produced a nationally syndicated Christian rock radio show called *Crosswalk*. Well did a good job, but in 1995 a new publisher hired him to edit the new *7ball* magazine. *7ball* was based in Nashville and had close ties to advertisers through its sister publication, *Release* magazine. With slick design, a more youth-oriented slant, and the benefit of synergy with the publisher's other magazines, *7ball* took off fast. At about the same time, several of the older labels filed for bankruptcy, owing *True Tunes News* significant cash. As a result, *True Tunes News* turned to the more affordable Internet for its future, leaving the printed magazine realm exclusively to *7ball*. As major Christian labels got more and more into alternative music, *7ball* was right there to spread the word.

The advent of the Internet was probably the most significant boost, though. Web sites such as *Lighthouse Electronic Magazine* sprung up almost immediately and offered reviews, interviews, and chat rooms. The sense of community, before limited to rare times when people could visit in person (concerts, festivals), now occurred day and night.

Their neapolitan style made Burlap To Cashmere a huge hit in the Christian market.

For better or worse, newsgroups and list serves popped up and allowed fans of a particular genre or band to have ongoing discussions. Bands were able to build significant mailing lists and keep in touch with fans. In general, as with the reduced costs for recording and manufacturing, the net was empowering bands and artists to remain independent longer.

The net also spawned the phenomenon known as Internet radio, still in its infancy. Nonetheless, the potential impact of low-cost worldwide radio broadcasting is staggering. Stations such as Christian Pirate Radio, RadioU, and TrueTunesRadio rushed to offer programming that would keep crowds listening.

The owners of True Tunes felt so confident about the potential of the Internet that they decided to close the store and move the whole company on-line.

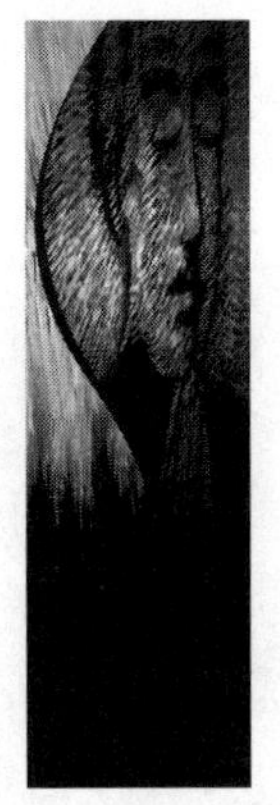

Epilogue

Beyond the Third Wave

Thirty years ago, it was unlikely that anyone foresaw what would become of this faith-music hybrid. Bands such as Agape, All Saved Freak Band, and Love Song certainly couldn't have imagined the scenario of today.

The early commercialization of Christian music met with criticism on several fronts. Many songwriters, singers, and bands felt apprehensive about making a profit from the fruits of their faith. Some bands, such as Agape, refused outright to do so. They'd come from the streets and lifestyle of hard rock and roll to faith in Jesus. Their music was an honest, gut-level manifestation of their experience. As formulas began to emerge, and audiences began to change from predominantly non-Christian to predominantly Christian, band leader Fred Caban believed that Agape had become some sort of Christian entertainment. Since that wasn't what he'd felt called to do, he shut down Agape.

Keith Green, though he came along much later, had a similar problem with Christian music. He'd spent his early years in a desperate search for fame and fortune as a rock star. His childhood record contract with Decca Records and subsequent hype as the "next big thing" in pop music had given him a taste for the limelight and enough experience in the business to know how it worked. When his life was changed by a radical

Sixpence None The Richer's Leigh Nash.

conversion to Christianity, he thought immediately that music, or at least the pursuit of fame and fortune, should be forgone in favor of service to God. In his case, that led to a music ministry as powerful a force of change for believers as it was for unbelievers. Green was able to draw stadium-sized crowds to hear his music and his scathing and confrontational preaching. He seemed to sense the complacency settling over the Jesus Movement folks, and he was vociferous in his critique of the emerging evangelical subculture that insulated itself from the heathen masses. He took a stand against set ticket prices and album sales. Concerts were based on a free-will offering, and his records sold for whatever people could afford to pay. This approach certainly flew in the face of the commercialization of Christian music. In many ways, Green brought the protest music of the 1960s back into the Christian music scene by refusing to accept the status quo.

On the other side of the table sat those who wanted to see Christian music become even more mainstream. Some pursued personal financial gain in this new marketplace. Others began to view the effectiveness of a given ministry in terms of how many people bought into it. Whereas the Jesus People of the 1960s would have been thrilled to put on a concert in a park and see a dozen people "get saved," these people wanted to see hit songs on Christian radio (listened to almost exclusively by Christians), record sales, successful tours, and eventually even product endorsements and video play. To be sure, many had good intentions. They believed that the music and the message of Christian artists were vital and compelling and would positively affect listeners.

A separate strain evolved alongside the hardcore ministry crowd and the mass-market mavens. It was comprised of Christian artists who wanted to practice their craft in the larger marketplace. Some felt led to spread the message into the secular world; others just wanted a career in music. Many didn't write about the nastier subjects and sometimes avoided offensive language, but they didn't think that their music was the place to give voice to their beliefs. In fact, much of their music was identified as Christian by what it didn't contain (encouragement of drug use, free sex, and open rebellion). Artists who did voice their faith in their music were quickly tagged as "Christian artists" and often ushered into the Christian ghetto. Many Christian businesses made a lot of money from the arrangement, thus furthering the divide. For many of the artists, though, it was infuriating.

With the fourth wave bringing both an increase of Christian thought in pop music and a quantum leap forward in the Christian subculture in terms of aggressively contemporary music being accepted, the scene seems to be ripe for a revolution of sorts. Unfortunately, the playing field may not be level. The machinery that generates billions of dollars from the sale of pop music is now largely invested in the gospel business. With EMI having a stake in Sparrow, Forefront, Star Song, and Five Minute Walk, as well as the largest distribution share in the industry, its well-oiled hum of commerce can be seen in the Christian marketplace. Provident and Word are in the same position. Even the most casual observers of the pop entertainment industry notice that their motivations and inspirations have far more to do with market share, demographics, and the bottom line than with quality, artistry, or content. Thus, the new yardstick by which Christian artists are measured is not their spiritual integrity, ministry content, or even skills but simply how many units of an album they sell.

This situation may not be good for music lovers. Good rock continues to emerge from the mainstream scene only because a small percentage of the market is enough to pay for it. Artists such as John Hiatt and Van Morrison are able to craft honest, mature rock for adults, and are even free to explore faith issues, because their niche is just large enough. That isn't the case in the Christian market.

As has always been the case, retailers and radio programmers wield an undue amount of influence in the Christian market. Programmers, by and large, seem to be almost completely uninterested in what people really want to hear. They know that a certain percentage of Christians in their broadcast areas will listen to their stations simply because they are Christian. They can play nearly whatever they want without losing that core. Then they have the donor base (many Christian stations are non-

Larry Norman, equal parts singer, story-teller, and humorist, is slowly returning to the touring circuit after years of self-imposed exile.

commercial and rely on donations), which tends to be comprised of the most conservative Christians who, in many cases, donate money to a radio station that meets their needs alone. Since their needs are for adult contemporary and inspirational music, that's what the stations play. Forget about excellent new rock music or even pop music by unknown bands on small niche labels. With a few exceptions, and maybe a late-night "rock show" once a week, Christian radio stations are far more interested in making regular listeners out of Christians than in playing music that would draw a secular audience.

Meanwhile, retailers struggle with shelf space, marketing dollars, and display area. They often don't have the time to treat a music section like a small record store. Instead, it becomes a top-40 rack of titles at mainstream Christian radio and the latest worship music. Since most Christian bookstores practically forbid an unbeliever to enter, they obviously care much less about connecting with people on the street than about becoming Christians' headquarters for books, jewelry, music, and even T-shirts and toys that promote the subculture at healthy profit margins. Due to the strictures placed on them by retailers, many labels end up signing acts most likely to recoup money the fastest as opposed to artists who write the best songs, craft the most relevant contemporary music, or engage the world at large with thought-provoking lyrics. So much of the best music still remains hidden underground.

In fact, when it comes to the marketing, distribution, and promotion of pop music, the Christian industry is right in step with the mainstream industry. Although proponents of the subculture find that exhilarating, many artists and fans do not. More and more people are looking to the independent scene for exciting music. Hundreds of artists either signed to tiny boutique labels or not signed at all are releasing high-quality, independently circulated CDs to a growing new underground. A few labels are even taking some of the best independent music and releasing it into the bookstore networks. With the explosion of the Internet, digital delivery of music, and greatly reduced costs of manufacturing, many believe that the future of Christian rock is brightest where the sun of the industry's attention doesn't shine.

Let's be honest: there's a lot of bad Christian music out there. There has been everything from saccharine-sweet adult contemporary beauty queens to swaggering Las Vegas showmen. Fans of Christian music have been subjected to prepackaged pop drivel just as every secular pop fan has been. But just like it makes no sense to ignore The Beatles because of Britney Spears, so too does it make no sense to ignore Daniel Amos or The Choir because of any of the schmaltzy acts in Christian music. Although enough Christian music is shallow, trite, and condescending, there are also hundreds of albums that are inspiring, transcendent, and gripping.

Sam Ashworth, son of Christian rock pioneer Charlie Peacock, emerged as a major talent with his band Sauté and is now a solo artist signed to Squint Records.

Until the past few years, the top-selling Christian music has been the least aggressive, adventurous, or challenging. Nonetheless, scores of acts in the underground have been making amazing music for over 30 years. Whether your tastes run toward the arena-sized pop of Audio Adrenaline or the roots rock of Third Day, or if you love obscure underground indie acts such as Mack the Coffeeman or Pedro the Lion, or if you are into "Christian rock," there is much music out there for you to discover. Every possible style — from death metal to gangsta rap to electronica — can be found among Christian artists.

Many artists of faith find great hope and encouragement in the recent success of Sixpence None the Richer, Creed, and POD. Maybe the seeming prejudice against all things Christian will wane under the influence of the almighty dollar. Others aren't so hopeful. Jesus taught that the world will hate his followers just as it hates him. Many believe that the prejudice will never completely go away, and they have resigned themselves to it. The artists, for the most part, just want to be heard. Finally, after 30 years, that is beginning to happen.

With the rise of the Internet, fans can now connect directly with the artists who move them. No longer must they rely on the gatekeepers within the church or the entertainment industry. The walls may not be down between the church and the town, but now there's a fancy new bridge getting people back and forth at will. Perhaps compelling rock by people of faith has its brightest days ahead. And, with every musical card already on the table, the public seems to be ready for the next wave of Christian rock. What could be more "alternative" than music that evolved in relative obscurity under the auspices of artists who knew better than to expect fame or fortune? They make the music because they have to. It doesn't get more real than that.

Further Reading and Resources

Books

Baker, Paul. *Contemporary Christian Music: Where It Came from, What It Is, Where It's Going*. Westchester, IL: Crossway, 1985.

Green, Melody, and David Hazard. *No Compromise: The Life Story of Keith Green*. Chatsworth, CA: Sparrow, 1989.

Howard, Jay R., and John M. Streck. *Apostles of Rock: The Splintered World of Contemporary Christian Music*. Lexington: U of Kentucky P, 1999.

Joseph, Mark. *The Rock and Roll Rebellion: Why People of Faith Abandoned Rock Music — and Why They're Coming Back*. Nashville: Broadman, 1999.

Livgren, Kerry, and Kenneth Boa. *Seeds of Change*. Westchester, IL: Crossway, 1983.

Magazines (Back Issues)

ACM
Activist
Campus Life
CCM
Cornerstone
Counter Culture
Cutting Edge
Harmony
Harvest Rock Syndicate
Heaven's Metal (HM)
Notebored
7ball
True Tunes News (and *True News*)

Other Resources

Brown, Bruce. "History of Contemporary Christian Music." CCM Communications, Nashville, 1999 (a script and a CD that can be downloaded at www.ccmmagazine.com/).

Di Sabatino, David. "The Jesus Movement." MA thesis.

www.allmusic.com (the All Music guide).

www.one-way.org/jesusmusic/ (a decade of Jesus music).

www.raisedbywolves.net.

index

Special thanks to the following for help with the index: Michelle Thompson, Pat and Sue O'Malley, Tessa Konc, Jeremy and Julie Elzerman, Jeremy Gudauskas, Sarah Madden, Kim Mundt, Amy and Joe Petit, and Jason Hartong.